The Ibu Chronicles

Life is Funnier Than Fiction

RACHEL BERGSMA

Dedicated to Vicky and Dennis Jeffers

Contents

Author's Notes

The Ibu Chronicles are excerpts from my Facebook blog, *Ibu Chronicles.* As my husband and I owned a tour and travel agency in Bali, I was asked in 2016 to join a Facebook Group about Bali; to give advice to tourists wanting to come and visit this magical island and learn more about this unique culture.

I started sharing glimpses of my life with my Dutch husband in Bali. (I am Australian.) Life became funnier than fiction, and my posts soon needed their own page, called *Ibu Chronicles.* Some excerpts are about our wonderful staff or even our neighbours, but most are about Ibu. **Ibu means Mother in Indonesian** (it also means Mrs and Madam), and our Balinese parents and business partners, Ibu and Bapak (Father, also Mr and Sir) ensure our life in Bali is never boring. Our tour office is located inside a traditional Balinese hotel in the mountains of Bali, Indonesia. The hotel is located next to a magnificent lake called Lake Batur inside a caldera of a dormant volcano. Ibu and Bapak have had the hotel since 1984. It was purpose-built as a weekend mountain getaway for Balinese from Denpasar, and for Balinese Government meetings and retreats. Foreign tourists did stay at the hotel, generally with a tour group, so they were looked after by their tour leader. Some random tourists just appeared at the hotel; generally, that is when we had to step in and help Ibu and Bapak, oh, and the tourist. Ibu is blunt, she is demanding, she keeps life interesting. I am sure you will learn to love Ibu as much as I do.

We only speak to Ibu, and the rest of our family and staff in Bahasa Indonesian or in Basa Bali (the Balinese language), so I translate in my writing. If they attempt English, I advise that in my writing. There is no political correctness in Bali, it is considered, by the Indonesians as a very western concept and not welcomed in Indonesia, so I write as we speak here in Bali. I always presumed PC was a computer. Mind you, when a tourist advised they had found a tablet on a sunbed at a hotel, I warned them to leave it alone, as we have the death penalty for possession of drugs here. Having only visited a western country once in a decade, I admit I am sometimes a little behind the western world. We use the term Bule, which is used by all locals to describe a non-Indonesian of any origin (although it means Crazy Albino). Some people are offended by this term, that is their problem.

Edition Number Two.

This book you are reading is now the second published edition. The first publication was put together very quickly (with no editing) as a fund raiser and was purchased by hundreds of people that had been to Bali. 100% of profits were used to buy rice and other staple foods for the Balinese in the village where our office is located. THANK YOU ALL.

This edition has been edited and some information added for those that have never been to Bali, some further explanations of those idiosyncrasies in Bali. I have attempted to explain as best as I can in the relevant anecdotes.

The Ibu Chronicles is now a three-book series, the prequels are the story of how we came to live in Bali. *The Epiphany* is my story, starting with my first visit to Bali in 1998, where I must say I wasn't won over by the Island of the Gods, vowing never to return. It is also the story of how I met my Dutch husband and my travel mishaps along the way. Oh, and an epiphany that gave me a much-needed boot around the ear. *The Measurement of Wealth* is the continuing story of living and running a business in Bali, Indonesia.

Bali's main religion is based on Hinduism and Buddhism. It is called Bali Agama. There is also a Muslim influence, as the country of Indonesia is predominately Muslim. Balinese lives are tightly intertwined with their religion, and it is a daily task to keep the balance between the Gods and the Demons. Balinese offerings are a huge part of daily life here, the main offering being canang sari, which is made daily. If you have been to Bali, you would have seen these everywhere. I refer to offerings in my writing, so here is an example of the Canang Sari (daily offering). The colours of the flowers used are white, yellow, red and blue/purple – the middle is green (shaved pandan leaf). The container (canang) is made from coconut palm leaves. Under that flower arrangement is a little gift, called poroson, and other little secrets can be placed under there... it's the magic of Bali; there are many mysterious wonders to discover here. There are also many comic moments living here, the Balinese don't take life too seriously and they have helped us to do the same. Life is Funnier than Fiction, especially in Bali.

Rachel Bergsma.

Chapter 1 - Working in a Traditional Balinese Hotel

10 June 2016 - The Toast

Toast, it is a simple enough thing to make, but it has been the bone of my contention for many years. It just rears its ugly head every so often to remind me it is still there.

Toast, yes toast, the bread kind, not the champagne kind. *How can you get it so wrong? Oh, yes you can get it sooo wrong.*

Let's go back, way back before electricity. No, I am not referring to the 19th century, I am referring to prior to the year 2009, in our village where we work, and lived at that time. Now we only live in the north part-time. The rest of the year, we live in the south of Bali, in an area called The Bukit Peninsula (Bukit), where we have electricity, but no running water, but that's another story. Bukit means hill.

The hotel would run a generator every night for two hours, from 7.00 pm when it got dark, till 9.00 pm when the kitchen closed. We lived behind the hotel and made precious use of that two hour window into the 21st century, to charge our phones and our laptop.

The exciting day finally arrived when the village acquired electricity full time. It was September 12, 2009. I know that date, as it was exactly two weeks after we moved out of the village, as we wanted to live in a village with electricity. *Ok, a village with beer.*

The marvel of electricity brought excitement to the idea that the hotel could at least, come into the 20th century. We would be pushing it to attempt the 21st century.

A fridge was the first thing that came to my mind. *Mmm, beer.*

Ibu disagreed.

Ibu and the kitchen staff are the old-fashioned Balinese that do not store food. Food is purchased at the market or picked straight from the garden and is cooked fresh every day. What is not used by the end of the day is given to the pigs. They would never use leftovers.

Me: "Ibu, I meant for the beer!"

Ibu: "Ah, yes, many guests complain that there is no beer. Okay, we will get a fridge!"

So, one day a nice shiny new Coca-Cola fridge arrived, and Ibu had the staff stock it with beer and water. And that night at 9.00 pm, Bapak promptly turned it off. I explained that you need to leave it on... I explained until I went blue... I explained how it would use more electricity to cool down again in the morning. This is just a perfect example of my challenges, I have let it go.

It is still to this day, turned off every night, promptly at 9.00 pm.

But the fridge is not my problem...*if Ibu wants to waste her money, then who am I to interfere.*

Toast is my problem.

I do not eat toast myself, as I am allergic to wheat, and there is no gluten-free bread available; however, our guests eat toast.

It all started when we wanted to have toast as an option for our tour guests. Toast with butter and jam. What a foreign concept to Ibu and the kitchen staff. What's wrong with rice for breakfast?

So, we bought toasters, bread, and butter. We gave a demonstration to all the kitchen staff, on 'how to make toast'. The staff oohed and aahed, as the sugary white bread (that's all that is available) turned a golden brown and popped up ready to serve.

Ibu was amazed by this contraption. Ibu loves buying new things that no one else in the village has. She had the only fridge in the whole village, and now she has these 'cook bread things'. Ibu thought it would be an excellent idea for all her Bule hotel guests, to also get toast, if that's what Bules wanted. That excitement lasted about two minutes and turned into blowing fuses in the hotel every morning, during breakfast service.

On the morning of Day One of Toast on the menu, I walked into the kitchen to see Nengah, the day cook, deep frying a piece of bread. She was holding another piece in her hand, that she had put margarine on. I watched her putting jam on the bread and then, BAM, dropping it into the fry pan, under all the oil.

I said calmly, *Okay, I admit it, that's bullshit.* I screamed, "Nengah, what are you doing?!"

She looked at me innocently and said, in the only English she has ever used to this day, "Toast."

And that was when it all started!

So, after many training sessions in 'toast', we seemed to be getting there. Well, we thought. The toast came out great, but many a time I would walk into the kitchen, to find Nengah standing there with a knife in the toaster, trying to pull out some toast she had gotten stuck in there.

Those lovely toasters lasted five weeks before they completely blew up. Luckily Nengah did not blow up.

Now, I cannot be too hard on Nengah. Nengah is a lovely lady, she can make a mean Nasi Goreng (Indonesian Fried Rice) with her eyes closed. She can make the best banana pancakes without disclosing Ibu's secret recipe, and she knows how to make any Indonesian/Balinese dish.

Nengah cannot read or write and has been in that kitchen since she was twelve years old, helping Doyok, the head cook, who has been in the kitchen for thirty years. And I do mean, they have been in that kitchen, they never have a day off. Nengah is not sure how old she is, and she does not know how long she has been there. I would say she is late thirties, maybe twenty-five years in that kitchen.

With electricity, came other marvels of the future, and one day Ibu introduced rice cookers. It took Nengah approximately five years to use one. Mind you, she has never cooked in one. I would see her each morning come in from some mysterious place in the hotel, with a huge cane basket of steaming rice, which she transferred into the rice cookers to keep the rice warm.

That mysterious place Nengah appears from, is somewhere I had always thought '*I will go and investigate one day*'. I generally got too busy and forgot.

Three days ago, I was looking for some unused furniture to borrow, and I stumbled across that mysterious place at the back of the hotel, through a secret passage and a secret wooden door. I felt like I was a kid in *The Lion, The Witch and the Wardrobe.*

Nengah has been cooking the rice in old clay pots over an open fire. *No wonder it tastes so good.*

Now, back to toast. We decided Nengah needed fewer electrical appliances, and the hotel needed fewer fire risks. So, we got a large steel plate to put over gas burners for her to cook toast on.

We seemed to be getting there... so we thought. I just walked through the restaurant to see a guest, not mine, but a hotel guest, holding up her toast and watching it fold over like a limp, greasy dishcloth. The look on her face of 'What the?' was too much.

I walked into the kitchen to see Nengah deep frying the bread again.

Me: "Nengah, what are you doing?"

Nengah: "Toast"

Me: "Nengah, no, that's not correct, you have done this every day for nearly ten years."

Nengah: "I forgot."

7 July 2016 - The Cheat Sheet

The Balinese have a calendar of ceremony dates, an auspicious calendar. There are many calendars here. There is the usual Grecian calendar, so we know what day of the week it is, in case you need to send your kids to school, so do not accidentally send them on a Sunday. Or you need to go to a government office. That is about where that calendar stops its function in this village. When you work in hospitality/tourism, every day is a working day.

A very old lady once told me that her son was visiting her in three days, then she pointed to the moon. She did not need a calendar, it was in the sky, she knew her son was coming on the full moon.

There is a calendar that tells you when it is a good day to do something, and when it is not a good day. Everyone in this village follows that to a tee.

So, today Ibu had me making offerings, and I have no idea what they are for. We generally make them for God, but we also make them for bad spirits.

It is disrespectful to ask what you are making; you are supposed to just do what your parents tell you. They know what is best for you. *I cannot imagine me growing up here, I was a 'why' child.*

So, I did not ask, I just snuck a look at the ceremony calendar, and it only shows that in two days there is a ceremony to salvage sharp weapons. *I don't own a weapon, do you Ibu?*

So, I was making the offerings out the back with the girls from the kitchen. (Not the usual daily offerings.) I had to refer to my notes for every part. *After nearly ten years, I really should know what I am doing.*

I went into the kitchen to find Ibu has a cheat sheet, so after nearly sixty years she still does not know what she is doing... that made me feel much better She looked at mine and told me it was a pathetic attempt, and she will do mine... *Seriously, how could I refuse?*

Oh, and the calendar today says it is not a good day for intercourse, poor Hubby.

15 September 2016 - The Smartarse

The taxman has given Ibu a black box. Ibu must have said black box attached to a computerised cash register. Ibu had some people come from Denpasar to install a computer and train the staff for one week. They were trained to use a new computerised restaurant ordering system. I had not been there when it was installed, nor when the training was done.

I arrived at work today, and the staff did not know how to turn on the computer, the staff that were trained for one week.

So, I showed them how to turn it on.

The staff then did not know how to open the restaurant program, the staff that were trained for one week.

So, I looked at the shortcut on the screen, the one of only two icons on the screen that said 'restoran', and double-clicked. Ta-da! *Now, can I do my own work?*

Ibu came out and said, "You train them, Rasch, you train them!" (she cannot pronounce my name).

Um, I wasn't given the training for one week on this Ibu, they are your staff, and I have nothing to do with your restaurant.

I told Ibu that I had never used that system or any restaurant system and that I had never worked in a restaurant. Well, I have, but back before computers. When I worked weekends after school. Where you just used a notepad and stabbed the order onto a spike at the kitchen window; the same system Ibu's staff have been using until now.

Ibu: "Please Rasch, please Rasch, just show them, you're so smart, they are idiots."

Me: "You can't call them idiots Ibu, you don't know how to use it yourself."

She followed me around nagging me to help. There was no way she would leave me alone. She goes into lockdown mode, and her fixation on one thing can go on for days. I told her I would have a look at it.

It was just a regular computer attached to a receipt printer. It was obvious how to open the software, being that there were no other icons or programs on the computer. It was obvious how to put the order in. Well, it was all obvious to me. For some reason, after one week of training, it was not obvious to anyone else.

So, as I do when I train my staff, I suggested we role-play and do pretend orders, and use the training software provided to do that. *You know, the icon on the screen that in Bahasa Indonesia says 'TRAINING'.*

One of the staff then asked me "What were you fed as a baby, as you are so smart?"

A little surprised, I answered, "I went to school and university."

Thinking about it now, I should have said: "Oh yes, we have smart food for babies in Australia, no need for schools."

Guess I'm not that smart after all.

9 November 2016 - The Wedding

We arrived in the village to see there was a wedding at one of the houses on the main road, as you come down into the village. *It does not look like a huge one, maybe a poor family?*

I walked into our office, and Ibu was sitting on the day bed. From the way Ibu was dressed, it looked like she was going to the wedding. So, I asked her, "Who is getting married?"

Ibu huffed and shook her head unapprovingly, as she does, and said nothing. Okay, I must be in trouble again, that's fine, I will go get a coffee then.

I grabbed my coffee and walked back into our office, greeted Bapak, who had just arrived, not dressed for a wedding. It looked like he was dressed to go to the Bangli Government offices. *I know all his outfits by now.*

Balinese may change outfits five times in one day, depending on where they are going.

So, I had a discussion with him about a few things we need to be done in Bangli, and then he left.

Well, as soon as Bapak walked out the door, Ibu sprang up off the day bed, with that look of 'I have to tell you something'. *I know when she gets close to my ear that she has been spying on staff, or she has gossip.*

It's gossip.

It's about the wedding.

Ibu tells me how it is a twenty-two-year-old girl from the village, marrying a very old American man. Ibu says he is eighty years old.

I tell her, "Maybe he's about sixty, I can't imagine he would be eighty."

She swears he is eighty or older, as he has a walking stick, he's all bent over, fat, and taller than my husband. *Okay, Ibu.*

She continued to tell me the whole story, and that this twenty-two-year-old was pregnant to this eighty-year-old. *He must be younger than eighty, if not, wow that's impressive.*

Then, after her gossip, she asked me with quite some consideration, "Why would she do that? Why would she marry someone that age?"

I answered, "Well, I haven't met her, but could it be for money?" *It just slipped out, oops, I'm a Bitch.*

Ibu contemplated my answer and walked off. You can tell when Ibu is contemplating, you can hear the cogs ticking.

Twenty minutes later, while I was concentrating on emails, Ibu snuck up behind me and was suddenly at my ear again, "Do you love your husband?"

Well, the last time I had heard that sort of question was when we first went to the Catan Sipil (Head of Civil Registry) over ten years ago. He asked Hubby if he loved his wife, while I was sitting there.

Anyway, Ibu continued and declared, "It won't work, this marriage, it won't work. You can't be happy unless you marry for love like Bapak and me, or you two."

Being that Ibu and Bapak spend every day together at work, and so do Hubby and me, I guess we have a lot in common. *Maybe, as Ibu and Bapak's marriage is still going strong after nearly fifty years, and Hubby and I have not killed each other after ten years, she thinks we are on a winner?*

Ibu announced, "Come to the wedding, and you can see for yourself!"

Well, I am a little busy, was not invited, don't know the couple, not interested in gossip, etc. I declined.

'Huff', huff', Ibu walked off.

Three hours later I bumped into Ibu in the village. She was walking into her home to get changed after the wedding. (Going to a wedding in the village is usually a one-hour visit, you do not stay long as it is a burden on the couple to have to talk to you. The couple generally have many guests all invited at different time slots, over three to five days).

Ibu grabbed me and pulled me down the small gang (lane) to her house, pulled me through the front door. *I mean pulls; she has my arm.*

Ibu started to take off her kebaya (Balinese lace blouse), and standing there in her bra, she said, "I think he's dead already."

I am like, "What? Who is dead?"

Ibu screamed, "The old man, the American man!"

I am like, "What the?" easily said in Bahasa Indonesian ("Apa?!")

"HE'S LYING DOWN, HE'S DEAD!"

I am still confused, "As in actually dead?"

"No, but he may as well be. He's so old he can't get through his own wedding. Who needs money that badly that their groom is a corpse?"

I was having visions of 'Weekend at Bernie's' and the groom being moved around the family compound (family property) positioned nicely for the meet and greets.

Then Ibu really started going on and on, how I was spot on, and how she told the mother of the bride what Rach had said about her daughter marrying for money. And how embarrassing this was for the family, and how no one does that in this village. What an inconvenience, if they then have a funeral, and how much that will cost, blah, blah, blah.

In between blah, blahs, and her walking into her little dressing area... I took the opportunity to step out of the house and walk very briskly up the gang... I could hear Ibu screaming out, "You were right, I told them all what you said!"

I started a slow jog.

As to the couple, I wish them the best. As to the family, I am very sorry.

Ibu, thanks a lot, not!

11 November 2016 - The Burnt Toast

It has been bucketing down here with rain for two hours, and the road in front of the hotel has turned into a river. I must leave for a meeting very soon, and I am a little concerned about driving in these conditions. Ibu went into the kitchen to burn rice cakes, so the rain will stop. That's what she told me, when she stood up and announced it.

Ibu has just opened the door into my office from the kitchen, walked in coughing and waving her arms through a cloud of smoke like she has just casually walked out of a burning building. Closed the door (poor staff left in there), and the rain stopped immediately. Ibu looked at me, as if that was perfectly normal, came over and rubbed my shoulders, saying, "Be careful," then walked off.

So, apparently this is what your Balinese mother does for you when she hears you must drive in monsoon rain on a potholed road by yourself. As usual she has not explained why, and I am not allowed to ask.

Now, I'm off to my meeting, and I smell like burnt toast.

15 November 2016 - The Sacrifice

I am in the office, and it is extremely difficult to concentrate. The hotel staff keep coming in the back door of the kitchen with various squealing birds. They have been dripping their blood on the different stages of the new hotel temple they are putting in.

Note to self: I really need to move my office away from the kitchen.

30 November 2016 - The Sleepyhead

The cheeky staff have been at it again. I was trying to have a conversation with Ibu, and she kept falling asleep on the day bed in our office...So, I let her sleep.

She finally woke, and said she had a sore eye.

I asked her why was she so tired?

She told me she did not know why she was tired.

I asked her, "Do you want some eye drops?"

Ibu replied, "Oh, no, Kadek already gave me *Arak."

I said, "What?!"

I looked over at Kadek, who was standing near the doorway, grinning like a Cheshire cat (he never smiles), and I asked him, "Why did you give her that?"

He shrugged and answered, "I don't know."

Ibu fell asleep again.

Another of Ibu's staff came in, and I stated to him, "Nengah, Kadek gave Ibu Arak!"

He replied, "Yes, good for us as she sleeps now instead of complaining non-stop, we can get work done now."

_____
* Arak is homemade alcohol, made from rice or palm flowers, with extremely high alcohol content.

1 December 2016 - The Eye

So, Ibu still has a bad eye, it was the topic of conversation for a good part of the morning at work. Ibu had been overseeing the renovation of the hotel temple, and it looks like some concrete dust had gotten in her eye. I discovered that fact when Ibu pulled a chair up right next to me and pulled her eye open for me to see, while I was on the phone to a client.

So, I have flushed out her eye and put an eye patch on it so she can rest it. Ibu does not rest well. A bit like me, she cannot sit still. Ibu continued to oversee the workers for the rest of the morning.

Ibu is continuing to annoy the staff. Ibu is continuing to annoy me.

4 December 2016 - The Doctor

So, Ibu's bad eye. Well, it started to get worse, and she was annoying all the staff with her whining and freaking them out with her eye patch. So, I rang a medical clinic in Bangli city and made her an appointment with an Eye Specialist.

Bapak took her to the Doctor. (This is an actual medical clinic, not the Witch Doctor.) I left work soon after.

I just rang her to ask her what the Doctor had said.

Ibu told me, "Oh, it's all better now!"

Relieved, I asked, "Great, it's not a cataract, is it?" (I had noticed some little growths near her pupil.)

"No, not a cataract!"

So, I inquired, "What did the Doctor say it was?"

Ibu answered, "He said, Bapak is not praying enough."

Bless their cotton socks.

15 December 2016 - The Table

This morning I walked around to the front of our office and saw we had guests standing there, patiently waiting for our guide to take them canoeing. I knew they were canoeing, as they were wearing lifejackets. *At least that means my staff showed up for work.*

However, the guests must have been standing there at least twenty minutes, as it was past the starting time. So, I apologised to the guests and told them I would go look to see what was going on. I headed off in search of a staff member.

We have twins that work for us on separate days, and I always mix them up. I can only tell which one is which when they smile, as one has a gap in his teeth. I was sure Cheery was the one working today. *Our manager, Nengah, does not start until the afternoon, so, I better sort this out myself.*

Ibu also has two staff called Nengah, we both have staff called Wayan, so that can also be confusing. Wayan is a first-born child's name in Bali for children (unisex name) born into the Sudra (low) caste. As there are only two other choices for boys' names, for your first born it is very common. Nengah is a second born name choice.

I saw Ibu, and I asked, "Ibu, do you know where Cheery is? The guests have been waiting."

Ibu replied, "Oh I think he's already gone down to the lake."

So, I walked down to the lake—no Cheery. I came back, apologised to the guests again, and I spotted Ibu's Nengah, so I asked him, "Where's Cheery?"

He replied, "Cheery does not work today, today Skinny work (Cheery's twin). Skinny is building Ibu a table."

Hmm? Ibu loves to use my staff.

So, I went around the corner, sure enough there he was welding up a table, with Ibu standing over him shouting orders. I said, "Skinny, the guests are waiting."

He looked at me nervously and said nothing.

We both looked at Ibu. Ibu screamed at me, "THE GUESTS WILL JUST HAVE TO WAIT! WHAT GOOD TO ME IS A THREE-LEGGED TABLE?"

19 December 2016 - The Phones

There seemed to be an issue with the phone at the office, and no one was answering. So, I phoned a staff member's mobile phone, and she was not at work. I phoned another, he did not answer. So, I sent an email at 9.00am this morning:

Good morning

I need someone to call me as soon as possible, please. It seems the phones are down again. I have sent Komang and Nengah a WhatsApp as well. I just need anyone from the office to call me as soon as possible.

Kind regards Rach

Email reply at 10.30 am, from Nengah, in English, sort of:

Dear Rach Ok Thank You We are really sorry our internet connection wash very slow

Great, that means Nengah is in the office. I called the office, no answer.

At 2.00 pm. I tried calling various phones, no answer, the main phone seemed to be connected to a fax. *We don't have a fax?*

I tried again at 3.00 pm, no luck.

It is now 4.30 pm - No one has phoned me back yet.

Note to self: check if we now have a fax, and teach staff to pick up the phone when it rings.

24 December 2016 - Email deciphering

It takes me a while to work out what my manager Nengah is trying to say, when he answers emails in English. Today's reply to me, after I personally sent him an email with the list of guest bookings for today, as one of our staff is sick:

Hi Rach. Thank you for your appeal Regards Nengah.

Tomorrow when I am drunk, he can try and decipher mine.

Chapter 2 - Not the Average Bali Hotel

2 Jan 2017 - The Faulty Towers

Oh, dear... I will not be up at the hotel, until the 5th, to see what Nengah has done, but he's at it again. He likes to take on the maintenance tasks in the hotel, himself. *Probably to avoid doing his own work.*

Last week I told Nengah to have someone from maintenance at the hotel paint a new grey PVC pipe white, in one of our booked hotel room bathrooms, so it would not stand out against the white tiles. I even showed him, caressed it gently to make sure he understood.

I came back to find he had painted all the chrome taps white instead.

Today I sent an email:

Maintenance: Room 9 & 10 - have they fixed and painted all the walls in these rooms yet?

Nengah's reply:

Yes, I have already fixed these rooms ready. I do only little paint on the head of the bed.

31 January 2017 - The Chickens

Ibu is shaking her head because I am talking to the chickens in a bag near the kitchen. The ones she is about to sacrifice.

Note to self: Check Ceremony Calendar before going into the office.

3 February 2017 - The Ultimate Spy

Ibu is the Ultimate Spy, she has been showing me how she pretends to sleep on the daybed next to my desk, but she is actually spying on the staff, with one eye on the CCTV screen.

Note to self: - Ibu now knows how the CCTV works, remember this when trying to hide from her.

19 February 2017 - The Roof

We had not been to the office for one week, due to significant landslides and flooding in the area. Half of the main road down to the village slid into the caldera somewhere.

We arrived at the hotel this morning. Greeted by Ibu and Bapak as usual. I always have a little hesitancy when I greet Ibu, based on what mood she is in. Ibu seemed fine, she asked why we were not at work for so long, why no guests, etc. I commented in English to one of the staff, so she would not understand, that tourists have been told, 'Kintamani is dangerous', so not to expect many tourists around.

One of our staff arrived, and Hubby followed him to open our equipment storage office, (where we store all our equipment - guests are greeted by our team and get equipment from that room, etc.) to find the ceiling had caved in.

We now have a swimming pool instead of an office, and everything is covered in mouse poo and thirty years of ceiling crap.

We have been through this before; we have learnt it is not a matter of just fixing the roof. It is a matter of Bapak consulting the auspicious Balinese calendar to see which day is a 'Good day, to fix the roof'.

The first time, in 2012, it was sixty-nine days before the roof could be fixed. That time we were a little gobsmacked as it was the wet season, and the office would have filled with water to the ceiling within sixty-nine days. However, I re-worded the question and asked if there was a date that we could move offices, as they had a similar room next door. Bapak looked up the calendar and it showed that a good date to move, would be in seventeen days.

So, we put tarps all over everything. Luckily, we could paint the new space, and move equipment in earlier. We just could not physically open for seventeen days, as the calendar said so.

So, today I was calm, while the staff pushed the filthy water out and down the steps, and everything was taken out to dry in the sun.

I knew the drill, so I went to Ibu to discuss a solution. As in, 'where is our new office you promised?' As expected, I got, 'Yeah, yeah, go talk to Bapak, he will let you know'.

Bapak was sitting at his laptop in our shared office, which I have been sharing with him since Ibu last moved our main office to the back of the hotel. Ibu moved us, as she wanted to renovate our office, however, instead of renovating it, she demolished it and built a room for guests. This was not in 2012, this was just another one of the times Ibu moved our office.

The new office space was supposed to be a temporary solution. I did not mind sharing with Bapak short term. I had to share, as the room she allocated us had no power outlets, and the Wi-Fi did not reach there. Ibu, six months later presented us with our new office, which was only 1.2 metres wide and four metres long. It was great for equipment storage, but we could not fit our desks in there, it did not have a toilet, it still did not have power outlets, guests could not be greeted in there. So, we went from a 5-metre x 6-metre office with a toilet, and a storeroom, to a storeroom, that Ibu thought would suffice.

As I approached our shared office, Bapak seemed very anxious. He needed my help immediately. He told me he had tried calling me for three days, but I had not answered my phone. *I'm not sure what number he was calling as my staff had contacted me many times?*

He could not work out how to log into Facebook!

So, as I was standing next to him at his laptop, leaning over to try and log him in, *(this is so important? So, not, Bapak)* Bapak let out the longest, loudest fart. *Bloody hell, instant karma for my evil thoughts.*

He continued to talk to me over this foul noise, which seemed to go on for an eternity.

After the fart, and working out that he had his password wrong, as he had forgotten what year he was born in, we finally got him into Facebook. *Phew crisis over.*

So, I approached the topic of the roof, "Yeah, yeah, I will let you know."

Off I went, as I had a meeting at the school. I had two VIPs coming that I was taking to see the school paving they had paid for. I left Bapak with his social media fix.

When I returned with the VIPs, we sat down for lunch. Bapak approached us to interrupt our lunch; now this is not a done thing in Bali, you do not interrupt or talk to people eating. *This time it must be important.*

Bapak had a new smartphone and had tried to upload some photos (one of us eating) onto Facebook, but the photos were just sitting there. I had no idea how to use his fancy phone, so I apologised to our VIPs and just clicked anything I could. The phone made some noises, and it uploaded the photos. *Crisis averted.*

It was time to take our VIP guests back to their hotel, so I said to Bapak, "I need to go home now. Can you please look up the calendar and let my Nengah know when we can fix the roof?"

Bapak answered, "Yeah, yeah."

So, in our formal way of talking in Balinese to your father, I asked for his permission to go home. He gave permission, wished me a safe journey, and then said in English with a giggle, "Kintamani Dangerous."

Obviously, yesterday was the day in the auspicious calendar to 'Fix Facebook'. I am still waiting to hear when it is the day to 'Fix the roof'.

Sabar Sabar (be patient in Bahasa Indonesian).

23 February 2017 - Roof Update

Bapak rang me today to tell me it was probably best that we moved to another room, as it will be a while before it is a good date in the calendar to fix the roof. He advised we could move any date... and there will be a ceremony once we officially have moved... on the correct date for a 'new office'.

So, I emailed my office manager:

> Nengah, I have spoken to Bapak, and we will move to the large back room, late next week, when we are not so busy.
> In the meantime, please arrange a new lock for the door etc.

He sent back this email, in English, sort of:

> Okey Rach That god idea Ibu have discusss with tukang* already, she tell me to start to take roof off in fiew days Thank you, Nengah.

I guess Ibu does not need the calendar?

This will be our fourth move, so I think Nengah and I will just stay with Bapak, until we build our own office.

I hope she waits till all our stuff is out of the office before the roof comes off... I guess it was 'God's idea'?

_____
* A tukang is a building worker.

26 February 2017 - The Toiletries

Last month I had a meeting with Ibu and Bapak about bringing their hotel into this century, and how in a certain price range, tourists expected toiletries. Ibu found this very difficult to understand; I mean I had already made them put in soap and toilet paper in the rooms, what more could tourists want? It is hard enough now for the staff to remember that bloody stupid toilet paper, I mean who uses that stuff anyway? Don't Bules wash? They have a hose, blah, blah, blah.

So, after Ibu calmed down about the loo paper, I again approached the toiletries. Her first reaction when I told her that in that price range you would put in the rooms a small bottle of shampoo, conditioner, soap, maybe toothbrush, toothpaste, comb, etc., was: "BUT WHAT IF THEY STEAL THEM?"

Today I brought her some samples, so she could have a look at what I meant. I handed her the plastic bag of small bottles of shampoo and conditioner, toothpaste and comb set I had gotten from a friend staying in a hotel. Ibu took the bag from my hand, tied it up and put it in the back room behind the kitchen. Without a 'thank you' or even a word, Ibu went off to the garden, where a mattress from a room was lying in the sun.

Determined, I went and retrieved the bag of toiletries, went out to the garden, and stood next to Ibu. I started to pull out the bottles one by one to show her and explained, "So this is what you need to buy."

She waved her hand at me as she does, a bit like shooing away a fly, shook her head and then stated, "The Bule tourists don't need that, they don't even have a bath!"

The wrong day to explain this after two guests with very long dreadlocks had just checked out and she was fumigating their room for bed bugs.

28 February 2017 - The Joker

Hubby and I were just having a quick coffee in the kitchen with Ibu, and she said to Hubby, "All the people in the village think you two take drugs!"

Hubby quite shocked, replied, "Who thinks that?!"

The look on my face must have been too much for Ibu to cope with. She bent over, held her stomach from laughing and blurted, "I was just kidding!"

Ibu is currently sitting down resting, as she exhausted herself from laughing at her own joke.

9 April 2017 - The TV

I have not been at work for a few days, trying to get a lot of the end of financial year stuff done, so I was working from home... *so no Ibu distractions.*

I got to the office today, and I went into the kitchen to get my morning lecture over coffee from Ibu. Today's lecture was, that people will think we have gone bankrupt since I have not been at work for five days... even though Hubby has been there... Yep, that's Ibu's way of thinking for you.

Lecture done and I went and set up my laptop on my desk to start printing off documents, and then I got called off for something.

I came back to find Ibu had moved my laptop from my desk and put it on the dining table, which is pushed up against the back wall of the office. The table is near the kitchen door, and bit of a high traffic area. Ibu had also had a small TV brought in and placed on a cabinet across the room. From where my chair had been placed, I was now facing the TV. However, the kitchen door was open against the table, so I could not see the TV from where she had moved me. *WTF! Oh well, too busy to move back, have some urgent emails to send.*

Once I sat down, she pulled a rocking chair up to the table, right next to my laptop, facing the TV and then walked off into the kitchen. *New chair, I have never seen that one before?*

I ignored what she was up to, stared at my laptop and start composing.

Ibu returned, turned the TV on, then sat in her chair on my left.

She turned her head around to me like a little puppy and said, "Now you can work, and we can be close."

I answered, "Ibu, but I am trying to work" and I signaled to the TV.

Ibu looked at me with puppy dog eyes and, "Yes I blocked the TV with the door, so you won't be distracted." Then turned back to look at her Indian soap opera, which was on the loudest I think a TV could go.

It's just not going to happen today.

I went to take a photo of her, but she jumped up, knocked the table, and ran into the kitchen screaming, "Arrghhh! I forget there's something on the stove!"

I am not going into the office tomorrow.

17 April 2017- The Skip Out

Well, what a big weekend that was, and I am not talking about an Easter drinking session. Now that I am writing this, I remember my Australian family Easters. I probably would feel just as tired at this moment... but not a drop of alcohol was consumed on my weekend.

So, Saturday was Kuningan. (Last day of a Balinese family ten day ceremony, where dead ancestors come to Bali and are ceremonially fed and entertained.) Ibu & Bapak were up early for the very last day of the ten days of entertaining and feeding their Ancestral ghosts. *Quite glad they've gone. I think everyone is, it is quite exhausting having that many house guests, whether they need a physical bed or not.*

I arrived at the hotel, to find all my staff were there. *Yay, happy dance.*

But, none of Ibu and Bapak's... not one.

I was only there to attend the ceremony. Ibu had the whole family there, all gathering around the family temple, in the hotel grounds. Ibu was sooo tired, Bapak looked stressed (not a usual look), and I went into stealth mode, telling them it would be okay, I would help.

So, off they went to visit the rest of the family temples in the village (we have a few)... *Well, I got out of that okay, now I don't have to Temple Hop...I will just start ringing the staff, and they will filter in after praying.*

WRONG.

So, I checked with my staff, we had six guests going canoeing, and Ibu had sixty-three guests that needed breakfast and to check out that morning.... *Umm?*

Thank God, the Chef wandered in. Then my wonderful work experience girl Made walked in and starting doing breakfast orders. One of the twins then stepped in and started serving the guests in the restaurant, and I felt all was okay... until I, me, personally had to check out guests, *Ummmmmmm?*

But we got through it, and we were proud of ourselves.

Ibu and Bapak returned at noon, "Thank you, thank you, thank you, etc., you are the best in the world, etc."

I left at 1.00 pm feeling proud and exhausted.

On the way home in the car, I got a call from one of Ibu's staff. (Yes, he came to work at 2.00 pm.) Um, one of the guests left and did not pay!! *Did we stuff that up?*

Then I realised. *Hang on, guests pay when they check-in.*

Turned out some low life Germans had snuck out without paying. (They convinced one of Ibu's staff that they would pay in the morning, a real fast talker.) I told them to get Nengah to look at the CCTV. He eventually found the footage and could see that they were sneaking past behind Ibu and Bapak in the early morning, before I started work.

Get this, they tiptoed behind them while Ibu and Bapak WERE PRAYING, and bloody left!

Poor Ibu and Bapak have no idea what to do... so, I told them I will go back in the morning, and we will work it out.

17 April 2017- The Coffee Pots

Back to work this morning, to find out there is a BIG CEREMONY. *Hang on, yesterday it was all over?*

No today is BIG CEREMONY!

Ibu had my ceremony clothes ready for me, and it was starting immediately.

Me: "Umm, Ibu. We have guests, and my staff haven't arrived yet."

"It's okay," she declared, "Dress them up, they can watch, and hurry!"

Our guests did get to witness a beautiful ceremony. The ceremony I, had to leave and be in, and I had no idea what it is for, it would be disrespectful to ask, and I am too tired to look it up. Our guests did not dress up in ceremonial attire, as they were there for canoeing.

I also discovered where my staff were, they were at the ceremony.

Due to the floods, we spent the ceremony standing in water, as there is no longer a water's edge to the lake. Well, standing in crops underwater, but it was a beautiful ceremony, and our guests took some photos, from the canoes, that they shared with me.

Then it was on the phone to Booking.com to try and track down these guests that did not pay and trying to find the CCTV footage again.

Then I had to accompany our guests to the village for their tour as Wayan, our part-time Guide/Driver had not come back from the ceremony. *I know it is over Wayan, where the hell are you?*

So, I quickly showed Bapak how to use the CCTV. Bapak sat down in his underwear (a white singlet top) and a sarong, at my desk to survey the footage, so I chose that time to leave... Bapak is now hooked, he was still there looking at the CCTV three hours later when I got back (but he's just fallen asleep at my desk). He is now also the Ultimate Spy, sort of, he will need to stay awake!

So, in the middle of German thieves, lack of staff, me having a BIG CEREMONY, two tours with only one staff person, and everything else that was going on... Ibu discovered there is a thing that keeps coffee and teapots warm, and she is hooked. She must have them.

So, I have Bapak glued to the CCTV until he falls asleep on my desk and Ibu insisting that while I am at a meeting at the Department of Employment in Denpasar tomorrow, I need to find her a coffee pot thingy.

I quickly looked up on google to confirm what she was after. I confirmed she wanted the glass pots that sit on warming plates. Ibu looked at the picture on the screen and asked me to scroll and find her more. I told her I did not have time; she would need one of her staff to search for her later. Ibu smacked me on the shoulder, "Look now, Look now."

Yeah, right Ibu, while I am also trying to get you a police report, and warn other hotels, of your bloody Germans.

Ibu followed me around the hotel, talking non-stop, about coffee pots until I left, "You get Ibu Coffee pots tomorrow, ya?"

18 April 2017 - The Coffee Pots Continued

So, today we headed off to Denpasar first, and the phone calls from Ibu started. Fourteen of them in fact, between 9.00 am, and 12 noon... that bloody coffee pot warmer is all she could talk about.

While waiting at our meeting at the Department of Employment in Renon, Denpasar, I called Bapak. He didn't answer, every time I rang I spoke to one of his staff and I attempted to ask: Has Bapak found the car park CCTV footage? (My staff have the day off.) Have Booking.com rung? Has the other hotel, that may have also had the bloody Germans, in their hotel, stealing paintings, rung? Has Bapak gone to the police?

Every time I rang, I could hear Ibu screaming in the background, "Has she found the coffee pots?"

OMG! The stores don't even open for another hour.

Every time I tried to make a phone call or send an email from my phone this morning, I got interrupted with a call from one of Ibu's staff. They would hand the phone to Ibu and all I got was, "Rasch, have you found the coffee pots?" Blah, blah, blah!

After our meeting, we went to three department stores and all out of coffee pots.

Now, we must drive for two hours up to Bangli for our next meeting, so Ibu will just have to wait until they have stock again.

Oh, Ibu and Bapak have decided they will not be pressing charges on the Germans as it is bad Karma.

Speaking of Karma, I want to know what I must have done wrong to deserve the bloody coffee pot calls.

19 April 2017 - The Condoms

Ibu's staff had been asking me for weeks, what on earth their guests are talking about when they ask if they have 'Stubby holders?'

So, Hubby was going up to the office and I gave him six stubby holders from our house, for Ibu, so she could see what they were, and she could borrow for now if guests requested them.

Hubby rang me to tell me Ibu got so excited, she had forgotten about the coffee pots and told Hubby, "Get fifty of them! Large and small!"

Hubby said that when Bapak came in and asked what they were, Ibu proudly told Bapak, "Beer Condoms."

20 April 2017 - Happy Coffee Pots

Ibu was thrilled we finally got her coffee pots, so we posed together for a photo with the new pots.

Hubby was the one that found them and went and bought them for her, but she said he could not be in the photo, because he was too ugly.

23 April 2017 - The Patience

Sabar Sabar; it means 'to be patient', something you must learn in Bali. *Although locals have not applied it to driving.*

Since living in Bali, we have worked out that you should only plan to do one thing in one day, if you need to drive anywhere.

Today my only plan was to go down to the Printers.

Usually, I would print at work, but the printer is being fixed, for three weeks now, Sabar Sabar.

Or, I would print at home, but our laptop broke, and the new one is not compatible with the old printer; the new printers for OS10 are not available in Bali yet, Sabar Sabar.

Now, I blame myself, as I am leaving checking the yearly tax documents a bit late. Still, I really needed to triple-check them as Bapak has also been checking his taxes and when I am at the office, he sings his, yep. "Seratus lima ratus lima ratus" (one hundred, five hundred, five hundred), with a little jig in his seat mind you. Sabar Sabar

So, I was done, everything checked. It was on the data stick, ready to go, and I opened our front gate to find my lovely neighbour across the road has concreted his driveway... and he thought it would be nice to do ours as well. *Sabar Sabar.*

1 May 2017 - The Bathrooms

So, yesterday a big part of my day was spent with Ibu and five building workers in a small two metre x three metre room trying to design a bathroom for the two new hotel rooms she is having built.

Now, Ibu insisted only a bath was needed in the new bathrooms, as locals use baths. It took me a lot of explaining that a shower was also needed, as Westerners use showers, and baths. Ibu could not quite work out my insisting on a shower, and not a seventy-centimetre enclosed corner shower box that she thought would work. *I mean the rooms will be beautiful, why spoil it with a bloody shower box that will feel like you are on a ship.*

Especially next to an oval Terrazzo bathtub (which she is also obsessed about, more so than coffee pots).

So, I was trying to explain how Westerners like to have a shower, and she would cut out her Western market without one. Although Ibu agreed with my suggestion of a rain shower, we had to go through the height issue of a shower. I mean she could not work out what was wrong with the showers she had installed in the other older rooms above the toilets. The way they installed the showers in the other rooms, after years of us insisting they were needed, was: You turn the tap on from the bath tap fitting. Yet the handheld showerhead sits in a bracket on the wall, one metre from the bath, above the toilet, and you must climb into the bath to turn it on. If you do not wish to hold the shower, you can climb out of the tub and stand in front of the toilet. That is if the water pressure is high enough. Otherwise, you may as well sit on the toilet to shower. When I pointed out this little obstacle in showering, Ibu argued, "What is the problem? There is a shower, why do Bules complain about everything?"

So, I explained to Ibu, that in the last beautiful room she had built, where there was a rain shower, Hubby at six-foot-four, stood in that shower, and it was at his chest height, therefore, Hubby would have difficulty washing his hair. Ibu went off on a tangent, as she does, and got fixated on talking about hair washing... asking me, "How do you wash your hair? How often do you wash your hair?"

This hair washing interrogation went on for so long that we decided to have a coffee break.

While sitting in the restaurant chatting over coffee, Ibu announced loudly, "See those tourists wouldn't want a shower!" and pointed into the garden.

I looked over, and there were three French guys with dreadlocks sunning themselves in the garden Bales. *I am glad they do not speak Indonesian.*

Ibu went on and on about how they would never wash their hair, continuingly pointing at them. I literally had to slap her hand down, as pointing and glaring at your guests, while yelling, is not exactly the done thing, in the world of hospitality. *Or any world, seriously Ibu.*

So, coffee break over and back to the hotel room, with more building workers (tukangs), all discussing this shower, toilet placement, etc. Five men and Ibu and me, all with sticks in our hands drawing out ideas of what would work, on the sand on the floor. (They do not lay cement foundations here, just sand.) There was me, pulling sticks out of their hands and saying to Ibu, 'Don't listen to them, they have never used a shower or a Western toilet in their bloody life!' 'You can't have a bloody shower face out the door.' 'You can't put a toilet in a corner up against the two walls as people sit on it, not squat on it!' I was literally miming sitting on a toilet at this stage. *We are not getting anywhere; I may as well go home.*

Suddenly, the room went darker, and a huge figure stood in the doorway—a huge man in an Army uniform carrying a rifle and a huge knife. *Gee, I didn't mean to upset the tukangs with my comments. I wasn't that rough pulling the sticks out of their hands.*

The tukangs scattered like flies, I mean this was the largest Balinese man I had ever seen. He was blocking the light into the room. It was a very dramatic entrance, especially if you have watched too many action films.

Nope, it wasn't me, it was that one of the French guests thought it was fine to walk up the street wearing not much more than bikini bottoms and a very tight singlet crop top. So, he explained in fast Balinese, why he was there. I did not understand him, until Ibu declared, "It's her guest", referring to me.

I was escorted to my office to see if we had booked this guest, who he referred to as a 'Joged' in the street. (Basically an erotic dancer - *they should not be in the street*.) Ibu followed us in.

I was being grilled by the Army guy, who had pulled up a chair and was sitting right next to me, at my desk, until I eventually charmed him. (Ibu giggling to herself.)

Then said girl walked back into the hotel, and past the window of our office; the Army guy yelled out in English, "Hey Girl."

Oh, boy!

He demanded, to me, "You go, go talk to her!"

I was like, "Ah, no way, she's not my guest, and she's French, she will bite my head off."

He laughed and said okay, he would talk to her. Luckily, at that minute, our guests came back from canoeing, and I used that as an excuse to excuse myself.

I returned later to see Army Dude was having a coffee and half-naked French girl was happily sitting in the Bale with her half-naked friends. *It is quite a cold day; dreadlocks must keep you warm.*

Ibu grabbed me and pulled me into my office with her 'whisper, whisper'. If Ibu cups my ear and talks right into my ear, I know Ibu thinks this is the only way to make sure everyone else will not hear, as she has a very loud voice. *But it is so bloody obvious, and it hurts my ear.*

Usually, she makes us hide behind a door as well.

Ibu loudly whispered, cupping my ear, "He likes you (the Army dude), he thinks you are funny and very smart, and that's good for us as we will have no problems here, so you go talk to him some more and charm him some more."

I looked at her with one of those looks I give her (that she taught me) and then thought for a moment, and said, "But Ibu, what about the bathroom, I have to leave in twenty minutes."

Oh, Boy, Ibu grabbed me and dragged me to the building site, so fast we were tripping over wood, etc., and told all the tukangs, "Whatever she says, you do!!"

Will be interesting to see what they have done as I had to leave shortly after that.

3 May 2017 - The Child

I had two little girls follow me around the village today. One girl told me she was from Karangasem originally. I had never met her before, she did not speak any Indonesian, only Balinese, Balinese that I did not speak. There are three levels of Balinese and I only speak, well attempt to speak, informal Balinese. I was not sure what level she was speaking.

I knew the other child well, as one of my kids practically raised her. She is seven years old and cooks and cleans for her elderly grandparents. Her parents visit her when they can, they work on Legian beach, in the south of Bali. Maybe once every three months they come up to visit, so we keep an eye on the family, supply drinking water, medicine, check grandma's blood sugar levels (diabetic), clothes, toothbrushes, etc.

This new little girl had befriended the one we knew; I would guess she is around five year old. As they followed me around the small gangs of the village, she kept worrying that it would rain 'chocolate rain'. The rain kept starting to spit lightly, then clear, she would ask me 'where would we go when the chocolate rain comes?' That was about all I understood, as her Balinese was so different. She continuously interrupted me as I was trying to talk with people, and I told her to hush it. She would ask, "Where do we go when it rains?"

I would assure her, "Anyone's house, it is okay, everyone is family here."

She continued to follow me around the village, and she kept climbing up into the offering boxes and stealing the candy. Candy is often put in canang sari and offered as a sweet treat to the spirits, God etc.

Then, as we walked past one house, she started going through their garbage. I grabbed her hands and dragged her into the house and asked the old lady homeowner, if I could use her water to wash this kid's hands. I scolded the child for going through the garbage and then asked the old lady if she knew who this kid was. She did not, she had never seen her before.

She continued to follow me, and when we stopped at one of our foster kids' grandma's house to have a snack, I rang my foster daughter and told her to come there after school. Grandma fed the little girl, she could not understand her either, and she is Balinese.

Then my foster daughter came and spoke to her (she has been learning medium Balinese at school), and we worked out that was what she was speaking. Grandma was not educated, so had not learnt any medium Balinese. Putu listened to her, and then she explained the story of this little girl to us. Her family had died in the recent landslides, she was displaced and scared of the chocolate rain that took her family and her home. The poor kid kept wanting to hold my hand all day.

I guess we have another mouth to feed. It is a bit like puppies, they just follow me home.

She has so many head lice I am scared to check my head.

10 May 2017 - The Toast, again

I walked through the hotel restaurant this morning, to see that 'What the?' look on a guest's face. *It is funny how people will pick up their food and turn it over a few times, just to make sure they are not imagining things.*

I went into the kitchen, and I said to Wayan, who is the hotel manager, and was in the kitchen, "What the hell is going on with the toast?"

He looked at me and gave me the same answer he gives me to every question I ask him, in English: "I dun know, yeah."

"Wayan, the toast is green!"

Wayan: "Oh, yes, we ran out of bread."

"But, Wayan, that is pandan cake, you are serving... with fried eggs?"

"Yes." Wayan said, proudly.

"Wayan, if you have run out of bread, then you tell the guest, you have run out of bread. A Westerner does not want to eat their fried eggs on cake."

Wayan, "Oh, we like pandan, it's very delicious."

Me, "Do you eat it with eggs?"

Wayan, "Oh, no, it's sweet, we eat as a dessert."

Now, that particular guest, that was served the pandan cake, was a young Australian girl, on a tour group, her first time overseas. I can imagine she grew up with light green kitchen sponges that they have in Australia, that looked identical to her 'toast'.

11 June 2017 - The Cheat

We have started our ceremony preparations today for the blessing of our new office ceremony. It involves making a rather large basket of various smaller offerings, called a Mecaru (offering for blessing the new office, placed on the ground) and there is a bit of an order to the placement of all the materials. Ibu has already given me a hard time for not remembering how to place things.

I just caught Ibu and my staff, on my computer, checking instructions on YouTube, on how to make the offerings, and the cheat sheet is out. *Sprung!*

14 June 2017 - The Offerings

Okay, got that wrong, Ibu is pulling apart my Mecaru for our Melaspas ceremony (cleansing and purification of our newly renovated office). And, I used the cheat-sheet... *I blame her for gossiping in my ear the whole time!*

I had to walk away, as now she has exposed the dead black bird she put in there earlier. *I can't look at that poor thing.*

19 June 2017 - The Bras

We had a donation for the women in our village, of a massive bag of bras, from some guests going on one of our tours, which we collected in Sanur. When we arrived at the hotel, I asked one of the staff to put the bag of bras in my office, so I could sort them for our guests to hand out personally to locals on their walking tour in the village. Ibu spotted the bag... "What's in that?"

I told her, "That is a bag of bras for the locals."

So, Ibu pulled one out and put it on over her jumper. I went and got one of the guests (who has read the Ibu Chronicles), so she could witness for herself what I put up with, and Ibu had already removed the bra. Ibu was all sweet and said to the guest, in English, "Thank you, thank you". Ibu explained to the guest how all the bras she had were so itchy etc., by scratching herself, of course.

The guest fell for it, so Ibu is getting a bra, or two.

Then it was time for the group to head out canoeing, but our staff member who takes them canoeing was missing... Ibu had sent him shopping. *I wish she would stop using my staff, but I know Ibu too well, there is something behind this.*

So, I ended up helping the guests with their equipment, until the staff member returned and then I went back to my office. Ibu passed me with a very guilty look on her face.

I decided I better get the bras sorted and get them out of my office before she wanted more. I sat down to slowly sort the bag out, placing my hand in the bag and gently pulling them out one by one. Then Ibu came in and sat down next to me, and started pulling them all out onto my lap and throwing them about until she found more that would fit her.

"Ibu, we can only have ten for the whole village, and we have already taken six." *Okay, little white lie.*

Ibu ignored my comment and continued to pull them all out. At one stage, I discovered she was sitting on two bras.

One of my staff, Made came in to see what Ibu and I were arguing about. Made is new, she said to me, "Sabar, sabar (be patient)."

I explained to Made that it is not about being patient, it is about dealing with a very naughty, cheeky Ibu. Ibu started piling all the bras on top of me and making strange faces, then pretending she was a monkey, then some other weird creature. I was covered in bras, Ibu seemed to have hidden two more under her leg and two behind her back, and then she started trying to put a bra on me. Made picked up my phone and started to take photos, as she thought the two of us were hilarious.

My other staff already know Ibu, so they are used to this behaviour. I guess for a new person, Ibu and my relationship may be a little bit strange, but at least now I have photographic evidence of what I put up with.

Chapter 3 - Cultural Differences

19 August 2017 - The Chinese Tourists

So, where to start, especially when Ibu gives me new material every day, such as today. I will save that for later.

It all started a long, long, time ago in a far-off land, well just a day I was not at work. A little cutie salesperson (according to Nengah, my staff member of ten years since yesterday) came into the hotel, to sell Ibu the idea of Chinese Groups staying at her hotel.

Well, I would not have fallen for her charm, in fact, I would have marched her cute butt, right out the door. But Ibu alas, did not know the Chinese tourists' reputation, and signed up for this great contract of, twenty Chinese tourists staying in the hotel, once a week, forever.

So, I arrived one day, to hear all about this exciting new group coming, who had blocked out ten rooms in the hotel, once a week for the next year. And, how on those nights, they would have the buffet, at IDR 65,000, all you can eat. (That's AU$6.50 including taxes.) I sighed, looked at Ibu, with the headshake she taught me, and said, "Well it's a bit late now if you signed a contract." *If only she had realised that is like offering Hubby a buffet, she will go bankrupt.*

Ibu looked at me, shook her head, and walked off, as if I have no idea.

Week One: Well, Ibu got the shock of her life, the Chinese filled plastic bags with food to take to their room, the buffet was emptied in a record ten minutes. Ibu could not work out how that had happened.

Week Two: The Chinese brought their little gas cooker and used the garden Bales for cooking up a storm, and a brand-new toilet seat was destroyed. Apparently, the toilet seat was good for cutting up the chicken they were cooking.

Week Three: Ibu Does Not Like the Chinese!

Let's fast forward to the other day. We arrived at work, and Ibu was 'Pusing' (dizzy/stressed), basically dizzy from the Chinese Group.

They had decided to go down to the lake, buy some fresh fish from a local fisherman, walk into the hotel kitchen and demand to cook their fish...Not one of the staff spoke Chinese, and their lovely guide was asleep. So, they marched into the kitchen, cooked their fish, left their dishes, a very messy kitchen, and very happy Chinese. They also left the incredibly surprised kitchen staff to stay back and work overtime (without pay), to clean up the mess.

The next morning, the Chinese had their breakfast; no buffet for breakfast, as Ibu had learnt that one. They must have still been hungry, as pop-mei noodles soon appeared, and twenty Chinese guests soon appeared in the kitchen again, demanding hot water, chanting in English, "Hot water, hot water!"

We arrived, after not having been there for a few days. Ibu was covered in traditional medicinal herbs and lying in my office, pusing again. She told us the story of the fish cooking and the hot water song. So, we taught her some words, in Chinese, such as, 'Bu Hao' (no good).

Having learnt some phrases in Chinese has helped us in tourism, and at McDonald's, and supermarkets in Bali, when you are pushed in front of, yelled over the top of, run over with a trolley, etc. 'No Good!' in Chinese seems to work. If not, just push them back, they are fine with it. That is how it is done where they are from. (My Chinese girlfriend taught me that one).

28 August 2017 - The First Haircut

So, continuing where we left off, the other day, with Ibu's headache from the Chinese Guests, we finally got to preparing for grandchild number thirteen's first haircut ceremony. Not my grandchild, Ibu's.

A child's first haircut is an important ceremony to the Balinese, held when the child is 210 days old. Ibu decided that I needed to learn how to do this by repetition, just like the Balinese learn. So, this was my tenth one. However, this was her daughter-in-law's big day, it was her fourth child, and she was to prepare the offerings, while I watched, and Ibu supervised...*I do have work to do, but this is more important.*

The preparations were already set up outside, the offerings just needed to be put together in the correct order. Ibu and I took turns holding the grandchild, so said child's mother, could put together the offerings.

Next to the offering set up, was a large oven, which was usually in the kitchen; however, today it seemed to have been moved outside, and part of this set up... My curious mind wanted to know; *When on earth did anything made in an oven come into the offerings?*

I had to know, and I kept peering in the oven, at the cake tin inside, wondering what amazing cake was going to come out of there. Ibu is traditional in all she does, so cakes have always been steamed above the rice cooking, not baked in an oven...*Has Ibu gone modern on me?*

I had some work to do, so I kept disappearing, only to hear my name screamed from outside, so I kept going back to observe, and smell the cake.

Now, the cake started to have a very distinct smell, it smelt delish, but the smell was familiar.

I was back at my observation spot, looking over at the oven, out of the corner of my eye...*I must be patient 'sabar sabar'. If I ask Ibu, what is the cake for, which part has the cake, what type of cake?...all those questions, then I have not learnt anything...I must just watch, observe and learn (or just shut up)*...Sometimes I feel like the Karate Kid.

I was a little chuffed that Ibu's daughter-in-law made mistakes in the layering of the offerings. And that Ibu huffed at her and did the headshakes and signal to the correct order of things. *I thought that it was just me that got it wrong.*

So, the offerings were completed, and I was nearly bursting and confused. *What about the cake?*

Which by now, I believed may not be a cake, but some amazing smelling bread. *Since when do we put bread in the offerings?*

Ibu walked off into the garden to rock the baby and the moment of truth came. The cook, Doyok, came out of the kitchen and opened the oven. I asked him quietly, "What is that?"...*I can ask him.*

He answered, "Pizza!"

I said, "Apa?" (What the? - Indonesian)

"Ibu said, make pizza."

Now, this is a guy who has worked in this kitchen for thirty years, has never left the village, has never eaten Western food, has never even seen a pizza, and does not speak one word of English. *Well, now he knows the word, 'pizza'.*

Here we go again, it is the Spaghetti Bolognese with fried chicken, and the Hamburgers with ham, all over again...

I enquired, "Since when did you start making pizzas?"

Doyok; "Yesterday."

"Has anyone ordered one?"

"Yes, yesterday."

"Did they eat it?"

"No"

"Then why are you making another one?"

"Ibu told me to."

Oh, boy.

"Ok, Doyok, please make the 'pizza', and I will come back to see what you have made. I will go to talk to Ibu."

So, while I was discussing with Ibu that if she wished to do a Western menu, she should consult with my husband, her adopted son, (who was a Chef), on how to train a Balinese, (who has never even tasted cheese), in the fine art of Western food... Ibu went off on a tangent about babies and me, and other stuff. Which we can save for another Ibu Chronicles.

I came back to find the pizza made... it looked quite yummy. The bread was a nice crusty loaf of bread. When you cut into it, it was like slicing a very dense crusty loaf of bread with cheese and some sort of orange sauce on top... but it was not a pizza. I have never seen a pizza fifteen centimetres high. Just like Ibu's ham and salad roll is not a hamburger, and spaghetti Bolognese is not made with shredded fried rooster.

I wish Ibu would learn to just watch, observe, and learn.

2 September 2017 - The White Balinese?

So, to continue from the other day of Chinese tourists, the first haircut ceremony, and 'Pizza ala Ibu' (oh, and trying to fit in a standard eight-hour working day), we pick up where we left off, which was after the pizza.

Side note: What I love about Ibu is she does not pretend to be anything she is not. She has never pretended to be poor or rich. She has never pretended to be nice. I really love that she has so much pride in being Balinese... she has never tried to make her skin white, to cover up that she is a hard worker. (Which in Asia, is often the belief - the darker the skin the lower the class of person, due to having to work in the sun.) Ibu never tries to look like the pasty white women on the Asian whitening cream commercials. Although she does not like her wrinkles, (what woman does,) she does not try to pretend she does not have dark skin.

Now, to continue after the pizza. I came out of my office applying some sunblock to my face; it was a 50+ and very thick. I stopped at one of the hotel wardrobes that was randomly sitting on the hotel garden path. It was blocking my path. It had a mirror. So, I checked that I had rubbed in the sunblock. Well, it was a good thing that wardrobe was there, and that I checked, not often do I look in a mirror. Well, wardrobes are not usually on garden paths. It looked as though I had tried to whiten my skin.

One of the young female staff cleaning the wardrobe, said to me lovingly, "cantik" (beautiful)... I, of course then rubbed it in as much as possible. *I just do not do the white pasty look very well.*

Ibu came out just at that moment, holding her Grandchild, and said loudly to the young female staff member, "Why do you think Rach is beautiful? Ibu has never thought that!"

Ahh, she's in one of those moods.

The staff member told Ibu her reason. Ibu shook her head disapprovingly, then started to walk around the hotel garden, rocking the sleeping baby, then yelled out, "The top of her head is white, and the bottom is yellow!"

She was, of course, referring to my grey hairs popping through. I have only gone to a hairdresser in Bali twice in ten years.

It was my turn to hold the baby. So, on the pass of the baby, I explained to Ibu that I had not had a chance to dye my greys, and Ibu declared, "I will do it, you should have black hair anyway!"

I exclaimed, "No way!"

"You talk Balinese, you dress Balinese, you act Balinese, you should have black hair, and then you will be Balinese," and Ibu walked off shaking her head, as though mother had spoken.

Hubby came out of the office at that time, to head down the garden path to the back of the hotel. As he was passing Ibu, Ibu blurted to Hubby, "You are ugly!"

Boy, she is on a roll today.

Hubby answered, "Okay, Ibu", and kept walking. He's gotten very used to Ibu calling him ugly over the years.

Then Ibu did a turn on her heel, you could tell one of her ideas had popped into her head, she gets that sly look... She followed Hubby down the path, past the wardrobe, "If you and Rach had children of your own, would they look like you?"

Hubby picking up speed, "Well, err, yeah, Ibu," trying to walk faster.

Ibu kept up the pace behind him, grabbed at his sleeve, "What, ugly with blonde hair and blue eyes?"

"Well, being that we are both blonde with blue eyes, I'd say that's a given, Ibu."

Hubby retrieved what he wanted from the back of the hotel. He did a quick left-right dodge around the garden furniture, taking a parallel garden path, to try and avoid Ibu. Ibu turned around and walked the parallel path, keeping up the same pace. They were now on opposites sides of the courtyard garden.

Ibu was walking parallel with Hubby at top speed now, his legs were one foot longer than hers, so she was doing well, and she had the wardrobe obstacle. Ibu yelled across the garden, "Well, that will just be one ugly baby!"

Hubby was not far from the turn, where the paths would meet... Ibu's kept up, and yelled, "So, Rach should get impregnated by a Balinese, so you have beautiful Balinese children!"

Hubby was on the turn, "I don't think so, Ibu!"

They were about to meet where the garden paths join again, and Ibu blocked Hubby's path, better than the wardrobe did, and Ibu declared, "No, it makes much more sense. What if you had a boy and it turned out really tall with hairs on its arms like you? (She pulled on his arm hair.) That would be just terrible... yes, a Balinese is the only way to go," and walked off, nodding her head that Mother has spoken.

Hubby replied with a sigh, "Okay, Ibu," and walked back to our office shaking his head.

3 September 2017 - The Walkie Talkies

Short and sweet; Ibu wants walkie talkies... I should not have told her to stop yelling at staff, or me across the garden...*this is my own fault. I just had to open my mouth... the guests don't understand Balinese, so why did I say anything?* ...This is the coffee pots all over again... I think nine times today she asked me to get walkie talkies.

I am on my way home now, it has only been one hour since we left the hotel, and she has already rung me to remind me to get walkie talkies. It is my day off tomorrow, and I bet she will ring all day.

I am turning my phone off tomorrow.

5 September 2017 - The Bule Tourist

A few *Ibu Chronicles blog* readers have made comments that they wished to meet Ibu, or stay in her hotel. Now, I am not saying do not stay in her hotel, the setting is lovely, some of the rooms are gorgeous. As long as you stay there when my staff are working, or even me, it's fine, we can protect you, from Ibu.

The hotel is designed for Balinese. It was built and designed for the Balinese Government; there is a huge meeting room. It is a government 'retreat' business hotel, which has an entirely different need and approach to foreign guests staying in a hotel. Now, do not go getting ideas that you will have a business retreat there. There are no Western business facilities... such as, do you need the big Gong in the meeting room to open your meeting? You wouldn't need the internet, would you? That would just be silly. Do you need to pray before your meeting? Don't worry, there is a purpose-built shrine just for that.

Also, Ibu does not speak one word of English. Okay, I lie, she can speak about ten words. She can scream them, not speak them.

Ibu can be as sweet as sugar if I introduce her to our guests on our tours. She does this, I believe, to make people think that I am imagining what she is really like.

Ibu avoids Bules (foreigners), but you can't miss her if you stay there, she screams across the hotel... she did want the walkie talkies, but we knew she would just yell into them, so we still have not purchased them... When she works out how to use a mobile phone without yelling into it, we can get her walkie talkies.

The reason we started taking the hotel bookings for 'Bules', is that the staff and Ibu just cannot understand the Western tourist...*we are a strange bunch.*

I would be sitting at my desk, and Ibu would see a white Bule tourist and scream at me, "You go talk to them!"

Well, Ibu I don't work for you, they are not my guests and just because we have the same skin colour, does not mean I need to talk to them.

The hotel made it onto Trip Advisor, and, oh boy, the reviews were terrible, all from Western tourists. In the end, I realised that like it or not, Ibu was going to have Western tourists check into her hotel. And they needed saving, Ibu and the tourists.

The location is a perfect spot to base yourself to climb Mt Batur volcano, the view over the lake is stunning. Hence, tourists would pass the hotel on the way to the volcano, and many just dropped in to check to see if there was a room available.

The tourists needed to have some sort of customer service that they were accustomed to. However, the staff needed training, so they did not run away whenever a Bule wanted to check-in, or even walked into the reception area. Four of the staff moved to jobs in housekeeping. They did not want to work in the restaurant or reception in case a Western guest checked in (and they speak better English than the other staff). That is how unusual we foreigners are. That amazing customer service and smiles you get at a hotel in Bali is not something a traditional Balinese person is accustomed to. In their culture, the visitor always smiles first. One of the things we do on our cultural tours is to explain just how different the two types of tourists are (domestic vs foreign).

Ibu is not one to put on any airs and graces, and change her way for the Western tourist market, like the rest of Bali has done so successfully. Ibu is Balinese, and Ibu will remain Balinese, her hotel is Balinese, designed for Balinese, and after thirty-six years she will not change. Balinese love staying there and always give it a 5-star rating.

The motto of our business is 'For tourists to adapt to the place they are visiting, not expect the place to adapt to them'. So, we fit in well, in 'The World According to Ibu'.

21 June 2017 - The Smile

We had smiling lessons with staff this morning... I really do agree with the staff, it does hurt. I have sore cheeks now.

Why can't we just be our usual grumpy selves? Why must the rest of Bali be so bloody friendly?

26 June 2017 - The Staff Meeting

Oh, how I do enjoy my staff learning... it would be great if Ibu could learn as well, but it is hard to change an old dog.

The smiling lessons continued this morning. It was a bit strange to be teaching Balinese to put their hands together in prayer position, nod, smile and greet a guest. They do it automatically to a Balinese person. However, when a Bule arrives, it is like little 'deer in the headlights', the little dears they are.... well apart from Pak Jero. Don't get me started.... *Okay, I am already there.*

Pak Jero, (Pak is short for Bapak, he is older than myself, so I must call him Pak out of respect) is Ibu's cousin-in-law and started working for Ibu about one year ago. Now, being that he is Ibu's family and that he is a Mangku (village priest), Bapak respects his position as a Mangku in the village. Bapak cannot tell him off, he asks me to do it. Ibu just works around him... unlike myself, who is a little less accommodating and a little easier to annoy when it comes to laziness... because he really is just damn lazy... Ibu says he is stupid, but I have assured her, he is not stupid... he is lazy.

Ibu had breakfast included in all rooms. We had done a promo for her, where guests could choose either the standard full rate with breakfast or a 20% discount no breakfast rate, which had her revenue up 216%. We introduced breakfast vouchers, introduced purely because Pak Jero kept just giving everyone breakfast. Then Ibu changed the hotel policy to no rooms including breakfast, just because it was too hard for Pak Jero to work out which guest had already had their breakfast; he was bringing some guests three serves of breakfast, without charging them.

I suggested if Ibu would not fire him, at least move him somewhere else, housekeeping maybe. It frustrated the hell out of me, but every time I tried to talk to Ibu and Bapak, they were like, "You tell him off, he is family, so we cannot."

He is not my staff!

Pak Jero had a habit of when you said anything to him, his answer would always be, "Yeah, Yeah, yeah" (in English), with a smile at least. So, I introduced a system where he had to put IDR1,000 (10 cents) in the staff tip box every time he answered, "Yeah, Yeah, Yeah."

It worked well, he only said "Yeah, Yeah, yeah" a few more times.

So, this morning I commented to Ibu when he answered 'sorry' instead of 'Yeah, yeah, yeah', "See Ibu, he is not stupid, he has stopped."

Ibu answered me in English "Yeah, yeah, yeah."

He was saying sorry, as I had watched him take a suitcase out to the carpark with a guest. He left the case at the first vehicle he came to in the carpark, and just walked off, did not say a word. The guest put her hands up in a 'What the?' kind of way, shrugged her shoulders and then dragged her case to the other end of the carpark to the right car.

Now, if he had taken the time to at least say goodbye to the guest, he may have noticed his mistake, or given her the opportunity to ask for the case to go a little further. *Oh, how I love CCTV.*

So, his excuse at today's staff training, was that he was already old, already fifty-five years old. So, I pointed through the floor to ceiling glass windows across the road to the onion field. I told him that I would go and get that Nenek (grandmother) from the fields over there planting onions, who is about ninety-five years old, and she could do a better job... I was serious... enough rant about Pak Jero.

So, our training continued, believing that all the guests had checked out. We were all in the lobby (which is glass on three sides) doing role-playing, when a guest walked past. She looked through the glass, put her hands together in prayer position, nodded at us and giggled. *See, even a bloody English woman gets it!!*

I did it back to her and then asked all the staff to do it as well, so the lady had nine people saying goodbye the Bali way. She left with a huge smile on her face. *See, that was not so hard, was it guys?*

Now, Ibu has a new staff member, and Ibu thinks that if any staff member can speak the smallest amount of English, then they should check-in guests. *Um? Ibu, this kid is eighteen years old, a Trainee, and started four days ago...*

Nope, Ibu is adamant that as he went to high school (okay, so only three of the other thirteen staff went to high school), I could train him up this morning, and he will be good to go tomorrow.

So, we tried some role-playing. I had three staff pretend to be guests. Ibu tried to repeat what I had said. She was waving her hand around, encouraging this new boy to try it for himself. The problem is, Ibu cannot pronounce any of the words in English. Hence, the poor kid was so confused. *If Ibu would just shut up for one minute, the kid could have a try.*

Listening to Ibu try to say, "Enjoy your stay", in English had me in hysterics.... this was a moment that we should have had sound on the CCTV. I had to keep saying to Ibu, "Sshh it," so he could practise correctly. Ibu continued screaming at him, "Try, try."

Poor kid. I wonder if he will return tomorrow.

Ibu was hindering my training session, so I said, "Ibu maybe if you go off and watch TV or something, he can learn."

Ibu replied, "Ibu wants to learn too."

"Okay, Ibu, if you want to learn too, before we even get there, here are some lessons for you" ....and I started to list them:

"Number One, when you answer the phone, do not answer 'YEAH' loudly."

"Number Two, if you cannot pronounce 'Thank you', just say 'Terima Kasih' as, 'TANK YOU' screamed with a frown at someone, just doesn't cut the mustard." (Well, the equivalent phrase in Indonesian.)

"Number Three, when you need a staff member, do not scream their name across the courtyard or restaurant full of guests."

"Number Four, when I am talking to guests do not scream out RASCH, RASCH, RASCH, repeatedly until I come."

"Number Five, turn the volume down when you watch the bloody Indonesian Soap Operas if you insist on having that TV in our office."

"Shall I go on Ibu??"

Ibu shook her head, screwed up her mouth like a cat's bum, and walked off. One of my staff, Made said to me in English, "This is a habit for Ibu."

Made loves that word, 'habit', ever since at one staff training sessions, I said, "It will all become a habit to you one day and very easy for you. For now, we will just practise every day."

So Ibu is off to practise how to say 'Enjoy' in English. It's a tough one for her, she got close, 'Enge', and I am off to hire a ninety-five-year-old onion grower.

5 July 2017 - The Spaghetti

Ibu do not argue with me! Spaghetti Bolognese does not have shredded fried chicken in it. Just because you cannot eat beef and the Chef cannot cook beef, does not make it right. Just don't serve it!!... *that is all.*

7 July 2017 - The Day Off?

Today I had a day off, a quick ceremony and sterilising of ten dogs.

Sometimes guests ask me what I do on my day off. Sometimes I glare at them. *Who has a day off?*

The vets met me up in the village so that we could catch and spay ten dogs. It was quite exhausting as we had to catch them, sedate them, and then carry them down the small gangs to the Balai Banjar (open air town hall in the centre of every village), where we had the vet set up at a makeshift clinic.

As I was carrying sleeping dogs, I had young kids following me, asking if I had killed the dog.

After the dogs had their operations, I had to carry them back to where I found them. The same kids kept asking if I had killed the dogs, no matter how many times I explained they were asleep.

I am a bit over kids today, I feel like sedating them and carrying them back to where they belong.

12 July 2017 - The Father (Bapak)

Bapak (Ibu's husband, age seventy-four), the only way I can describe Bapak is, he is 'My happy place'.

I share an office with Bapak, so I spend more time with him than with Ibu. Bapak is a humble man who does not say much, however, when he does it is always profound. *A bit like my husband who does not say much, but when he does you laugh, usually at him, not exactly with him.*

Bapak is my guru (teacher), he has taught me so much and still does.

He was a teacher for many years, a Guru Agama (a religious teacher). He taught our current Bupati (regional Mayor), he was also the village head for ten years and the Wakil Bupati (Regional Deputy Mayor) in his time... now he is just Ibu's husband.

Today we had a problem with our driver, Ibu and Bapak's relative. Not sure how he is related, but being one of four bloodlines in the village they have many relatives.

He picked up our guests, and even though they had booked a tour package, including meals at Ibu and Bapak's hotel restaurant, he tried to convince them to go to another restaurant, where he would get the commission... He was driving Bapak's car, so it was a bit of a blow to the family.

So, Bapak was shaking his head with disappointment and Ibu went into her normal stress relief mode of shopping. She was following twenty metres behind my Hubby, listing off her shopping list for Lotte Mart (wholesale supermarket) for tomorrow, with Hubby walking off in every direction trying to ignore her. That was when I thought, *I should take a photo of this, Ibu following Hubby around the grounds of the hotel, screaming his name out and her shopping list, Hubby, trying to pretend he was busy and ignoring her.*

Then Ibu 'Cottoned On' (not a term the Balinese would understand but since Hubby learnt that English term recently, he loves it).

As I walked out with my phone, Ibu turned on her heel and yelled out to me "Rashel I know what you are doing! Bapak has Facebook and he told me how you put photos of me on there!"

Well, wasn't I a little surprised, so I sunk back to my office.

I thought I better look at my personal Facebook page to make sure there was no evidence... but then realised Ibu has spies everywhere and probably in the Bali group I post in. So, I looked up Bapak's Facebook page, which I helped him set up six months ago, and he already has 323 friends. (I have 200 friends, joined in 2007.) *Bapak is the biggest sweetheart, so I can see why he has more friends than me.*

Bapak is addicted to Facebook. Ibu has already told me off for Bapak's addiction, as it was my fault that he was staying up every night on Facebook for the first few months.

Bapak was the reason behind our canoeing. His idea was if we got the water licence for the lake, we could stop a greedy person from putting jet skis on the lake. So, if we got the only water licence and put gentle canoes on the lake, we could save the Holy Lake. Has worked so far for nine years, go Bapak!

Ibu continued to follow Hubby around for thirty more minutes, screaming out his name, while hotel guests sat on their porches, watching, and looking bemused. All the staff were laughing at Ibu chasing Hubby around the hotel. I contemplated getting CCTV footage to post on my Facebook page... but Bapak was sitting at the CCTV screen, so, I thought not... especially after I saw Bapak's Facebook page was pretty much dedicated to his love of his Ibu.

18 July 2017 - The Stomach Ache

Today Ibu was disturbing my work because she had a stomach ache. She was on my day bed screaming out, "Raschel Sakit Perut, Sakit Perut!" (Rachel, stomach ache, stomach ache!)

I told her to stop it, she just wanted attention.

She turned onto her front with her bum up in the air, so I smacked her bum and told her to stop acting like a baby.

I give up. I am going home to work.

Update: I just got home, and Hubby just called me, to tell me that when I walked out, Ibu did a huge fart and announced, "All better now, time for food."

Apparently, she is now eating a huge plate of food.

25 July 2017 - The Obat (Medicine)

So, I went up to the office today. The only reason I went in, was to have a meeting with Ibu. (That's only a 2.5-hour drive.) However, Ibu would not talk to me as she was in one of her moods. She had sore eyes; she refused to use the eye drops I gave her, or the ones the Doctor gave her. She would prefer traditional medicine, which is ground-up stuff, looks like clumpy sand and she has plastered it all over her forehead.

All that stuff falling in her eyes has nothing to do with why her eyes are not feeling better. *Don't I know anything? Geez, Rach.*

Chapter 4 - Mt Agung Volcano

21 September 2017 - Let's Be Serious For A Moment.

So, Mt Agung's belly is swelling at an alarming rate. The Government have decided it best to evacuate all those living within a twelve-kilometre radius of Mt Agung crater, that's about 175,000 people, and 30,000 cows.

Agung means supreme. Most people refer to Mt Agung as a 'he,' I refer to Mt Agung as a pregnant 'she,' who should know better than to be smoking during her condition. I have taken up smoking as well. *Well, that's a big fat lie, I never quit.*

However, I am now smoking daily, as opposed to just when I have alcohol. *That's a lie too.*

I always had a ciggie with my early morning coffee, and then I could go sixteen hours or more without one, and have one after dinner. My staff had never seen me smoke before this, so they find it quite strange and ask me constant questions about it, such as, "How many packets do you smoke a day?"

A Singapore Doctor once asked me that same question. "How many packets do you smoke a day?"

Packets? Geez.

I told her, "Only a few cigarettes, not packets, but a lot more when I drink alcohol."

She told me, "That's not a smoker, that is just something to do your other hand.*"

I couldn't wait to tell Hubby that one.

It used to be called social smoking, like social drinking, but it is so unsociable now to smoke. If we had more money, I would also do more unsociable drinking, meaning I would be drinking alone.

I told Hubby I will give up smoking as soon as Mt Agung does, she is being unsociable as well.

29 September 2017 - The Evacuation

The village has not been evacuated, they are not in a lava flow area, they are protected from lava by the crater rim of the caldera. There is a high possibility of ash fall out of course, this will all depend on the wind direction when Mt Agung does erupt and to what extent she erupts.

It is a constant reminder of 1963, every time you arrive at the caldera when you see the trees. Such an ancient place, however, there is such a contrast with the relatively young vegetation. There are so many pine trees and even ghost gums, planted to rejuvenate the area after the ash fallout of 1963. The trees that survived that fallout and remained standing, remind me of something out of Lord of the Rings with their magnificence. When the locals returned after 18 months, they placed temples under those giant trees of the past, with just a chair for God to sit and admire, as God must have wanted those trees to survive.

In October 1963 Mt Batur also erupted, and that black scar captures your eye every time you take the winding steep road down to the lake.

Today we went to up to check on the elderly. Kedisan has a high aging population, all of whom remember 1963 Agung eruptions. We, of course, wanted to check on the school and the general knowledge everyone had, being that no one has computers and there are only a few smartphones and televisions.

Our main concerns were:

The elderly that all live alone; their families work away, many in Kuta and Legian.

The children: so, I went to the school today to check on preparations there.

Our staff, and their families, and, of course, what was everyone else doing to prepare?

I will start with the elderly. I dropped in on some that I knew were living alone, and one old dear, nearly 100-years-old was preparing her offerings to go to her land and pray. She told me, "Last time I ran, and this time I will run".

Being that she lives alone, and with severe arthritis (although she works every day in the fields) was a huge concern to me... I spoke to her in detail. (She speaks old Balinese, so this was a difficult task.) I managed to convince her to let me contact her son. Three hours later he arrived, after leaving his beach bar in Kuta. He did not mention anything about the loss of business from fewer tourist numbers, that many westerners on social media, claim Balinese are complaining about. I have never heard a complaint from our villagers. They accept the slumps of tourism, they appreciate the highs, and they know the tourism business is fickle. He waved me down in the street to thank me and was taking her, against her will, to their house in Denpasar.

I dropped in on a few more elderly and discussed with them, whether their adult children had plans to get them if needed, and if they had been in contact. I rang and spoke to a few of their adult children on the phone, and they were ready to come at a drop of a hat, no discussion about their loss of income they may face in the future, no complaints at all.

It was sad to hear the older ones retell their memories of the last event in 1963 and how falling volcanic rocks burnt their skin, and all their crops were destroyed. All the trees that had died and how they had to leave to find work; back then it meant basically walking as far as Singaraja to find work (eighty kilometres away).

I showed them pictures of the correct masks they would need, and how to prepare their homes, bring the dogs inside, etc. A lot of information is out there, but many cannot read. I explained to a few old ladies that their scarf wrapped around their face would not be as efficient as a proper mask, but if it was all they had, they should wet it first. Many homes I checked on were empty. They had already been collected. It just shows that their adult children want to make it easier for the rest of the community. To leave if they need, without a huge number of people all needing to go at once. The road down to the lake is not fully repaired from the landslides, so it is only a single lane at present.

While I was with one old lady in her grass hut, there was an earthquake, which had me out the door very quickly.

No one from our village has gone to the allocated evacuation camp to use up space reserved for those from the danger zone.

Next, the children; I went to the school. The children stayed later after the bell rang, to pray and then to sing. It was a sobering moment for me, wondering what stories their grandparents had told them over the years and how they were feeling about this. The teachers told me they were scared, but the children seemed happy as usual. I discussed with the headmistress the mask situation; unfortunately, she had surgical masks for the children. I had to explain these were not sufficient and may give them a false sense of security. I explained how they could make goggles from plastic coke bottles, and maybe tomorrow this could be a project. She will go to the village head to see when correct masks will be coming. Again, I showed all the information I had downloaded for her. I feel she has a better understanding of how to prepare now.

The villagers were all going about their days. Many stopped to talk to me as I walked through all the small gangs of the village, checking on people. It was very quiet, there were not as many people as usual, but many wanted to tell me how they knew to cover up, etc... so, that was great... the masks they did not know about... so, that was not so great... I will work on that one tomorrow.

Balinese are community/family people. They do not complain (well, not to me), they believe suffering makes them appreciate the good times. With at least 300 people from the village working on the beaches or as drivers, they aren't worried about their businesses. They are worried about their families and their community; they are working together to help each other. The Balinese way is for the good of the community, not for the individual. Balinese all over Bali are taking time off work to take donations to the camps, using their space for complete strangers, taking strangers into their homes. Balinese are survivors, they are resilient, Balinese are why you visit Bali.

There was another volcanic earthquake when I reached the hotel. Bapak wanted to learn how to say 'earthquake' in English. It took him ten tries, but he proudly got there in the end... he just had to drop the S, he kept saying 'errsquake'.

Bless him, seventy-four years old, so he remembers the massive 1963 eruption. Both Mt Agung and Mt Batur volcanos blew that year.

I have given all the staff masks, (and masks for their families) as well as Bapak and Ibu. They are putting locks on all the doors to the office/kitchen etc., prepared for if they must evacuate... They have not locked the hotel since it opened thirty-six years ago.

10 October 2017 - The Indian Soap Operas

Just a quickie: Was having a break from mask fitting in the village and trying to do some work. Ibu has her new mask, but I forgot to pick up her reading glasses that I took in for repair, so I am in the poo, again. Ibu is watching TV in my office (her Indian soap opera). She is rubbing it in that she cannot see without her glasses. So, I will feel guilty, she is standing right in front of the TV screen, thirty centimetres from the screen, like a toddler... but the volume is the same as usual (full), so I cannot concentrate. *Aduh!*

Aduh is a word I use regularly, really there is no equivalent as good in English to this word. It is the way it is pronounced; it is just magical. I guess Geez, or Oh, Boy, or Arrghh, are similar, but can never be as good as Aduh (ArrrDoo)

Note to self: Pick up Ibu's reading glasses, see if Nengah can break the volume dial on that TV.

14 October 2017- The Masks

So, yesterday we had a Cultural Tour, this was an excellent opportunity for me to tag along to incorporate some more mask research in the village.

I numbered the different sizes (six sizes). I took one sample of each size on the usual tour route with our guests, so I could have them help me with this mammoth task of everyone having correctly fitted masks for ash fall out. We have 850 masks now, however handing them over isn't as easy as I first thought. Having already taken the opportunity to go up to check children's faces on the last canoe tour, I am onto the next priority, our elderly. I was not going to fit the whole village. This was just to check random faces from different families, being that there are only four bloodlines in the village, many faces fit into four categories. The initial idea is that IF the ash comes, they can go to our office and ask for a Mask Number [insert their mask number]. That was the idea.

So, I set out with our guests on the tour of the village, weaving through the rabbit warren of ancient streets, they asked if I ever got lost in there... they got to meet some of our wonderful elderly characters, and I was able to have these lovely elderlies try a mask on for size.

As suspected, the women in the oldest bloodline had heads the size of children, the men also from that bloodline had small faces. We did have some masks that were intended for the children in the years three to six classes that fitted the adults, so we will need to track some more of those down.

One new discovery was that the villagers were quite used to surgical masks, yet these are N95 masks, so the two elastic straps go over the back of your head. We came across my favourite Grandma (Nenek) in the street, and she invited us over for a coffee.

When we got to her house, she grabbed a mask from me with pride. She knew how to fit a mask, what on earth was I on about?! She proudly placed it sideways with the headbands over her ears and then could not see, it did give our guests a giggle.... Eventually, Nenek went off to make us coffee, fed up with the mask, the silly thing it was.

I had met Nenek's husband in the street earlier (all four-foot of him) and when he tried on a mask, he said: "PAS" (Fits). Yet, it had a gap of two centimetres at the bottom.... *hmmm, when elders know best, you need to tread carefully.*

I managed to find one that fitted him, he went off to the fields with not a care in the world, yelling back, "Tidak, Apa Apa!" (No worries in Indonesian).

Back to Nenek: When Nenek did have her mask on, sideways, she mimed for us all how she would wear it when she went to cut grass in the fields for her cow, even if the ash did come... *Oh, dear.*

Nenek also pointed up and showed our guests her fantastic view of Mt Agung right from her porch. And said to me, "Tell the guests, no worries, I will know it is coming before anyone else. See, I have the clearest view of Mt Agung, not a problem."

She is correct, it is better than the CCTV they have set up on YouTube.

A little concerned about my findings... trying not to show it to the guests. We went back to our bikes to ride to the next village of Buahan, for that million-dollar view. It was strangely quiet, riding down the main street of Buahan, usually such an active village.

We stopped in front of a friend's place, Made. Made came out from a hut where she was peeling onions, to tell me her village was now at KRB 1 (Evacuation Zone One). Everyone was allowed one suitcase and left every night to sleep in the camp... This was a bit of a surprise, being that her village is one kilometre from our village.

Made explained that the earthquakes were unbearable now, you could not think, you could not sleep, the roads kept lifting with the earth movement...*Oh, dear.*

I had some masks for her, but her hands were dirty, so she asked me to just to open her shirt and tuck them into her bra, so she could retrieve them later.

Her concerns were not at all with an eruption, but with potential landslides, having just cleaned up from the landslides in February. Only just getting their farming land back, as it was underwater and rubbish for six months, I could see why her concern... the lake water level had been up to their homes, flooding all their crops. Due to the landsides on the other side of the lake, and the westerly winds, they had ended up with bits of people's homes washed up against their homes, a lot of dead fish and even a car. Also, when you look up at the edge of the caldera shadowing over their village and their farms, you can envision their fears.

A little bit of a chat with her about the kids' needs in the camp. The kids wanted pencils, paper etc., which we had back in our village prepared for our kids, yet her village is now a priority so, I promised them to her, and then we headed off.

Well, we intended to leave her village, after a few happy snaps. Yes, our guests took some. However, some random marine policemen in the brightest blue jumpsuits *(looked like straight out of a packet, first time worn)*, whom I have never met before, tracked me down and said they had come to have photos taken with me—*no idea why. Very random. I would not do well at being famous.*

So, after their little photo-shoot, we were finally able to move on back to our village, through the vegetable farms. Riding past the beautiful newly planted chilli crops growing on the lake's edge. The whole quiet ride back, had me thinking about this land beside my wheel and how it was finally given back by Dewi Danu (the Lake Goddess). *She must have needed it for something, as she took it for nearly one year with the floods, and now they may have to leave all their crops behind.*

Off to our final stop at the school; the kids were supposed to be quietly reading outside while we used a classroom for our guests to have a test on what they learnt that day, *only joking, well sort of.*

We do not encourage children as a tourist attraction, but the kids slowly snuck in one by one, until we had a full classroom. I was explaining the caste system on the whiteboard to the guests, and the kids had told Hubby they had never learnt about that. So, Hubby told them they should listen. It ended up being a lesson for thirty kids as well... We used this school visit as an opportunity to deliver the masks for the Year One & Two classes, to be locked in the school cupboard until needed. I will deliver the rest on the next tour.

The kindergarten also received their masks, which we collected from a kind tourist staying in a hotel in Legian at 6.00am just that morning before going up to the village. So, overall a good outcome, a tour, mask hand out and research all in one!

We stopped on the way out of the area for our guests to take some photos of Mt Agung, our guests not realising until that morning, how close they would really be to the supreme (Agung) mountain. So many images appear on Facebook of Mt Agung, from quite a distance, we are a lot closer than we would really like to be right now.

The outcome was that I could determine the needs of the elders concerning these masks. I will write up instructions for the village heads, and I will print a step-by-step chart, with pictures that they can use. They can hold a meeting with the elders to show them correct fitting AND explain the one-time use of a mask if it is full of ash, then don't put it on again... Glad they have that task and not me... evacuation etc.... we are getting there! Sabar sabar (be patient), pelan-pelan (slowly).

17 October 2017 - The Masks Continued

So, today was another successful day. I tagged along again up to the village, on a canoe tour, so I could go off to the village and get more done while our guests were canoeing.

When we got to the hotel, I borrowed the minivan, as I had all the masks in the back, and I left to go to the school.

That was the plan anyway, I just needed to drive 500 metres up the main street. The village head's son was getting married, so there were a lot of cars lining the main street. Unfortunately, our village is not designed for cars, so this caused a small issue for me to get to the school, as they had parked across the whole main street. There was not enough room for me to drive through, nor anyone else that lived in the next village that may need to use the road to access their village (the only access road).

Asking the Pecalang (today in the role as parking attendants, they are our traditional guards), if they could just move one car, so I could get through, was more difficult than I first thought.

No one that was on the street directing the parking of cars knew how to drive a car!

Eventually, I was through the temporary carpark, being the main street, and on to the kindergarten for more instructions on fitting their masks. Then to the school to ensure classes Three to Six got their mask in the correct sizes and further instruction. The older children in the village fit into the adult category, but now all children under twelve had masks!

So, feeling a sense of accomplishment, it was time to go and check on the neighbouring village, Buahan. I could not go in the other direction back to the hotel anyway, it would stress out the valet parking guys.

On our Cultural Tour, last week, our guests met Made, whom I have known for ten years.

Made calls me 'Grees'. Even when I had a name badge for years, she still pronounced my name 'Grass', she spells it Grees. I have no idea why, even when her niece has sent me messages on Messenger, where my name is clearly Rachel, she writes Grees as well.

Made seemed very scared about the quakes they were having. Last week Made was eager to tell our guests about the quakes, using hand gestures, as she does not speak English. Mimicking the road moving up and down and the house shaking vigorously at night. She told us how everyone in her village had gone to sleep in the Evacuation Camp the night before. Apart from her, as her husband was away for work. I had promised Made some textas and colouring books donated for our village. Made's village was now a priority over ours, as kids were sleeping away from homes already. So, I headed there to drop them off.

When I arrived at the village, I thought everyone had already evacuated as there were not many people around... I soon found them. I could see farmers up on a very steep bank of the caldera. Their waists had ropes tied around them, the other end fastened to a tree, so they could farm the steep land of the caldera... ropes required in case of another earthquake, so they would not be shaken off the hill. The rest were in a makeshift bamboo and woven grass hut, preparing for a ceremony to ask the Gods to stop the quakes.

Made, kindly took a break from preparations for the ceremony, to have a chat with me; we walked off to the edge of her farm. I was telling her about how on Facebook last night, a few tourists were saying locals in Seminyak were saying the mountain is asleep, nothing happening. Well, Made wanted to talk, she wanted to tell those tourists what was really happening. So, I said I would interview her on video and post it on our Facebook page. *She wants to have a little vent, like Agung and me.*

I will hopefully be back up there on Thursday to continue with the elderly and older children's mask fitting/instructions. I will go and check on Made again.

17 October 2017 - Breaker, Breaker

Today I arrived at work to find Ibu in some sort of whimsical trance, collecting flowers in the garden, so I let her be.

I walked into the office I share with Bapak, and all I could hear was CB radio chatter. We now have a CB radio set given to us by the Government, so we know when to evacuate! We are the point of call for the whole village. *Not sure why it is not at the village heads' office? I guess they do have a lot of days off.*

Bapak, unfortunately, could not work out how to turn on the portable hand controller (an actual walkie talkie, not for Ibu). I showed him how to turn it on, and it said in English, "Power on."

He looked disappointed that it was not in Bahasa Indonesian.

Then he put it on his desk proudly, next to him so he could be the first response.

About ten minutes later the walkie talkie said, "Battery Low", in English. Bapak looked at me. I had to show him that there is a little charger holder that he is supposed to keep it in.

Poor Bapak, I think he just wants it to talk to him in Bahasa Indonesian.

27 November 2017 - The Mt Agung Eruption!

Da, Da, Da, Dah! I felt like that needed a drum roll... We arrived at the office, and Mt Agung has gone and erupted again. Not a small steam cloud, this was an amazing sight to see. *Hopefully, a once in a lifetime experience.*

We stopped on the way up to take a video of that ash billowing into the sky. It was amazing how it looked as though someone had put up a glass wall four kilometres high, to prevent ash from falling on our village.

Ibu grabbed me as soon as I arrived and dragged me to the laundry (*Ibu literally pulls me places, by my arm, sometimes not letting go as she knows I will make my escape.*)

We had tour guests in the restaurant who were having breakfast, and I really needed to go and chat with them about their tour, since a volcano has erupted and all that. But no, that was not important to Ibu.

So, Ibu had bought a very large clothes dryer, and had it proudly placed up on bricks in the middle of the open-air laundry. The problem was that the dials were all in English, no one had ever seen one of these big white boxes before and no one, including Ibu, knew how to use the bloody thing.

I gave Ibu and housekeeping some quick instructions on how to use it. Including, better to put the sheets in for one load, and the towels separate due to drying time, do not put the cat in there, etc. Then I tried to excuse myself to get back to our guests. Ibu grabbed my arm again and proudly stated, "I bought it, so when the ash comes, they can still dry the clothes."

I did not have the heart to tell her that as the laundry is open-air, the dryer would just suck in all the ash. I needed to get to my guests. The ones that were currently sitting in an open-air restaurant watching a 9000-metre high ash cloud approach them.

I again tried to excuse myself, but Ibu wanted validation that her purchase was a brilliant idea. *Obviously, she needs to have an excuse for spending so much money. Ibu, since you won't let me go, you will get the truth.*

I said, "You know, they use more electricity than even the washing machine."

Ibu paused and pondered that one. Then, with such a proud look, "Yes, when the ash falls down here, they can still dry the clothes."

I broke free from Ibu's clutches again and tried to excuse myself, my guests had been sitting out there for a while, but Ibu refused to let me leave.

At least twenty minutes had passed, and I had not been able to get away. Ibu had blocked my exit path. "Yes, but isn't this great, Rach, isn't this great, when the ash comes, they can still dry the clothes."

Ibu was practically chanting, "Bagus Ya, Bagus Ya," (Good yeah, Good yeah,) "Bagus ya Rasch?"

I tried again to escape, and she grabbed my arm again.

Okay, you asked for it Ibu.

So, I said, "Ibu, you know when the ash comes, you won't have any guests, so there will not be any sheets to dry!" And, with that, I walked off.

Sorry, Ibu, you pushed me to my limit.

12 December 2017 - The Rain

So, we currently have an erupting volcano called Mt Agung.

Bali has a lot of nature's challenges, especially where our office is located. We have floods, earthquakes, landslides, cyclones and we have Mt Batur, also an active volcano, which currently has a bit of a rotten egg smell about it. We have the lake, which can also produce that rotten egg smell to tell our canoeing guests to get off there fast, and unfortunately, can kill the fish. The road down to our office is narrow, steep, and winding. It is still being repaired after the landslides in February, when half of it disappeared into the Abyss.

A large tree came down two weeks ago and blocked the road at a lower point, the only road in. We deal with it.

The roof of our office, actually, two different offices over ten years, caved in due to heavy rains. And again, on 27 November 2017, (when we were concentrating on the enormous erupting cloud in the sky) we arrived to find our bike storage room was a swimming pool. Luckily the water stopped just at the boxes of masks for the village, so they remained dry. *Miracle, maybe?*

We knew when we opened the business that we were up for the challenges of Mother Nature. My Facebook memories came up a month ago, reminding me of a comment I had made on 14 November 2009. It said, 'Contemplating what happens if the volcano blows, as our office is at the base of it.'

We do not have a 'Business-as-usual attitude' because it can't always be business as usual. I had to laugh, I was sitting at my desk during that time of frequent quakes, and a tourist rang the office. Nengah answered the phone. A tourist had asked, "Is it safe to climb Mt Batur tonight? I heard there were lots of earthquakes."

Nengah answered, "Oh, no very safe here." He talked a bit more then he hung up the phone. Just as he hung up the phone, an earthquake occurred, and he sprinted out of the office.

When he came back, I sat him down and explained that we cannot use the word 'safe'. He is not a safety expert. It is not our place to measure someone's safety. We must give them the facts to help them decide on their own measurement of safety... He hasn't used the word 'safe' since. Mind you, we have not had any quakes since either.

We are used to working with Mother Nature, adapting to the change, we have been doing it this way for ten years. We have not always got it right. We have had some funny tours in the pouring rain, where guests are provided with coloured ponchos and look like Teletubbies riding past the villagers; the villagers yelling out to the guests, "Hujan Hujan!" (rain, rain!) *You would think the villagers by now, would be used to our crazy guests riding in the rain.*

I guess if the ash cloud prediction is incorrect, then we can always give our guests a nice mask to match their ponchos and leave the area if necessary. *Otherwise, the villagers will really think we are crazy.*

Chapter 5 - Back in Business

3 February 2018 - The Greeting

Due to Mt Agung's constant earthquakes for four weeks, then six weeks of ash fallout, we have been closed, so I have not been up here for two months.

I arrived at work this afternoon to be greeted in the restaurant by one of our new staff with a big smile and Balinese Greeting, *wonderful.*

Then twenty minutes later, I heard the same staff member say to a guest, "What You Want?"

Oops, not so wonderful.

So, I wrote on my 'tips for staff' on a whiteboard that I have behind my desk:

What you want/What do you want? (in English) – Sing Dadi (cannot, in Balinese).

What would you like? (English) – Bagus! (Good, in Indonesian)

This was so I could discuss it with them later, as I was a tad busy.

This turned into a bit of a distraction. I was trying to send emails and Ibu was standing over me reading the board behind me, and trying to say it out loud.

Ibu kept saying "Whap do you Like?"

No, Ibu.

Then she tried "What would you like?" but could not pronounce the words, 'What' or 'Would'. Ibu said, 'Whap and Whoop'.

Bapak joined in, and he could not pronounce it either, so he suggested: "What will you like?"

No, Bapak.

Ibu kept practising until she got it. I gave up trying to concentrate on my work, as she had brought in all her staff to try it as well. They all stood in front of my desk trying to read the board over me.

I really wanted to capture her on video saying it wrong, as, 'Whop Woog you like' and 'Whop Whoob you like,' as it started me giggling.

So, I thought, why not video her. She perfected it just when I hit

51

record...*glad no-one videoed me when I was learning Balinese.*
Note to self: Find a new location for that whiteboard.

4 February 2018 - The Hair Salon

I slept in the hotel last night. I will try again to get some work done today, pay wages and then go back to the south.

We are not handling Ibu's hotel bookings, as it has been so quiet that we trained one of her staff to look after the bookings, so she would not have to pay our company.

Nengah has taken over my desk, for the time being. We had just been chatting about how he can spy on Ibu from my desk and from the CCTV. I glanced at the CCTV screen, and I could see Ibu in the restaurant. She was dyeing her hair in the restaurant handwashing basin, as you do. There were no guests in the restaurant, so I just let her be.

So, after Ibu dyed her hair in the restaurant this morning, she was a little bit distracting, as in:

"Can you check my sugar levels?"

She is not a diabetic.

"Can you check my blood pressure?"

I am not a Doctor.

Ignoring her for a bit, I was trying to get some work done, and I glanced a few times at the CCTV, and noticed a Westerner had been in reception for a long time. I said to Nengah, "Who is working reception?"

Nengah replied, "Kadek."

"Nengah, there is a Bule in reception, but no staff."

Nengah went to help... He came back, "I found Kadek, he is making flowers for Ibu."

Ibu butted in with her, "WHAT'S GOING ON?" scream.

I explained that a tourist was standing in reception but no staff...

"Arrgh", Ibu shrugged, "Whatever! Kadek is making flowers for the Bupati (Mayor visit). What did that Bule want?"

I answered, "Maybe to check in?"

Nengah interjected, "He wanted to look at a room."

Ibu, asked, "Arrghh, Rasch, when you do travel agent again?" Then she started mumbling to Nengah about Bule tourists, and she hoped he didn't want a room and blah, blah, blah. (She thinks they complain too much.)

I ignored her, then twenty Chinese guests wanted to check out. I knew she would want my Nengah to do it, so I got in quick. "Nengah is busy, he can't do that."

Ibu casually, "It's okay, their drivers will check them out."

Obviously, running a hotel has been going well, since we stopped handling bookings for her and training her staff then....hmm?

At least the flowers are lovely.

9 February 2018 - The Coming Home, Take 2

For years, we have tried to move back to the village for peak season, so we do not have to drive up and down. I have stayed in the hotel a lot of the time, but when it is full, I cannot stay... *even when I do have a room booked. Aduh.*

It is not as easy as just moving, as we have five dogs. Without the dogs, we could live with Ibu and Bapak again at the back of the Hotel... but we got kicked out due to having dogs. Ibu does not understand our relationship with our dogs, we have a cat as well.

When we first lived in the village, Hubby had six cats in the hotel; I am not a cat person. The cat will not be coming with us, it can stay in our house in the south of Bali and be a guard cat. The dogs, however, they are coming, well four of them are, our special needs dogs. One very large rescue dog is firmly planted on our front doorstep, we cannot touch him, but he follows us on walks, and he is the best doorbell. The other dogs we have are rescues that cannot be adopted out. We end up keeping the special needs rescues as they need a lot more attention and much more challenging to find adopters. *They fit in well in our dysfunctional family.*

Ibu just does not understand this. Ibu's comments have been, "Just put them in the paddock up there," (three kilometres away) and waved her hand up the hill. Or "They can just roam the streets," or, just a huff and a shaking head.

Ibu had a dog, Rocky. Rocky passed a few years back; he was twenty years old. I was there with him, nursing him through the last days. Ibu, well, Ibu thought I was just nuts, and why didn't I just leave him alone to die, next to the kitchen, in plain view to any guests from the hotel courtyard. He was too large to pick up, and it was pouring with rain, so I made a shelter over him, and sat in it with him. Ibu still thinks I am nuts for doing that... we have very different ideas about animals, she still can't stand it when I talk to the sacrifices.

Enough about the dogs, although, finding a house is all about the dogs and not about us.

One day we mentioned to Ibu that we were looking at houses to rent in the village to come back to live there. This was when we got the normal Ibu speech, 'Well just live in our place, or that place is ours, or you can have the old restaurant,' etc. etc. Ibu had us going all over the village with her, 'I have an idea, go look at this place.' However, with the dogs, no place Ibu offered would work. *One of the places I wouldn't even let dogs live in.*

Meanwhile, we were trying to look at homes other people owned, and she was diverting us to anything her family owned. We were offered a few homes by people in the village that did not use them, as they lived in Denpasar. Lovely offers of basically rent-free. (We just pay to fix the fence, etc., to keep the dogs in.) They only used them about once a month when they had a ceremony to come up to. So sweet, even when I asked, "Where would you all sleep when you came up for a ceremony?" They were all happy to sleep on the floor of the house we were in. Hubby did not want ten people sleeping on his lounge room floor every month, so we turned down the very lovely offers.

We didn't find the right place, and Ibu wasted a lot of our time sending us to the 'perfect place' or 'just wait I have the perfect place' or 'in a few months you can have the perfect place.'

Peak season came, and we didn't have time to move. *Just, perfect, not.*

So, we are trying again this year... stay tuned for this one. We plan to be there before June... I have Nengah looking, sworn to secrecy to not tell Ibu... if he finds us something, we may have to sneak into the village in the middle of the night.

17 February 2018 - The Hair Medicine

So, after the other day of Ibu dying her hair in the hotel restaurant, today I walked into the restaurant kitchen and found Ibu using a restaurant kitchen saucepan to pour water over her head, over the restaurant kitchen sink. She was pouring it over her hair, it was then pouring all over the dirty dishes. I asked her what she was doing, and she told me it was 'medicine for her hair'. *That's fine Ibu but in the kitchen sink of a hotel restaurant?*

I then noticed a powerful smell of bleach, "Ibu this smells like Bayclin?" (bottled bleach for cleaning floors, etc.)

Ibu answered, "Yes, Ibu ran out of shampoo, so giving it a good clean."

I said, "That might strip off, all that dye you put in last week."

"No, I only used a little bit."

"Okay, but in the kitchen sink (of the restaurant)?"

"Yes, it's raining outside, it's too cold to go to the bathroom."

Ibu logic... I guess it is better that she used bleach instead of shampoo, being that it was all over the dishes!!

17 February 2018 - The Drinkies

Most Balinese do not talk when eating, Ibu follows me eating and asking questions. I will even move to another part of the hotel, and Ibu just appears.

Ibu just wanted to chat today. Today's conversation was about 'drinks'. Not alcohol, this was about; 'What do I drink daily?' Again, not alcohol folks, I wish I had that, daily.

I arrived at work, I first walked into the kitchen hesitantly, as you never know what mood you will find Ibu in. But I need coffee to start my day, so

I always brave it.

Without even saying good morning Ibu announced to me, "I am going to make some Jamu, a big bottle and you can drink it too. I will make it with turmeric, honey and ginger and lemon."

Phew, she is in a good mood.

I replied, "Thank you, I already make it every night."

Ibu questioned me, "When do you make it? How do you make it? When do you drink it?"

Here we go, she's in a chatty mood.

"I just use Turmeric, honey and lemon."

"Honey is so expensive, where do you get it from?"

"I know it is, we get it at Lotte Mart."

So, the conversation went on and on about honey, and the price and the quality, and then of course, "Buy me some honey!"

Boy, I knew that was coming. Why do I even open my mouth?

Now, Ibu does not mean we pay for it, in fact, we have never paid for anything for her, but she does send us shopping a lot.

It continued with me going from the kitchen into the office, Ibu following, "Rasch, so, what do you drink when you first get up?"

Me, walking out of the office, Ibu following, "Rasch, so, what do you drink before bed?"

Me, giving up and coming back into the office, "Do you eat first?" Blah, blah, blah.

I was trying to get some work done, but Ibu kept following me. I even moved my laptop to the reception and sat on the reception guest chairs, but she followed me there.

I went back to my desk. Ibu went and got her breakfast, and then she came back to continue the conversation. She stopped for a few seconds to pray and get in a mouth full, and then she started again. *Why didn't I take this opportunity to find the staff's black hole??*

I was stupid again and mentioned drinking a young coconut after my run every night. Now, do not go thinking I am a fitness fanatic. When you have five dogs to walk, and then all the neighbourhood dogs join, it always turns into a run; run this way, run that way.

"So, do you drink yellow, or do you drink green?"

Seriously, this conversation went on for about two hours, she just kept following me around asking questions about what I drink. I should have just said 'beer'.

Then, the cogs were ticking in Ibu's head, I heard them when she took a breath. Ibu asked, "Why do you make Jamu every night?"

I replied, "It helps reduce the lump on Sibran's head."

Now, don't worry, Hubby has had the lump checked. It is nothing serious. He has a fatty lymphoma on his forehead. He can get it cut out cosmetically, or we just shrink it with Jamu, or I could just hit it with a book.

So, Ibu walked into the kitchen and I heard her say to the cook. "Did you know that Jamu is the reason why Sibran's cancer on his head is shrinking? It gets rid of cancer!"

So, Ibu has cured cancer, and I can finally get some work done.

Two hours later, I caught up with Hubby, he put his hand in his pocket to pull out the key to the school, and a wad of money fell out. He asked me, "Why did Ibu stuff money in my pocket to buy lots of honey?"

18 Feb 2018 - The Sign

The other morning, Ibu rang me at 6.00 am, put me on hold, then hung up. I knew it was her and not the staff, as she has no idea how to use a phone.

She rang again and screamed, "Rasch! Rasch!" and then hung up.

She rang again around 7.00 am and screamed Hubby's name a few times and then hung up.

Eventually, she managed to make a call and hear me, and then once she knew I could hear her, she went on and on and on, about something. I had not had my third coffee yet, so I put the phone on the kitchen bench, put the kettle on and just yelled out, "Ah ha, yeh" a few times. *I learned this trick years ago, with my real mother.*

I got the gist of what she wanted, she wanted a sign made in English. I told her to give it to Nengah, and he could email it to me, and I would check his translation before they printed it. She was happy and hung up.

No email ever came.

Yesterday I thought about that call, and went to Ibu and told her I had never received an email. Ibu said it was fine, as Nengah used Google Translate and made it for her. *Great, why so many calls to me then? Aduh.*

I thought I would go and have a look at the all-important sign.

I went and had a look in one of the hotel rooms, and this was the sign Nengah made:

ATTENTION !!!!!!
Please before leaving check the luggage Complaint's left behind after leaving the hotel are not the responsibility of the hotel When doing activities outside the hotel area, valuables can be deposited in the save box hotels Thank you

I read it a few times. Then I went and asked Ibu if she had safety deposit boxes. She stated, "No, Bapak will buy a safe."

But the sign is already up?

I think I will just leave the sign as is, until I can clearly work out what she means, and what she can provide for the guest. And, as it is stuck on the wall of every room, with sticky tape. I tried to remove one, and the wall paint came off. *Aduh*

2 March 2018 - The Working Day

Working with Balinese can be a challenge when you come from Australia, where the work ethic is strong, or anywhere, really. You must put that all aside if you are going to last, working in Bali. *Or you may kill someone. They have perfected the art of time wasting.*

I thought I would just recap one morning this week. A typical day, not an 'Ibu being overly Ibu' day. See if you can spot the differences to working in a Western World.

I got to work, Ibu seemed friendly, did the normal pass Ibu at the toilets, the usual chat. 'How are you, are you healthy?' The toilet is one without a seat that you bucket the water into, so the floor is very wet, one reason my uniform has a sarong. I did have on pants the other day, and I did have wet pants for the rest of the morning.

I had my breakfast, then went and had a pleasant meeting with Ibu about plans for the tours, for when we move back. Ibu was normal and reasonable and only mentioned the 'not-suitable-house' once in conversation.

Bapak walked in with a pancake and said, "Makan" (food/eat), to which I nodded and said, "Selamat Makan" (like Bon Appetite). We could not talk to Bapak until he was finished. It is rude to speak to a Balinese while they are eating.

Ibu and I agreed on how the reception/lobby should be changed, and where our tour desk would go. Ibu agreed that I could organise that. She would allocate me her twin to move the desks with my twin. (The twins have been working for Ibu part-time and us part-time since Agung erupted, and tourism is still quiet.)

Then Ibu remembered that the taxman had come to visit. This is an unusual thing to happen, we have never had a visit before (unless taxes have not been paid). A few days prior I had received a phone call from the tax office. Our account rep at the tax office said he wanted to come in that day and just check we had a physical office. I explained I was not up there, and that the office was 'under renovation', so I was sharing with Bapak. However, I told them he/they could go to the hotel (usually, there is a team when someone goes out of the office, big teams, government workers love getting out for free coffee and snacks) and that the staff or Bapak would show them around. I had rung Bapak and told him they were on their way, and he said that was fine, he would be there to greet them.

It turned out that Bapak went out as soon as he hung up the phone, and Ibu was there to greet them. Ibu told me how she explained to the taxman how we would be moving our tour desk back to the front. That she had demolished our office. *She failed to say two offices.*

And, that this was temporary, so we were sharing an office. *She failed to say this has been temporary for nearly two years.*

Then she very excitedly explained how she told the taxman how we do so much in the village, the school, masks, goggles for when the ash comes, blah, blah, blah. I am not sure why Ibu thought the taxman wanted to know all of that, but Ibu seemed very satisfied with her meeting with the taxman. I could just imagine this poor guy trying to get out of there, just wanting to eat his pancake and drink his coffee with the rest of his team. I mean there was no other reason to be there, he had ticked his box - yep this is where they rent an office, not a fake address.

So, probably like the taxman, I was relieved to finally be able to excuse myself. I needed to go down to the village heads office (local Mayor's/council office). So, I formally announced to Bapak and Ibu where I was going, to get permission to excuse myself and head off. We do not just leave the house, office, anywhere, without formally asking our parents or our hosts' permission to leave, (and explain where we are going) or it is rude. *I only do this with Bapak though, as Ibu rarely gives me permission to leave.*

I arrived at the village heads' office. I was just about to step through the front door, my hands in folded prayer position, ready to bow my head and say, "Om Swastiastu." (This is how you enter all small government offices, or it is rude, including a police station, if Indonesians only, you say 'Permisi' instead.) One of the staff, Putu, spotted me, who I was there to see, and yelled out from her desk, which was behind the reception counter, "Rachel get me a bra!"

The Deputy Mayor and another Government officer were sitting in the reception/visitor's waiting area, having a cigarette and coffee. I smiled and greeted them, all the head bows, etc. They seemed oblivious to the bra demand. I went to the reception counter and told the receptionist that I just need to speak to Putu briefly and asked if she could come out to the visitor's area.

Putu came out, and I tried to explain to her why I was there, but she had other ideas. She opened her blouse and told me that the bra she had on was too small and she needed a bigger one (in front of the Deputy Mayor and others, who don't seem to care). I explained that I didn't have any bras and agreed with her that her bra did indeed look too small, and it looked uncomfortable, and that the one I was wearing was a little the same. She grabbed my breast to have a feel and agreed that we both needed bigger bras. The Deputy Mayor and others did not seem to think this was strange in any way.

Finally, she asked me what I wanted. By saying abruptly. "So, what do you want?"

I explained that I needed the phone number for the person that owned the house that we had the childcare centre in, as we wanted to rent it again. Then another village head walked past and asked what we were talking about, so I explained to him the purpose of my visit. The phone number, not the bra fitting. Then another one yelled out from behind the desk jokingly, "Fifty million!" (meaning the price of the rent on the childcare centre, which is ten times more than last year). Then the Deputy Mayor wanted to have his say. Still smoking, he said we should put a flat-screen TV in there, in the house. Not sure what he was on about, so I just teased him and told him he shouldn't watch Indonesian TV, it rots your brain. He sheepishly said, "Just at night."

I told him he should read a book.

Finally, after everyone had chatted about bras, TVs and rent, I was given the phone number, and I left.

I arrived back to the hotel; I asked one of the twins to help me install a lock on my desk. *I am not sure which twin, but he comes and helps me.*

Then he and his brother were to move the desk to the reception area, but he had disappeared. I went in search of either twin, and found that all the staff had disappeared. *Ahh, it's 11.00 am, every staff member has lunch at 11.00 am.*

I mean every staff member, no one at reception, no one in the kitchen, no one answered the phones. I walked around to the area behind the kitchen where they took their breaks, numerous breaks. All the staff held up their plates of food and in unison said, "Makan." (food/eat)

I smiled sweetly and replied, "Selamat makan," then they continued to shovel it down in silence, all squatting, even those on chairs. *Makan Dulu. I cannot disturb them now. Aduh*

You do not ask a Traditional Balinese to stop eating to work. 'Makan Dulu' is 'eat first', just like 'Kopi Dulu' is 'Coffee first'. *I had Kopi Dulu down pat, long before living Bali.*

Finally, they finished their lunch, and their cigarettes, and slowly, and I do mean slowly, started to get back to their tasks. However, no twins returned to me, so I went looking for them, to have them move the reception desk. (These two are our muscle men, six foot tall and very strong). I could not find two twins, just one, no one knew where the other one was. *This is common at work, staff disappear for a while, there is a black hole somewhere in the hotel, I will find it one day.*

Then, one of the girls from the kitchen came out and asked me what I had done with the tape measure that I had borrowed earlier. I told her I put it back on the fridge, where one of the twins had gotten it from, for me. Well, I was told it was not there. So, I did three laps of the hotel, retracing my steps and had at least ten out of thirteen staff ask me at every turn, where the tape measure was. *It seems like it is so urgent, they need it right this moment, so everyone must stop what they are doing to ask me where it is.*

I finally went and checked for myself, on top of the fridge, there it was. *Well, that was a good twenty minutes we all managed to waste, better than the black hole.*

While doing my lap work, I did manage to find another staff member to help one twin. *I most likely came across both twins on those laps, I will never know. He will do.*

So, they pulled the desk apart (not necessary), carried it over and dumped it in bits on the floor in the middle of the reception area, and just stared at it. At this stage, we had two reception desks, one in pieces (it's a sectional) in the middle of the reception area and nowhere for guests to sit, and it was a mess. A car pulled into the hotel driveway, and five official-looking men got out. *Oh, great, bad timing.*

It turned out they were from the bank. So, the five bank men mastered the obstacle course into the reception area and stood at the end of the hotel reception desk, announcing they were there to discuss guest credit card payments. No appointment, they just dropped in. *Probably wanting free coffee and snacks.*

We really needed to get this reception area cleared. So, I left the Bankers for a moment to go and round up more staff. *With more staff, we should get this done quicker.*

This did not go as well as expected, the staff could not work out that you have a front and back to a desk. *Drawers need to open guys, can't be against the wall guys.*

Then another staff member walked in, announced, "Oh, that needs glue," and walked back out.

Then we seemed to have more staff, all trying to work out how to put this desk back together, that they pulled apart. It was turning into what seemed like six Mr Beans all trying to work together. *I mean, this is not IKEA furniture, this thing has two parts and a top. C'mon guys!*

It was lucky I had those five Bankers, as they did a great job putting the desk together and really helped set up the Hotel Reception. They agreed with me that we needed a new painting as well. I liked where they put the pot plants.

I wished the Bankers had stayed five minutes longer, as, when I returned to admire the reception, one of the staff, the old man Pak Jero, had hung up all the things he could find, on any nail on the wall behind the reception desk. Where I'd had a whiteboard removed. We are talking hung on any angle, an old, ripped calendar, some handwritten notes, any nail on the wall he had hung something, as in punched the paper over the nail. I took them all down and put them in the drawers of the desk, which were empty. *As, who uses drawers? Silly me.*

I went to find a twin to pull out all the nails.

Hubby came back and asked which twin helped me. I told him I had no idea. He asked if it was the grumpy one. I told him they are never grumpy to me. I told Hubby that I really wished he had not paid for one to get a haircut and have his little goatee cut off, as now I could not tell them apart. *I am sure during the day they both help me, just not at the same time.*

So, that job was finally done, but then someone had then gone and died in the village, *well that slows things down just a bit.*

At least Mr 'I'm so old' Pak Jero had to leave, so he could not hang anything else up. I did not ask who died, I had a bit of stuff to get done and I had wasted a ridiculous amount of time on reception.

As I had no staff, they all had to go off with Hubby to pay their respects to the deceased, I decided to pump up a canoe that had been repaired. I did not really have a choice. Well, I could have just left it, but it was still sitting on a path in front of the entrance to our storeroom, blocking the path to two hotel rooms, where the staff had just walked out and left it there, pump attached and all. The canoes cannot be put away unless pumped up, as they sit on racks.

It was a hot day, so I took it over to a tiled area in the shade at the end of the hotel, away from guests' rooms... I was using the foot pump to pump up that canoe and I heard, 'Hello, Hello'. *Stupid me, I forgot this is quite near to the cemetery.*

The whole village was walking down the street to the cemetery yelling up to me, 'Hello!' ...Now, I am talking nearly the entire village, 500 of whom I had not seen in a while.

So, it was, 'How are you? What have you been up to?', and a lot of laughs at me pumping a canoe.

Then, of course, a quick bury of the body, and they were all walking back. So, the other half I did not talk to on the way down, were now on their way back.

Canoe finally pumped up, and I was very sweaty, as though I had done a bit of a workout, and I was about ready to go home. It was only lunchtime though, my lunchtime, not staff lunchtime.

Nope, the deceased's family had come into the hotel, and all wanted to catch up. One had started going through the photos on my phone. My phone does have a password, but she was quick. *I put it down after using it and she had it.*

She came across a photo of me, you know the silly ones on Facebook that show what you would look like as a Hollywood star. *Ok, I know, I was bored on the long drive one day, and everyone seemed to be doing it, I buckled.*

She was in my Facebook account now, then she showed Ibu. *Great.*

Then it was getting passed around to all the staff—*any excuse for them to stop work.*

I'd used a photo of when I was thirty years old, so, then I was asked 'why I was so beautiful back then?' I replied, it was 'Pre-marriage', and it was touched up with makeup.

Lots of laughs and a discussion, that I should wear makeup, etc., then everyone gestured to a family member who does makeup for a living, as in I should let her do my makeup. I looked at her makeup. *Hmmm, not sure if I could pull off the blue eye shadow, bright red lipstick and white pasty stuff put on with a trowel look. Thanks, but no thanks.*

I commented, "I can't stand that thick stuff on my face, I do not know how you wear all that gunk."—roars of laughter.

So, when I finally got my phone back, the twins wanted to see a photo of Hubby when he was younger. *For this, both twins show up? Ok, and then back to work.*

I showed them a photo 'pre-marriage'. Ibu made a gesture like her arms were snapping like a crocodile. *Not sure what that one is all about, she has a thing with wild animal impersonations.*

Then did her usual, 'you are so beautiful, Sibran is so ugly'. *It's that 'I should have married a Balinese thing' again.*

All the staff that could possibly stop work had to come in to see this one, and comment how fat he looked. Then I remind the kitchen staff that they were supposed to be cooking lunch for the guests that were sitting in the restaurant.

So, it was a typical morning at work. It has been a long time since I worked in a Western world, I wonder if I could still fit in?

8 March 2018 – The Toothpaste

The cook at the hotel does not have a mobile phone anymore (it's broken, he goes through a lot of phones, Hubby gave up giving him new ones), so we cannot ring any last minute orders.

So, I rang the hotel phone. No one answered, so I sent an email to the hotel:

> Please tell the kitchen we have a tour tomorrow, it is now with 3 guests, not 2..

I got back a reply to that email, later that night, that just said:

> Sorry Rach Ibu need you to bay a toot past for the guest maybe tomorrow you've free time

As soon as I arrived yesterday, I went straight to Ibu and said, "I got your message last night, we can go shopping for you tomorrow to get the toothpaste." *Always best to suck up to her first thing, makes it a much more pleasant day ahead.*

I confirmed with her that she was sure she did not need toothbrushes as well? "No, No, just toothpaste," she declared.

She thanked me, and then I went and gave the cook the order. (No one had told him I emailed). *It seems like Ibu will not give me any material to write about today.*

Later, Hubby went in to get some money from Ibu to buy the toothpaste, and he had a similar conversation with her. He explained that last time he had bought her little packs with toothbrush and toothpaste together.

"No, No, No!" Ibu demanded, "Just toothpaste!!"

Hubby was a little bit more thorough than I was and told Ibu to look at the box, as it clearly stated on the box, 'Toothbrush with toothpaste'. He asked if maybe she had later bought some separate toothbrushes?

Ibu put on her glasses, read the boxes, and screamed out to the Security Guard "Why didn't you tell me they were a set?"

Hubby was not sure why the security guard was involved. He still does not realise the dynamics of her staff. I have come to realise that the Security Guard is the only one that listens to her or comes when she calls.

Basically, Ibu was just venting and had most likely forgotten which member of housekeeping told her they needed just toothpaste.

So, Hubby had money in his hand to buy toothpaste AND toothbrush sets for Ibu. All sorted. We were about to leave, guests heading to the car, we were having to drop some guests off in Seminyak before going home, as our driver had taken our other guests. And Ibu's driver had not returned. There seemed to be no one else available in the whole village.

It was a nice peaceful day, Ibu left me alone.

How wrong was I?

Ibu came running out, "Rasch Rasch! Did you buy me a painting for reception from Tegallalang?"

Um, no Ibu, don't you think I would have given it to you?

I nicely replied, "No, Ibu, I haven't exactly had the opportunity to go to Tegallalang."

Ibu yelled, "Yes, you did! You went through there the other day with guests!"

Geez, she doesn't know about the toothpaste, but she sure has her spies out, as to my movements.

I replied, "Yes, Ibu, with guests."

Ibu declared, "Well, you could have just taken them in the shop with you."

I calmly explained, "Ibu, the shops are closed that early in the morning."

"They are open now, go now, take these guests with you, they can look at paintings!"

"Umm, Ibu, we are not going through Tegallalang."

"Well, you can go tomorrow, after Lotte Mart!"

"Um, Ibu, that is an extra one-hour drive each way for us, and from here, it is only thirty minutes to Tegallalang. You could go."

Huff, huff, "No, you go, take your guests now!"

I walked off doing my Ibu head shake. I mean she only wanted two paintings, two metres x two metres each, they could go on the guests' heads, not a problem.

When I finally got in the car, after making the guests wait, due to Ibu, I apologised for the delay, explained what had happened and said to them, "Imagine if I got in the car just now and said: You want to look at painting? Just looking! I can get you cheap price if you want to buy. Then we go look at woodcarving and batik, we go to coffee plantation, I get you cheap price. I have friend."

9 March 2018 - The Coming Home, Take 3

We have had our mind set on using our old childcare centre as our new peak season home, as it is a three-bedroom house, being that the bedrooms are the size of closets. That is fine, we do not have much. My home office in our house in the south, is in the walk-in-robe, with the clothes.

The childcare centre is perfect, as it has a large walled yard that we want for the dogs, of course. However, a five-metre strip of the wall has fallen down. So, we thought, that is fine, we will pay to fix it, as a bonus for the landlord. The children have all moved to the new kindergarten. We will eventually paint over the murals, we may keep the one with clouds.

The landlord agreed that we can have the house for a year, and that they will organise to rebuild the wall and we just pay her for that. That saves us time in organizing etc. *Happy Dance.*

We agreed on a price, for one year, including the wall, which was about the price a family of four would pay for the buffet lunch at the Mulia Hotel in Bali. It still amazes me the price people pay in Bali to consume food and drinks at these high-end places. I am not a 'Foodie'...Okay, I am a 'Drinkie'. *If we had the budget, I would be an alcoholic.*

Many years ago, a friend had his 40th birthday at KuDeTa Restaurant in Seminyak. I rang Hubby from the bathroom to tell him that the bill on our table of six people, was the same price as one year's rent on our house in the South, seventeen million rupiah. This is just an observation, not a judgement on anyone, just giving price comparisons. If I were on holidays and had the money, believe me, it would be champagne and wine every day. *Okay, I lie, if we had the budget, I would just drink champagne and wine every day, no need to be on holidays.*

When it comes to prices in Bali, it seems some people pay Bule prices, especially tourists when shopping, and some expats when paying rent, etc. We do not, we pay local prices. I discovered this one day when Hubby dragged me shopping in Poppies 1, Kuta. I despise shopping, he tricked me as it led to the beach, where I was promised beer. When he asked the price of some shorts, the lady said, "For Balinese, it is fixed price."

Hubby and I are both blonde and blue-eyed, I guess we are no ordinary Bules. We try to teach people on our tours all about this, it really is about the tourist, not the local. Extremely hard to put on paper, there is a lot to it, but once our guests understand, it is like a light globe going off, and everything just looks different to them. I love those light-globe moments. Sometimes I do not, as sometimes people's light globes indicate they are thinking back to moments where they may have been ripped off, and a lot of thoughts go racing through their minds. I look at it this way. If you were willing to pay it, then how can you say you were ripped off? Move on, negative thoughts are not good for the mind and soul.

So, back to the house, all agreed on, then I got this message on WhatsApp from the landlord:

'What date did you want to move in again?'

I sent back: 'Well it was going to be 22 April, but since you are fixing the wall, it can be 1 May.'

I got back: 'Okay, we will need to check the calendar and see when it is a good day to fix a wall.'

Here we go again!

14 March 2018 - The Painting

A pleasant surprise today, got to the office to find Nengah had painted our office. It needed it, washing off all the ash residue took off most of the paint.

I guess he also wanted to change the wooden furniture. He did not use any drop-cloths, so now the desk has a new pattern to it. But it's all matching, including the printer and the chair.

Note to self: Tell Nengah we do not need him to paint the house after all.

Chapter 6 - Ibu-Ibu

24 March 2018 - The Ibu Dua

When learning Indonesian, counting and measurement can be an interesting one, as they use a different method of classifying plural objects, grouping inanimate things. Unlike English, where we can just add an 's' on to most things, in the Indonesian language you can use the word fruit (buah) or word tail (ekor) as classifiers of inanimate objects or not. However, I am not always talking about bananas or puppies, but I could be, so I had a few interesting conversations in the beginning, when I believed I had mastered the language, only to discover I had not...

An old man once told me he had four tails at his house, he was referring to four puppies. He could have actually told me he had four tail puppies and it would mean the same thing. But, if he had told me he had say, 4 spiders, he may have used the word for tail as a classifier. For example, four spiders would literally be said four tail spider... and I would have stood there arguing, that spiders don't have tails. Or the staff would ask me if I wanted the three fruit tables moved, and I would argue just move that bloody table... not the one with fruit on it. The storekeeper would ask me how many seed eggs (the word seed is used as a classifier for a small individual piece), and I'd say I just wanted chicken eggs, none of those strange ones... They do eat some weird eggs here, so I was trying to clarify... but failing miserably... I had to learn to just stop and think, and to also not be so quick to argue... Eventually the language sank in, mind you it took me years to stop asking Wayan to cut the hair instead of the grass. Potong rambut (haircut) potong rumput (cut grass).

Just as the language can be confusing to non-Indonesian speakers, it can be just as confusing to Indonesians to speak English, so I think many do an amazing job. The 's' for plural can be very confusing to a local learning English. They would say, for example 'dua buah kilo' (two fruit kilo), for two kilos, say, of rice. I get away with 'dua kilo', I drop the word 'fruit' and they know what I want.

Nusa Dua, which is in the South of Bali translates as Island Two. It is not an Island. Confused? The name comes from the two small Islands in the bay next to the area.

The first time my birth mother met Ibu, Ibu very confidently told her in

English, that she, Ibu, was Mother Number One (Ibu), and that my birth mother was now, Mother Number Two (Ibu Dua).

Ibu Dua is easily described. She never goes anywhere without her handbag and her lippy on. She must have a cup of tea wherever she goes. She does not drink or smoke, yet she seems to get herself into situations I generally get myself into when I have been drinking. I on the other hand do not carry a handbag, have never worn lipstick, and have never drunk tea. We always agreed that we did not have much in common.

However, when Ibu Dua first visited me in the village many years back, and she saw the room we were living in, she exclaimed, "Oh, you are my daughter."

Which was much better than, "Are you sure you are not a Capitalist?" which she had said years prior.

So, Ibu Dua is my birth mother. There are actually more Ibus, blame that on my father remarrying five, or it may be six times, who can keep up. There is a whole book to be written on that one, stemming back to before I was born. *Someone else can write that story.*

I have just booked Ibu Dua into Ibu's hotel for two nights at the end of May for Galungan.

I have warned Ibu Dua, that there will be an Ibu-Ibu Chronicles.

7 April 2018 - The Personal Assistant

I got to work this morning to find that Ibu had put up some signboards from the 1970s on the wall behind our tour desk. *Okay, I can deal with that, until we get our new sign made.*

I then went to the tour desk to plug in my laptop, as I was going to work from reception, since the hotel was quiet, they had no reception staff to bother me and, so Ibu & Bapak did not disturb me. Only, to discover that I could not pull out the chair. They had moved the reception desk in, so the tour desk was now basically a cupboard, and the chair was trapped between the desk and the wall.

So, I was back in Bapak's and my office, and within five minutes the hotel phone rang. No one answered it, so I answered it.

Then I was running around the hotel trying to find Ibu and Bapak, as it was a Mangku and someone had died in the village.

Then Ibu came in and answered the next call, talked to the caller, scribbled some notes, hung up and walked over to me. I was busy typing on my laptop and Ibu placed a pen and paper in front of me. I mean, while I was typing, she put the paper under my wrists, just to make sure I saw it. "Sibram, write this down!" (She often calls me by my husband's name and pronounces it in various ways.) Ibu read out her dictation, and I wrote down what she said, as she had scribbled her notes in shorthand. *I guess I am now Ibu's secretary?*

Ibu left satisfied with that. I tried to get back to work.

The hotel phone was ringing again, and I was not answering it...*Okay, I answered it.*

Then I was off to find a staff member to help that caller. For some reason Ibu had staff off doing really important stuff in the hotel, like planting some onions out the back, as opposed to answering phones.

I knew I just had to wait another twenty minutes until it was the guests' check out time, and then I would be grabbing housekeeping to have them move that tour desk back before they were too busy cleaning rooms, or planting onions.

Then Ibu walked in and asked why I was not working at the tour desk like I said I would. I explained that the desk was blocked. She stated, "Oh, just have the staff move it later."

I took the opportunity to ask her about the sign she put behind our tour desk.

She answered: "What sign?"

Ibu has either lost her memory, or she really has no idea what is going on in her own hotel. I'm off to have the desk moved. Oh, wait, the hotel phone is ringing again.

I'm working from home again tomorrow.

26 April 2018 - The Genius, No More

I may not be a genius anymore. So, after many years of planning, we have a new tour program, where guests can do traditional classes. Our Balinese offering making classes have started with some free trials.

Although the guests have thoroughly enjoyed them, I have made a terrible mistake. My mistake was trying these classes out on smart people. Our first class was a more extended class, on our over-night tour. We offered it to our guests for free, as a 'let's trial Ibu,' and see if she can last without slapping anyone's wrists, as she does with me, or yelling at them etc.

As the guests were friends of mine, they could give me some honest feedback, and if it were a major fail, not a problem, we would just drink beer instead.

This was not exactly the right group to start Ibu on, as she immediately started commenting on how smart they were. *That's fine, okay, the next group may not pick it up as quickly as this lot.*

So, we tried the shorter class with the next tour group. Let's see how they go. *Hmm, okay this group is picking it up just as quick, I mean their son can solve a Rubik Cube blindfolded in some ridiculous time. I really should have chosen a different group.*

Ibu again, commented, "How smart the Bules are!"

I can't believe I paid Ibu for these classes, only to have her find out my secret, I really should have thought this through. Why didn't I think about how exposing Ibu to other Bules, she would work out that I was not a genius?

For the last trial group, I was a little relieved when one person did make a small mistake. Ibu did have a little go at her, but the class ended with Ibu saying, that she had worked out that all Blues are smart, not just Rasch! *There goes my secret, I have had them all fooled for over ten years. In fact, I took so long when I first start making offerings that now Ibu knows I am a bit slow...*

Would any idiots like to do a Balinese Offering Making class?? I need my reputation back.

12 May 2018 - The Toast, Yet Again

Okay, so today one of Ibu's staff was buttering bread and putting it on the grill plate. I caught him doing it, and even though I said stop, he continued until all four were buttered. *It is amazing how they ignore you and continue.*

I have had that before, I once told Nengah (the kitchen Nengah) to STOP, as she was putting tap water in the pancake mix. She just kept going, even though I was repeatedly saying STOP. She even continued to make the pancakes with me following her saying, "No, No!"

Then all I got was, "I forgot."

It is like robots without a bloody off switch.

So, I tried to explain to the staff member that what he was doing was frying bread, and that it was not TOAST! Ibu butted in, "No, put in fry pan."

NO IBU!!!!!!!!! This is my main problem...Ibu.

I calmly, while exploding on the inside, as you never get anywhere if you raise your voice here, explained that if you put it in the frying pan under oil, it was more like French Toast.

Ibu heard 'French toast', and she said, "Okay, we make like that for the French guests."

OMG! That is the worst thing I could ever say. It is the hamburger with ham all over again. I am such an idiot.

So, Hubby joined in on this one, trying to explain that French toast is made with egg and milk and the French will not be ordering it. We tried to explain, for example, French fries are just called French fries. Nope, Ibu had never heard of French fries. *We nearly put them in her head, but luckily, she is too French toast focused.*

Ibu had decided! Ibu started to make French toast... but she did not have milk. No matter how much we explained that milk was a key ingredient, Ibu was determined, and she was in one of those lockdown moods, where you just cannot get in. Ibu grabbed the sweetened condensed milk, which would be fine for sweet French toast; however, Ibu grabbed salt, and pepper. I literally had to slap her hand away from the pepper.

Ibu made her French toast... and then announced, "Bapak will be the taste tester."

Poor Bapak, he doesn't even eat bread. Hubby and I left the kitchen, we had a house to paint...*there is no point when Ibu is like this.*

13 May 2018 - The Pie Warmer

I arrived at work and saw the coffee pot warmer had been removed. A very large pie warmer had taken its place. I did not think much of it as Ibu had a large government meeting that day, not that they eat pies, they must have had some use for it. *Maybe it belonged to the group, as they were setting up in the meeting hall?*

Nope, Ibu had bought a pie warmer, so she could keep toast warm in it.

I only discovered its intended purpose, when she asked me to write a sign in English that said, 'Please choose 2 pieces of toast or 1 pancake.'

Ibu obviously had a travelling salesperson come to the village... they can smell her a mile away. Anything different, anything no one else has, and Ibu wants it. How a pie warmer salesman, sold a pie warmer, to a Balinese woman in a village, who has never seen a pie in her life, just goes to show their sales brilliance.

Now, after a LOT of arguing, I managed to convince Ibu that no one wanted a piece of toast that had been sitting in a pie warmer for hours. And, her amazing pancakes, which are more like a crepe, unfortunately, would turn into rubber Frisbees when they sat in there for a while... *Those pancakes are a secret wheat-free recipe she will not share with me.*

So, after explaining it could not be used for toast and pancakes, I wondered what she would do with a pie warmer.

One week later, that pie warmer was still sitting there, so, I asked one of the staff, "Did Ibu buy this thing brand new?"

"Yes," he replied, "For KFC."

I clarified, "For what?"

"For KFC, fried chicken."

I remembered a previous argument with Ibu. It was about BFC (Bali Fried Chicken), and that she should let the little shops popping up all over Bali do their Deep-Fried Chicken. Ibu should stick to running a Hotel and a Restaurant. So, I calmly explained to the staff member, that we should send the toast warmer/pie warmer, *now known as the fried chicken warmer,* down to the warung. (Ibu also has a warung up the road.) I commented that this was a restaurant, and everything must be fresh, the warung could have cooked chicken that sits there all day. He looked at me with a 'well, you know Ibu', look. We both nodded in agreement.

So, later that day, we had to pop into Ibu's warung up the road, as one of the staff there had the key to the childcare centre/our house, and we wanted to get in. Low and behold, some travelling salesperson had also sold Ibu an ice cup machine. This fancy machine puts a plastic seal on a plastic cup—*Gee, great for the environment Ibu. Great in a village with no rubbish collection Ibu.*

There was one of Ibu's staff, standing out the front trying to sell these cups of coconut ice. *To whom? Who the hell is she supposed to sell them to?*

The warung is on the main road near to where all the homes are. Tourists rarely get past the aggressive guards up the road, and the only people walking around are old local people with no shoes and a load of grass on their heads, and not a cent in their pockets. *That travelling salesman better not come back when I am there!*

15 May 2018 – The Arrival

We collected Ibu Dua from the airport and brought her to our house in the south.

It was a long night. Ibu Dua fell asleep reasonably early. After I explained to her that the large gecko in her room was called Fred and that we've never really asked him to leave. I would try, but otherwise, he was there first.

Before going to sleep and having her, 'Just one more cup of tea', Ibu Dua wanted to show me these amazing magic sponges she bought online from China, they could get any marks off walls! *You have been up for 20 hours, on an International Flight and you want to show me sponges at 9.00 pm?*

Just like Ibu, once she has something stuck in her head, there is no stopping her. So, she proudly got out her white sponge (she only brought a bag of ten of them) and went looking for a mark on my walls.

To her dismay, she could not find any marks on my walls. I asked her, "What made you think I would have dirty walls?"

Ibu Dua replied, "Surely, with all these dogs, there must be slobber on the walls."

I proudly declared, "I do not have slobbery dogs," and let her continue to find a mark. I soon realised if I did not find one mark for her, we would be there all night. I finally found a small gecko poo mark. *Thank you, Fred.*

She was so pleased and proudly showed me how you just lightly rub over the mark. Major fail! Ibu Dua said, "Ah, well I didn't want to rub too hard as one lady online said they took off all her paint, but I have never had that happen, they are just amazing."

Her online shopping may be like Ibu's travelling salesman.

Once Ibu Dua finally slept, poor Hubby could not go to sleep yet. We had run out of water in our tanks. We do not have mains water, but a neighbour had water. So, Hubby needed to hook up a long length of connected hoses to a neighbour's tap fifty metres up the street. The mains water only comes on occasionally from 10.00 pm until 3.00 am (not at all at our house, but the neighbour has a pipe from another house). So, Hubby was up all night filling tanks and buckets all over our house. Ibu Dua was not aware of that, and I woke to a large scream as she bumped into him in the middle of the night, on the way to the loo. She then proceeded to talk, well whisper to him, but she is just like Ibu, a bit deaf, so a very loud whisper. *I did not hear Hubby utter a word; she may have been whispering to herself.*

It is okay, she lives alone, she talks to herself all the time. She talks to everything, she reads her phone out loud, she talks to the dogs. *I talk to the dogs as well; they are such good listeners.* I am sure in her home she talks to her plants.

Anyway, we got through the night. This morning I went to have my coffee. Ibu Dua has learnt over many visits that the Number One rule in our house in the morning is DO NOT talk until we have had coffee! Kopi Dulu! So, I walked past her, and she put her finger up to her mouth to make the 'shh' sign and then stood there watching me make coffee with a look on her face, that she was just busting to say something.

I proceed to make my coffee, but it was too cruel. It was like watching a child on Christmas morning trying to patiently wait until the moment they could open their presents. I finally said, "Go on, I know you are busting to talk."

Well, she did not have the best night's sleep. *Well, none of us did there Ibu Dua.*

She went to the loo and was frightened to bump into a man in the dark. *Yes, well, that would be your son-in-law Ibu Dua.*

Then, while she was in the loo, a bat got stuck in her hair. I had thought the 'bumping into Hubby' reaction went on a bit long, but it was 3.00 am, and I just put a pillow over my head and tried to go back to sleep. Welcome back to Bali Ibu Dua.

19 May 2018 - The Conversation

"Hello, Hello anyone there?" Calling to speak to Ibu on the phone takes patience. *Sabar Sabar.*

Ibu does not have her own mobile phone, so I must call the hotel.

I needed to talk to Ibu about my Manager. I decided to call before he started his shift. So, I called early this morning. I called, and no one answered.

Then I called again a few minutes later and got a fax line.

Then I called, and Ibu answered, she must not have been able to hear me, so she hung up.

I called again, Ibu answered. I did manage to speak to her for a few seconds, to ask her how she was, etc. She mentioned Lotte Mart and shopping and then she put the phone down and walked off. Then I could hear someone pick up the phone and hang it up.

One hour later, I called, and I got Ibu again. I asked her if Nengah was there yet, as I wanted to speak to her privately about Nengah. She put me on the phone to Nengah. *Aduh. Oh, well, had to talk to him about our tours, so had an excuse to talk to him.*

So, after talking to Nengah I asked him to have Ibu please call me straight back, as I was now running out of phone credit. I knew she was in the room with him.

Two hours later, no call from Ibu, so I called again. I got Pak Jero. He answered the phone with a grumpy "Yeah."

Great, all my staff training has gone out the window.

I asked, "Is Ibu there?"

He answered grumpily, "She is busy."

I asked, "Is she in the hotel?"

"Yeah, she is busy."

"Can she please call me back when she is not busy?"

"Yeah, Yeah, Yeah."

At least when Ibu answered the phone this morning, she answered with a friendly 'Halo.'

I called again, one hour later, and I got another staff member, who answered, "Halo."

I asked if Ibu is there.

He replied, "She is praying."

I asked for her to call me back...

Still waiting... Sabar Sabar

Note to self: train staff again on how to answer a hotel phone, and to take a message.

20 May 2018 – The Cool Shades

I walked into the kitchen at work this morning, forgetting to take off my sunglasses. They are prescription glasses. Ibu spotted them and wanted to try them on. She got the shock of her life when everything went dark. I explained she had to go outside, so she went into the restaurant. Nope, still could not see. I explained she needed to go into the garden, in the sunlight.

Ibu walked to the back garden and exclaimed, very loudly, "Oh, I can see!"

"Ibu, shh, there are guests in the restaurant."

She walked back, giggling her head off that the guests had heard her.

Ibu then proceeded to walk back inside to look in the mirror, complained it got dark again, and that she could not see the mirror. This went on for a bit. Finally, she announced, "They are too small for your face, so I should have them!"

Ibu believes we have the same prescription. We do not, unless of course, she likes my glasses.

Being real Armani's, I am a little disappointed, but I will get them back eventually. When she keeps bumping into things in the kitchen.

Oh, Ibu Dua used her magic sponges on our kitchen cupboards while we were at work. I think she was incredibly happy that something needed cleaning. *They do look sooo good.*

21 May 2018 - The Training

Ibu's training style and mine are vastly different. All the staff that have been trained by Ibu, seem to understand her training method, and apply the same method to any new staff. Hubby and I do not in any way understand her training method. I once said, at a staff meeting, "If I cut off all our heads and spun them on this table, Hubby's and mine would face one way, and all of the staff's would line up facing in the exact opposite direction." *Being Balinese, I presume their heads would face Mt Agung.* (In Bali, Mt Agung is always North – no matter where you are on the Island – now, that's another story).

I was busy painting the childcare centre the other day and went to the hotel to grab a quick staff lunch. I looked in the kitchen for the glass cabinet that for years has had little bowls of yummy bits and pieces for staff lunch. I looked everywhere, but could not find the glass cabinet, so I asked the Chef. He said, "Oh, now we buy lunch from outside."

This is a restaurant, and they are buying food off the street carts?

I asked why that was, and he looked at me and said, "Training."

Training, now that word has been a constant source of amusement to Hubby and me over the years. It started many years ago when we had five high school boys come to train with us for three months. We had two with us, we put two in the kitchen, and one was with housekeeping.

On day two, of the boys' training, we walked into the kitchen to have our coffee, that coffee, that without drinking, I do not function. The staff know not to talk to me until I have had my coffee. *Kopi dulu.* All the staff have kopi dulu before they start work, even if they are two hours late, kopi dulu. I went to grab a cup from the coffee cup cabinet as an automatic morning ritual. There was no cabinet. I looked around blankly, and the Chef pointed to the other side of the kitchen. I asked why it was over there and was told, "This is the students' training."

Hubby and I looked at each other, as in we do not really understand it, but okay, we will just go with it.

Over coffee, Hubby and I discussed it. We concluded that maybe Ibu thinks if the boys take out every cup and glass and move the cabinet, then wash everything and put it all away, they will never forget where everything is. Also, everything will be washed. It made sense, sort of.

The next morning, we went into the kitchen and remembered the cabinet had been moved. In a robotic, 'I have not had coffee yet' motion I went to where the cabinet had been placed in the new position, the day before. It was not there; it was back in its original place. Hubby said to the Chef, "What the hell?"

Chef answered, "This is training."

Ok, so, those boys will never forget where those cups are.

The next day the cabinet was moved back across the kitchen. *FFS, what the hell is going on here?*

Me, "What the?"

The Chef answered, "This is Training."

Now, come on, they are supposed to be training in kitchens, not furniture removals?

This became a daily ritual for those boys, until I said something to Ibu, who got a bit peeved. Okay, a lot peeved, that I insulted her training method and told me in no uncertain way, to train them myself.

So, four weeks ago, Ibu hired some new staff. I was busy, yet every moment I walked past her, she went on and on about me training them. *They are not my staff.*

Ibu had not actually mentioned to me she was hiring new staff. I only knew about new staff when I walked into the kitchen and found the whole kitchen rearranged. Hubby walked in and looked around, then looked at me and said, "Training?"

We laughed and sure enough, in walked two new staff into the kitchen.

I have not had time to train them yet, so the kitchen has had a makeover every day for the past four weeks. I can't even find a spoon now.

These two will be able to put furniture removalists on their CVs. However, I am sure they applied for jobs as kitchen hands.

24 May 2018 - The Milo

Yesterday we only went up to the village to work on the childcare centre, to get it ready to become our temporary 'winter home', and to borrow Bapak's pickup truck. We had a lot of stuff to do. Such as get a hole in the bathroom filled with concrete. A big hole, to reinstall a toilet that was put in by one of the twins and was balancing over a one-metre-deep hole on a piece of thin wet wood. *My own fault for asking someone who has never used a toilet to install a toilet. I will try the other twin.*

It was getting late, so we went back to the hotel at about 5.00 pm, to get the pickup truck and say goodbye. Ibu was in one of her lockdown focus moods, the focus being Milo. I walked through the kitchen and noticed a staff member crushing up small cubes that looked like beef stock cubes. Turned out they were Milo snacks. Someone had put in Ibu's head that she could make Iced Milo drinks with her fancy ice cup machine she had bought. I had to explain to her that the little things he was crushing were milo snacks for kids (cookies), not drinks and that Milo required milk. "That bloody milk!" (Ibu thinks milk is as annoying as our dogs. She cannot understand why so many Western meals need milk.) Ibu demanded, "Go to Denpasar and get me Milo and milk!"

I told her I could go on Sunday, but we were a tad busy currently. She screamed we could go on the way home. I explained the supermarket would be closed by the time we got home. Ibu was not impressed.

Now, to those that have moved furniture, or moved to a new house, you know how much work and time is involved. Ibu has never moved to a new house, since she got married 48 years ago. She has the staff move furniture all the time (especially kitchen staff), so, she could not see why I could not fit shopping for Milo in.

I said goodbye, see you tomorrow, and then Ibu started to cry and would not stop. Her lip quivered like a three-year-old, and she cried, "Please buy me Milo, I need it tomorrow."

So, this morning we got up extra early, packed up the truck and then had to make a detour in our three-hour journey in the rickety pickup with no AC, to find Milo.

We finally found it (it came with milk powder in it, so weird) and then we got stuck in traffic, so it took five hours to get up to the hotel.

When we arrived, Ibu was not there. Ibu was at a ceremony and not back yet. So, we went to the house and unpacked the truck and back to the hotel, still no Ibu.

I was exhausted, so I decided to stay at the hotel. Hubby would drive back to the south.

One of the staff just told me Ibu is not due back till 9.00 pm. So, I just gave the kitchen staff the Milo, which they just put in the kitchen pantry, they did not even know she wanted it. *Aduh*!

26 May 2018 - The Joker

Ibu was in one of her joking moods again. Telling Hubby that I had a different boyfriend in my room every night when I stayed in the hotel alone, and that is why I stay, not that I am tired.

If Ibu is going to whisper a secret to someone, she really shouldn't yell their name out constantly first.

29 May 2018 - The Pizza, obviously

We went into the kitchen the other day, and one of the twins was making pizza. *He was not smiling, so I do not know which twin.*

He does not usually work in the kitchen, but it seemed that there were no other staff around, so he stepped in. *Finally, some training has sunk in.*

I still get the Twins mixed up; the other day I paid the wrong twin, and then I gave the wrong twin the key to our house to do some work. That key has since disappeared. So, I was locked out of our house for two hours yesterday, as Hubby had the other key and had gone to Ubud. My fault apparently, as I used a whistle as a key chain and the twin with the key said that his kids must have thought it was a toy. So, the key is somewhere in the village. I will just have to listen for it.

So, back to the pizza. I looked down on the kitchen bench to see what for a minute resembled a pizza, but not quite. There was a strange bright orange substance on it, and the twin was placing normal pizza ingredients on top. I asked, "What is that?"

He replied, "Pizza."

I said, jokingly, "What is it, Bali Pizza?"

He replied nonchalantly, "Hawaiian."

Hubby walked in and said, "What, the hell is that?"

He replied, "Pizza."

Hubby asked, "What type of pizza is that supposed to be?"

The twin again replied nonchalantly, "Hawaiian."

Hubby exclaimed, "But, that base is still too thick!"

This one was only just over an inch thick, so, we should consider this an improvement.

The twin ignored him and started to put on the cheese. Hubby said, "Well, at least that is a great amount of cheese."

Personally, I think Ibu will go bankrupt with that amount of cheese.

I jokingly said again, "This must be some sort of Bali Pizza, with that weird orange sauce."

The twin again replied nonchalantly, "Hawaiian."

Hubby and I looked at each other. It was that '180 degrees understanding of things' look. We gave up and walked out.

I went and found the Chef and tried to explain to him that the base needed to be thinner and asked what the orange stuff was. He said, "Sauce."

I asked if he made it.

"No, Ibu bought a jar."

I went to find the jar... I found it. Now, some of you that live in Bali, or have been here many times, may start to realise that the locals refer to things by their brand name. For example, they do not say nappies/diapers, no matter what brand they buy for their baby, they are all called Pampers.

So, I am presuming Ibu must have said she wanted Prego sauce, which is a brand here. Well, she got Prego sauce. I believe that may have been the first brand she was exposed to. It was Capsicum Chunky Garden Vegetable Pasta Bake sauce. It did not even have tomato as an ingredient.

I really wanted to hang around to see the guest take a bite.

Note to self: Must move pizza training up on my long list of staff training.

31 May 2018 – The Village Arrival

So, Hubby picked Ibu Dua up from Ubud and brought her to the village. I went looking for Ibu and told her Ibu Dua had arrived, and she blew me off.

Ibu Dua thought maybe Ibu had her nose out of joint that she had arrived, I mean she has been Number One for a long time. It was the day before Galungan, a particularly important ceremony, so I just presumed Ibu was busy preparing offerings for that, and that she was in one of her moods. I knew that mood was guaranteed to switch soon, and I assured Ibu Dua it was not personal.

It turned out Ibu was not that busy with offerings, Ibu was busy with her new idea.

Now, I had no idea what Ibu was up to. I walked around the back to see Ibu using her grandson as a measuring tape. Yes, as a measuring tape, she had a long plank of wood laying on the ground, she was lifting him up to sit him down on the plank, then marking a spot, lifting him again to sit, and marking another spot. That seemed perfectly normal to everyone observing.

I had no idea what she was making. Still, I went to get the camera anyway, as surely this was going to be interesting.

By the time I had returned, the grandson had been replaced by a real measuring tape. I still had no idea what she was making, and I wrongly presumed it was something for the ceremony, silly me.

I asked her, and she said it was for people to read a book on and fall asleep. *Umm, a bit of a strange concept, sleeping on a plank of wood?*

I shrugged it off, as most of Ibu's ideas are strange to me.

A few hours passed, and I spotted Bapak feeding his fish near Ibu Dua's room, so I called him over to say Hello to Ibu Dua. It took him a while to realise who Ibu Dua was. *He has only met her about five times, us white people all look the same.*

He greeted Ibu Dua and then asked how old she was, as you do. He commented he was a few years older, welcomed her, said we were family, and off he went.

I then went to find Ibu. She was still in a mood, the staff were cutting up the plank of wood. Not sure if they were using the grandchild measurements or the tape measure ones.

One of our foster kids' grandfathers came to the hotel to welcome Ibu Dua. He was much more eager to see her and catch up than Ibu. He greeted her and asked her how old she was, commenting he was a few more years older and then sat down to have a good old chat. He wanted to invite us both over to his house for Galungan, as all his children and grandchildren were there, and said that his wife would be so happy to see Ibu Dua again. So, that made Ibu Dua feel more welcome, that someone remembered her, it has been three years, and that they all wanted to catch up.

Then I saw Bapak and the staff, come around the corner carrying a huge metal thing. (It was like a large metal U, approximately three metres high). *Maybe it was for a marquee for the ceremony?*

Again, I had not been informed of anything, so I was going with the focus on the Galungan ceremony again.

I excused myself from Ibu Dua to follow them all, to see where they were taking this thing.

I asked Ibu again, in between her acting as foreman on the placement of said large metal object. While she was telling her grandchild quite sternly that his body was not required for this part. I was finally told it was 'A Swing'. Now, where on earth this idea came from, I do not know? Why money was being spent on this thing and not fixing the rooms, I do not know? Hey, I never understand her way of thinking, I just go with it, generally.

After seeing the nearly finished result, I cannot really understand how you could fall asleep on it without falling off, but hey, I just need to let it go.

After the swing was installed, I asked Ibu to come and say hello to Ibu Dua. Ibu said she was too busy and proceeded to cross the street, right in front of Ibu Dua's room, to go with Bapak to pray at a small Temple. *Hey, I can't argue with that one.*

Ibu Dua later commented to me, that Ibu gave her a funny look as she returned from the temple. Knowing Ibu, I have a niggling that she may have done the prayer at that time to make Ibu Dua think she was busy with important things, although Ibu Dua had seen the swing arrive.

Ibu finally seemed satisfied that she could leave the staff to finish the swing, prayer was done, she came to Ibu Dua's room to say Hello.

She was as sickly sweet as she could get, but soon there was a genuine love there. Ibu greeted Ibu Dua and asked her how old she was, told her Bapak was a bit older than her and that she was only 63. Ibu was doing her best with a little bit of English. Ibu Dua was doing her best with a little bit of Indonesian and I was so confused that I kept speaking Indonesian to Ibu Dua. I was trying to translate for them both. Ibu asked all the questions that she should really know all the answers to. *I mean she's only known her for a decade.*

I answered many of the questions on behalf of Ibu Dua, without translating, as I knew the answers. *Well, I should, I have known her for my whole life.*

'So, where is your husband?' I answered he is dead, knowing divorce would just confuse the issue, and especially the number of wives he's had. That got confusing, as then it was, 'How many siblings did I have?' I advised, I am Ibu Dua's only child, and she should already know that. Well, boy, did I get it for being the only child, and still getting it... that is more of a story for later.

Ibu went on and on and on, firing questions one after another: "Does Ibu Dua live alone?" "What would happen if she got sick?" "What happens when she dies?" "Will I go to Australia?"

Then Ibu declared, that Ibu Dua must live with me, as I am her only child, it is my responsibility, she is old, blah, blah, blah. *Oh boy, and you wonder why I never tell you stuff about my 'other family', Ibu!*

So, I was trying to translate all of this, and I said to Ibu Dua, "Ibu thinks you should live with me."

Ibu Dua very quickly replied, "Oh No, that wouldn't work!"

Maybe, a little too quickly.

That was hard to explain to Ibu, that my mother really could not live with me since we would drive each other insane, was not really something I could say. So, I said, "Hey, she is not old, she is fitter than me, she plays tennis three times a week."

Then Ibu commented that, 'Yes, she does look very fit and healthy. Racsh obviously does not take after Ibu Dua, Racsh takes after Ibu and is unfit and unhealthy for her age'.

Aduh.

So, after the interrogation, Ibu Dua was finally welcomed back to the family.

1 June 2018 – The Eat, Pray, Crash

Ibu Dua was going on a bike tour the next day, and I suggested she practice on a bicycle, not in front of the tour guests.

When Ibu Dua first came on tour many years ago, I suggested she practise when the other guests were there. Bad move. On that first tour, many years ago, I was casually chatting to the guests when I heard a scream. Ibu Dua came flying towards us from the back of the hotel, down the garden path, with some speed, screaming, "There are no brakes!"

I had very quickly realised it had been that long since she had been on a bicycle, that she was trying to use the brakes on her pedals, that did not exist. So, I screamed out, "They are on your handles!"

The message clearly did not get through, and still screaming, "NO BRAKES!" she went flying past us, out the driveway, across the road and came to a halt upside down in the cabbage patch. *It's moments like those that there is no denying it, she is definitely my mother.*

So, we were going to practise this time, with no guests around.

After a few wobbles, and changing her to a children's bike as she is very small, she was off, braking and all.

Ibu Dua got quite good at it and was riding around the hotel calling out, "I feel like Julia Roberts!"

Ibu, Bapak and Pak Jero (fifty-five-year-old staff member) were in a bit of shock. *I mean, she is seventy-two, and in their mind, I should be planning her funeral.*

Ibu and Bapak's grandchildren were all called out into the restaurant to see the 'Grandma ride a bicycle'. *I am amazed they did not phone more family members, to come down and witness this miracle of youth.*

Pak Jero kept calling out, "She's so smart, so smart."

Not sure what was going through his head, but I never do. *Did he think she had just learnt to ride in that short time?*

So, Ibu Dua was ready and racing to go...

3 June 2018 – The Ibu Way Or The Highway.

Or in our case, small gangs (lanes). Ibu made it very clear, that she was not impressed with my lack of responsibilities that I am supposed to adhere to, as an adult child of an 'elderly person.' Trying to get it into Ibu's head that Ibu Dua isn't exactly elderly, she is fitter than me, was not working. So, Ibu was in one of her moods with me.

Last night, I went to Ibu and asked how much she would charge me for her driver to take Ibu Dua to the airport when she left. None of our drivers wanted to do the trip. I knew our rate and her rate, and I knew it would be peak hour, so I was willing to pay a bit more than she usually charged me, so the driver got a fair rate.

Ibu upped the retail price by IDR 50,000, going on about traffic and the toll road, etc. I got shitty and said, "That's more than the normal rate on the board for tourists, well Sibran will just drive her" and walked off.

I can be in a mood, too, Ibu.

4 June 2018 – The Ibu Dua Departs

The next morning, when I walked in to the hotel, Ibu and Bapak just snarled at me, as I said good morning. I said, "Fine", in English and I muttered some other stuff. *It is great that they do not understand me, as I can get it off my chest in English and go on with my day.*

The time came for Ibu Dua to depart, to go back to Australia.

Ibu Dua had spent one week at the beginning of her trip, with us at our house in the south. Ibu Dua commented that the last two days staying in a hotel, nearby to us, not in our house with us, was much more enjoyable. And, that although Ibu insisted Ibu Dua and I should live together, she had thought that idea was mad. Now staying close by to us, she realised that if she lived in Bali, in a house close by, she could cope with that. *Does that mean Ibu Dua is moving to Bali?? We will see. Probably not, unless she wants to live with Ibu.*

Ibu Dua was packed up and was ready to check out. We went to the cashier, and Ibu came out to ask what Ibu Dua was doing. I explained that Ibu Dua wanted to pay by credit card. *Oh boy!*

Ibu started saying that I should pay for her as she is old. *Ibu Dua probably should have milked this old thing more while she was here.*

So, Ibu looked at Ibu Dua's food and room bill and said she could not pay for her food, that it would be free, and she would take that up with me later. *Aduh.*

We already had a discounted room, but Ibu discounted it some more, telling Ibu Dua that I was crazy. Ibu Dua proudly commented to Ibu, that she was crazy as well. *A bit of a bonding moment when your birth mother realises you take after her after all.*

Ibu made a lot of hand gestures and made a lot of comments, getting very vocal, and although what she was saying was in Indonesian, I think Ibu Dua got the gist of it. *Ibu can mime like Marcel Marceau on drugs, she should be on the stage.*

She went on and on about Ibu Dua's crazy daughter and her ugly husband. How I should be looking after my old mother better. I should be going to the airport with her. *Only a 6-7 hour return trip.*

How we are family, and we need to look after the elderly. Ibu told Ibu Dua, with one of those mother-to-mother looks, that she would talk to me and scald me later. Ibu and Ibu Dua hugged, some tears, and then Ibu Dua started to leave. I reminded Ibu Dua, that maybe she would want to give me a hug goodbye as well. It was not that she did not want to say goodbye, Ibu Dua had been distracted by Ibu's over the top performance. *Ibu can make you forget everything you were doing; it happens to me daily.*

A big hug and some tears and she left... Well, we thought.

Hubby took Ibu Dua to the Hot Springs, as her flight was not until later that night, but returned thirty minutes later, as it was a public holiday, and the place was full.

Ibu asked me, "Why is Ibu Dua back?"

I told Ibu, with a very straight face, "Ibu Dua has taken in everything you said, and on the way to the airport decided to return to live with you, as she is family, and older. And now Ibu must look after Ibu Dua until she dies." *Gotcha Ibu!*

Then the time came for Ibu Dua to leave, for the second time, and suddenly light globes were going off in Ibu's head. She got extremely dramatic, as she had realised that it was Ibu Dua going to the airport. For some reason, she thought it was an older couple that we had as guests that I had asked for a driver for. *Not sure why they needed to pay more?*

So, after Ibu making her huge scene in front of Ibu Dua, again, about her leaving and I should pay, as her child, for everything, blah, blah, blah, Ibu Dua departed, and I was sat down for 'the talk.'

When you are nearly fifty years old, and your parents want to give you a lecture, it does make you feel young. *Okay, guilty.*

I did not get any lectures growing up, so maybe I had some catching up to do. The whole family were called down for this one, Ibu's grandchildren had front row seats. Ibu and Bapak, talking over each other. They explained that they had not realised it was Ibu Dua wanting to go to the airport, and that I should have explained that better. I apologised. I have learnt that it is easier.

I pointed at Ibu's chest and said, "Next time Ibu Dua is here I will only refer to you as Ibu Satu, and my birth mother is Ibu Dua, stupid me." *Every married female in Bali is called Ibu, and we have never had this problem before, obviously, my fault.*

The grandchildren thought this was hilarious, they had not heard the Ibu Satu & Dua thing before. Ibu reiterated that when Ibu Dua was here, I must always call her Ibu Dua, and Ibu, Ibu Satu. Ibu was repeating it over and over. They like to repeat things to make sure you get it. I know that's how they train staff, you know, move the cupboard, move it again, why not move it again. Okay, just one more time, in case you didn't know how to move it. No wonder Ibu calls Bules smart when they do her offering class, as they seem to get it straight away, no furniture moving required.

The grandchildren were laughing so much that Ibu got a little confused on her 'who is Ibu Satu and Dua', which made them laugh some more, then the rest of the family got in on the laughing. *Maybe they think it is silly that Ibu got confused? I mean there were only seven Ibus in the room right now, and we know who everyone is.*

So, once it was set in stone, 'The Ibu Rule', then came the lecture of the 'Old Person Rule.'

Now, this one was too long to write, but to give the shortened version; basically, Ibu had a plan. Ibu and Bapak will give us land. We are to build a house here for Ibu Dua to come and live with us, so she can die here and be cremated. It did not matter how much I tried to explain that Ibu Dua has family in Australia and that they may want to be involved, it was decided. *Maybe she thought the Australian family could have a Bali holiday at the same time as a funeral?*

Ibu basically said if I was not willing to move back to Australia to live with Ibu Dua there, then this was the only solution they could come up with. Ibu Dua will live here until she dies. It has been decided. I was having visuals, of the process here in our village with the dearly departed, and I was not really up for it. I mean I know, being dead, at least Ibu Dua would not be talking my ear off, but I really did not want her lying on the kitchen table for a few days, no matter how quiet she was. She's not that heavy, but we live in a maze of small gangs. I did not want to carry her down the gangs and do a Weekend at Bernie's. Nor did I want to go and dig her up every 210 days until she is cremated, and I am pretty sure Ibu Dua wouldn't want that either! *Oh, why couldn't I have had an older brother to give all this to?*

Now, really it is quite lovely that they care, but Ibu Dua will probably outlive me. She certainly does not want to spend her last years living with me. *She has not done anything to deserve that.*

In the end, I just agreed to follow Ibu and Bapak's long term funeral plan for Ibu Dua and said I will start saving.

Note to self: Tell Ibu Dua personally about her funeral plan, before she reads the Ibu Chronicles on Facebook.

Chapter 7 - Kampung Living

7 June 2018 - Living in a Kampung

For those that have been to Bali, you may have heard the word 'Kampung' before. You may have heard hotel staff or Balinese friends say, "We are going back to the kampung."

A kampung is basically a village, generally a basic village, you would not call Sanur or Legian villages a kampung. Many Balinese live in quite modest homes in the south of Bali. They make the journey, sometimes cramming the whole extended family into one vehicle, or even on a motorbike, to go 'back to the kampung' for a ceremony.

We have many families back in the kampung this week as it is Galungan. An extremely important ten-day event where families come together, including their dead ancestors. I have heard the analogy of Galungan being a Balinese Christmas. I can see why, I could compare it to my Australian family Christmas, especially when the families go back to a rural area. The family all get together, travelling back to the original family home. They get very drunk, eat far too much, argue a bit, get nagged by their parents, even though they are adults. The grandchildren from the city spend a lot of time bored with their country cousins, as they are told to stay outside and can't play computer games. The children and teenagers all get up to old fashioned mischief, while their parents prepare lots of meals and get drunk. *Yep, sounds a lot like an Australian Christmas, minus the dead ancestors.*

We are back in the kampung. It has been nearly a decade since we lived up here, and we are living part-time in the old childcare centre/now our house. It has a lovely vibe about it, as Ibu Dua pointed out, probably from ten years of little children occupying it. *Boy, little children are dirty, seriously, it has been one month, and I still can't get the place clean.*

I have removed most of the names written on the walls, and washed the walls, but it still feels dirty. Sorry, little Wayan and Made but that crayon turtle and your other drawings just had to go, they were collecting dirt.

I can't blame the kids entirely, as the house walls were covered in a fine film of ash from Mt Agung as well. If the kids had not played with a ball inside so much, there might be more glass in the windows. Newspaper just does not cut it when the neighbours burn their garbage... *we will need to get some glass.*

I painted a lot of the walls, left the mural, as we may need to use the place for children again. I thought I had painted most of the white walls. I woke the first morning to look up and see a rainbow sticker on one of the walls. I had not seen it before, it made me smile. *Not sure how I missed it, but it can stay.*

I also woke up the first morning, and before even getting up, I could see out the window, there was Mt Agung. *Who the hell moves closer to a volcano that is on high alert?*

We are 13.7 kilometres from the crater, I went and looked it up straight away. Agung kindly welcomed us that first morning by erupting at 4.39 am. It was just a minor eruption, and the wind direction was in our favour, but geez, or Aduh.

The childcare centre was purposely built for children, and not a 6.4 ft Dutchman. Hubby must duck under the doorways, and the kitchen bench comes up to his knees, but many people in the village do not even have a kitchen, so we won't complain. The toilet was not designed for children, I am not sure who it was designed for. In fact, I now feel five years old, as I must climb up to sit on it. It was put on top of the old squat toilet and my feet dangle (they do not touch the ground). We probably should have used a plumber instead of one of the twins to put it in. We built a concrete step, but it needs to go a little higher still. Sitting there swinging my legs, it makes me ponder how children go to the toilet comfortably (western toilet) when they are small. I now believe parents really should cut them some slack if they want to use their potty for a bit longer.

Some other things are too high, such as the kitchen tap, it is one-metre above the sink. *To keep out of little children's reach?*

The power points are at head height and none are placed in a practical spot, but we don't have many electrical appliances. There are only four power points in the whole house, that will do.

Hubby installed a hand-held shower, but I can't reach it. It does not really bother me, as we have no hot water, so I am not using it anyway. I am back to the old *mandi, water boiled on the stove, and then poured from a little plastic bucket with a long handle. And it is cold up here at night, but that's just me being a Princess, it is currently 11 degrees at 6.30 am. Now you may think that's not cold, but you cannot buy a heater anywhere in Bali. I know, I looked. When your windows are made from newspaper, your walls and ceiling are not insulated, and you have no carpet, it gets a little chilly. *If the old ladies can do it, then I can do it. I am fitting in; I have the socks with thongs (flip flops) thing down pat.*

The dogs are also being Princesses, wearing jumpers and jackets (thanks to Ibu Dua bringing them some), so I am not the only one. I try not to be a Princess, but the word got out very quickly. One of the old ladies across the road seems to have told everyone that I slept at the hotel for a few nights, so I could have hot water. Whenever I see her in the street, she asks if I am sleeping here tonight. I know she must have said something, as last night when I went to the hotel all wrapped up in winter woollies to grab some dinner, Ibu asked me if I was too scared to shower because we did not have hot water. I reassured her that I had bathed, but had not washed my hair as it was too cold. She agreed it was too cold to wash your hair and said she will probably use one of the hotel rooms. *I am getting in on that action. Must suck up to her a bit more.*

I know it was the old lady in our street that must have spread the word, as I heard her telling people in our street. She does that a lot, she asks me a question, and then repeats it immediately to all the old people sitting in the street, quite loud, like an announcement. *God help me if she ever gets a loudspeaker.* I guess they are just too tired to get up and ask themselves, and so they rely on her. There are a few old ladies that daily poke their head over the front wall and ask me questions. *Maybe they have a roster?*

'Have I eaten? Have I bathed? What am I doing?' It is a bit like having lots of Mrs Mangles (Australian TV show, Neighbours). One old lady passed me over some rotten bananas yesterday, when I answered I had not had lunch yet. *Thanks, Grandma.*

It is stunningly beautiful up here, though. I mean, I was here all the time during the day, when there were ceremonies or for work. From the hotel I was always in the hotel grounds in the morning and I had forgotten about the morning mist over the mountains, listing to the temple prayer and music as the sun rises in the village.

Saturday is Kuningan (the last day of the ten-day ceremony, which started with Galungan) and everyone will be back in the kampung to send the dead ancestors back to the Heavens. I mean, they can't stay here forever, this gets expensive, feeding then, bathing them and entertaining them. Sunday will be quiet again when everyone goes back to where they live in the south.

Oh, and our neighbours in the south must have thought we moved up here permanently, as when we went back down to the south last week, we found they had erected a marquee in front of our gate, on our driveway. *That's okay folks, like good Balinese, we do not complain. Well, not in person, I have the Ibu Chronicles to just let it out.*

It was a lot of walking back and forth to put furniture in the car to bring up, as we could not get our car into our carport, or even close to our house.

We may go back down to the south as well on Sunday, and see if we can get into our driveway. Not sure if Sunday is a good idea though as there will be thousands of hung-over Hindus leaving their kampung.

A mandi is a tiled box in the corner of the bathroom, used to scoop water over yourself to shower and when going to the toilet, to wash your privates.

8 June 2018 - Santa Is Back In Town

Once a year, Santa and his wife come to town and bring our village and us, lots of presents. Santa arrived yesterday bearing very, very generous gifts. Santa and his wife must be two of the most generous people I have had the pleasure to get to know. They have been a huge contributor to our school and our village, they live in Australia.

This year Santa spoiled us. Ibu even got a gift. I had no idea that they had not met Ibu before, and upon Ibu meeting Santa's wife, Ibu told us that Santa's wife was the Number One most beautiful in Bali. Ibu explained that if you have dimples when you smile, then you are considered the most beautiful in Bali. Ibu and I do not have dimples when we smile, Ibu pointed that out.

Ibu did the normal Bali questions, 'How old are you?' etc., and then Ibu found out that Santa and his wife had a Medical Clinic in Australia. Well, Ibu went on and on about how she had never been to a Medical Clinic where the people were so beautiful and friendly-looking. Ibu said that she was far too scared to go to a Doctor in Bali as they were ugly, mean, and scary, and she thought she would get sicker by going to them.

So, Ibu took the opportunity to get a free consultation and asked me to ask the Doctor why she kept forgetting things. Ibu wanted to know if there was a pill to fix her memory loss. I told her that the Doctor had said, 'No, there are no pills, and she will probably have to be locked up in a mental hospital very soon.'

Ibu looked shocked and was speechless for the first time. It took a few seconds to click I was joking, but Ibu soon realised, and then tried to push me over, laughing her head off, telling the beautiful Doctor that I was crazy. *I learnt that from you Ibu, I too can be a Joker.*

Ibu was a little disappointed that the diagnosis from this very beautiful Doctor, was, "We all start to forget things when we get older."

10 June 2018 - Strike a Pose

Yesterday was Kuningan, and that meant dressing up again in Traditional Adat (Customary) clothing.

Now, I have been a little busy going back and forth in between houses, moving stuff, cleaning, and working as well, so I had not washed my smalls. So, the night before, I asked Ibu if I could borrow a white or skin coloured corset, she has so many. Ibu brought out a handful of corsets for me to try; every time I put one on, she announced it fitted. *Not sure she has ever had a bra, or a corset professionally fitted, but I am pretty sure that certain parts belong in certain places.*

A few were just so tight. *Okay, I know a corset should be tight, but I need to breathe.* They were all made for a slightly less endowed woman, the one that came anywhere close to fitting didn't exactly fit. I tried my best to get those girls in there, but I guess wearing them under my arms for a few hours can't hurt. I put my top back on and walked into the restaurant to show Hubby, Santa and the Doctor, and we laughed our heads off. I mean, Madonna seemed to wear that look quite well. I walked back into the office and showed Ibu, by pressing my finger in the middle of one of the pointy cones, where my girls should have been, there was just air in there. Ibu gave both pointy cones on my chest a firm poke as well, and then pulled the corset down further and said, "Tomorrow remember to pull it down."

Well, although pulling it down did flatten my pot belly somewhat, I was still left with the pointy Madonna look. *It will just have to do.*

So, the next day the Doctor and I walked around the village, dressed in Adat, and no one really noticed, until we got to the next village and my girlfriend Made came out to say Hi. Made laughed her head off, poked where my girls should be, and then proceeded to poke the Doctor's corset (who she has never met before) and found hers to have some filling. Made poked mine again, then gave them a good feel to try and work out where I was hiding my girls, discovered them, squeezed flat under my arms, and laughed again. Made gave the Doctor's another feel just to reiterate how a corset should fit and then started to chat about the weather.

10 June 2018 - Washing Your Smalls

Have you ever noticed there are no washing lines in Bali? Well, some expats may have bought one at Ace Hardware, but you won't see a Balinese with a Hills Hoist (Australian washing line).

I finally got around to washing my smalls, and I am using a rope on the kids' swing set. I must have it quite low to the ground, as we cannot have clothing worn on our lower body, up near our heads.

Hubby suggested I wash today, as the builders next door are not working, or they may question all the eye patches hanging on a rope.

13 June 2018 - Not a Problem

Our tour guests were doing a Balinese offering-making class with Ibu. Mt Agung volcano decided to erupt. Ash was bellowing 4000 metres into the sky, thirteen kilometres behind them. Ibu said to the guests, in English. "No worry, ya? This normal," and continued with the class...

14 June 2018 - School Graduation

Had a beautiful morning with our school graduation, Hubby handing out awards, me crying, as I do every year. And then someone went and died. No, it was not one of the kids, a person that had been sick for a long time. It gets a bit busy in the village when this happens. I mean everyone must drop everything and carry the deceased down to the cemetery. I mean drop everything, so all the people that work down south must stop work and come back up to the village.

There were so many people to catch up with, that I have not seen, since, um, last week, when someone else died. This is the group that work on Kuta and Legian beaches. You know the ones; you may have been to Bali and heard their 'war cry' on the beaches, "Want massage? Paint nails, buy bracelet? Where you from?"

I see a different side of these people, I mean the last time we went to Kuta beach, everything was free. Yes, we have spent a whole day on the beach, with food and beers, and never paid a cent. When you are from the same village, you are family, no one would let us pay.

Payback for free stuff today though, it is tiring on their knees, walking on the sand all day annoying tourists. Today I had so many beach vendors up in the village wanting knee compression bandages, magic pills for achy muscles and generally just a good old fuss over. The problem, besides me not being a Doctor, was that when you are in a funeral procession, it can be quite difficult to check someone's knees. The traffic makes it even more difficult. *Bloody people on public holidays in a hurry kept tooting at me as I was lifting sarongs and trying to walk at the same time.*

I did not check the deceased, but I felt like I checked everyone else. *Good thing I went to medical school. Oh, that's right, I did not.*

So, it is finally over, everyone has headed back to the beach to make it for the sunset rush. You know, they believe that when the sun sets, the demons from the ocean mesmerise you and can steal your children from the shore. *I know many tourists on Kuta beach that get possessed by demons at sunset, they are forgiven, they can't help it.*

18 June 2018 - It's A Good Day For

Many years ago, a guest said, "It's Good Friday."

I was having a coffee and enjoying the beauty of the scenery and agreed "Yes, it is a Good Friday."

Later they mentioned it was a good thing they were having fish for lunch as it was Easter. *Oops.*

Back then, the Christian holidays really didn't get a mention in Bali, I mean you couldn't even find a Christmas tree. I remember putting on Facebook that I had forgotten it was Easter. My Aunt commented, 'God wouldn't have been too impressed that you had forgotten.' *Oops.*

Well, in our village there are lots of 'good days' for certain things, and then there are days that are not good for things. You may already know that there are good days for weddings and funerals in Bali, or you may have just thought that everyone liked a certain day, but no, it must be on the 'right day'. There is a calendar that will tell you all of this, it is hard to read, it is in Balinese, but we do not really need to read it, as that's what our Mangkus (village priests) are for.

Yesterday must have been a good day for burning. And, oh, boy, did they burn. I rode my bike to work, and by the time I got there, I had been through four clouds of smoke and smelt like burning plastic.

One year, when we were living up here the first time around, we discovered there was a 'good day 'to cut your hair. You were not supposed to cut you hair on another day. Being a hairdresser isn't the best vocation to choose in this village. The way we discovered this, was one day all the staff were lined up at the back of the hotel, cutting each other's hair. At first, I thought they had just decided to all get haircuts at the same time but was soon told it was a 'good day' in the calendar for a haircut.

Being very traditional up here, they follow that calendar to a tee, thus the reason we had to wait sixty-nine days until it was a good day for our roof to be fixed.

There are good days to make iron, but it may not be a good day to sell iron. A good day to fix the fence, but not make a new fence. Good days to fix the roof, good days to slaughter a pig, good days to work on a house, good days to farm, good days to make weapons, a good day to make a snare to trap vandals, the list goes on and on, and on.

So, the other day Hubby said he needed a haircut, but not to upset the balance of things, I thought I better look up when was a good day. I could not find one, I told him I'd get back to him, I'd ask my Mangku when I next saw him.

Then, earlier this afternoon, I was outside walking one of the dogs, and I noticed a row of men lined up in the gang (street), cutting each other's hair. I came back inside and announced to Hubby that he was having a haircut.

I gave mine a trim as well, as you do not know how long before this day will come around again. So, we've both had the chop, and then I thought I better double-check the calendar. I looked up today, and it says nothing about a haircut. It does say 'it is not a good day to do anything important'. *Well, at least I got that right, didn't do much important today at all.*

19 June 2018 - Chunky Joe, Where You Go?

The Balinese language has different dialects from village to village. A girlfriend in the next village told me I needed to learn her dialect. An Indonesian girlfriend in the south, had always commented that I speak Indonesian with a Balinese accent. When the Bupati (Regional Mayor) has visited, Ibu has insisted I speak High Balinese. (There are different levels, with different words.) I only speak informal low Balinese. She has given me a phrase to say, three seconds before he has arrived. *Geez, sometimes I can't even find a word in English, give me a break Ibu.* I have too many languages in the cupboard in my head. Some days I go to the cupboard, and the cupboard is bare.

Chunky Joe (how it is pronounced, not sure how it is spelt) is Balinese for, 'where are you going?' in our village. In my girlfriend's village, just a few kilometres away, it is pronounced 'Ke Joe' (again, not spelt that way). In our village in the south, it is 'Kulky Joe' (spelling?). All of which you hear quite often.

In the south, the Balinese in our village call us, 'Bangli', meaning we speak Basa Balinese (Balinese language) from the Bangli region.

Now, in the culture here, it would be quite rude for someone not to enquire as to where I was going. I mean, does one of your family leave the house without a word?

So, the other night, after two nights of dog fights in the street all night, and no sleep, I decided it was time to do something about it. I grabbed a huge bowl of dry dog food and was heading off to solve the problem. I mean the fights are from a hungry wild dog coming from the mountains, trying to move in on the other dogs' garbage. It was after dark, (it is dark by 6.50 pm) and I opened the front gate. Only to startle a man sitting on the front wall of the house opposite (three-metres away) with his walkie talkie. (Pecalang – our local guards) "Chunky Joe?" he enquired.

I explained that we had not had any sleep and I was off to feed the dogs to solve the problem of fights. The Pecalang promptly announced to whoever was on the other end of the walkie talkie, that the Bule Mama was off to feed the dogs in the street to stop them fighting. Copy that. *I guess when the old lady has gone to bed, someone must make a night announcement of my movements.*

The person he was speaking to, must have been a long way away as the antenna on his walkie talkie was nearly two metres high.

So, that sorted, report of my movements attended to, I headed down the very dark gang. I could see some shadows of dogs, but they were moving further away. I mean, what human is out walking the streets after dark, she must be scary. I passed a house, and on the porch, were some people chatting, "Chunky Joe?"

Obviously, they didn't get the memo.

So, I explained it all again to them.

I started putting dog food on a few entrances to homes, then continued up the gang to the mountain base. I could hear a motorbike coming up behind me, the light getting closer. A man in the dark of the night, said, "Chunky Joe?"

I could not see who he was, I was a 'deer in the headlight'. I explained again what I was doing. *Geez, could the first guy not have announced it on the loudspeaker for me?*

So, the guy on the motorbike, no idea still who he was, said he would follow me and shine his headlight, so I could see. I walked further up the gang, nearly at the mountain base now, the headlight shining into the darkness with a giant shadow of me on the trees. I placed a large pile of dog food at the tree line and thanked the guy. He turned and headed off into the darkness.

I turned to walk back. I could see the lights in the distance of the homes, but I could not see the road. I knew I had to be careful, as the road was only two metres wide, and it was being repaired, so on the edge, somewhere in the darkness was a one-metre deep ditch. I then heard another motorbike pop out of one of the side gangs, but no headlight, "Chunky Joe?"

It was two kids on a motorbike, with the headlight off, probably as they were not supposed to be out after dark. They seemed to know where the ditch was, so after explaining again to them, who I could not see, only hear, as to what I was doing, I followed the sound of the motorbike back to our house.

I decided to walk past our house to the garbage dump and put the rest of the food there in separate piles, so maybe the dogs would not need to eat garbage. I was again startled by the Pecalang with the walkie talkie, as he nearly fell off the wall, while he said, "Chunky Joe?"

So, I had to explain my intentions again, which he promptly reported to whoever was out there listening. Copy that.

I returned. I explain to the Pecalang that I was now going inside the house, he reported that as well. *He seems quite pleased that he has something to report tonight.*

It was a very quiet night; the dogs did not fight.

The next night they started fighting again. *This is going to get expensive.*

I may have to write up a memo for the Pecalang, with a schedule of my dog feeding, so he can send it out to everyone; will save some time.

25 June 2018 - Pulling Teeth

A saying that came to mind, as we were trying to find a beer in the village after 6.00 pm tonight. If we do not go down to Ibu's hotel, finding beer in the village is a bit 'like pulling teeth'. Well, to Hubby, it seemed that way after I sent him on a beer run. He went to many of the little warungs in the village, that either did not sell beer or wanted to charge 5-star prices for a dusty bottle off a shelf that sees the sun most days.

Now, Ibu does not charge me tax, but she isn't the neighbour in the south, who illegally sells it from her house, so beer isn't as cheap up here, and it is hard to find a cold beer, or any beer in this village. We also wanted something a little closer to our house and cold. Okay, to be honest, to avoid Ibu knowing how many beers we can drink.

We had a couple of beers at the restaurant at Ibu's hotel a few weeks ago, and the twins commented that they had never, in five years of working for us, seen us drink. We have had a few friends visit lately, who have stayed at Ibu's hotel, which has made for a few nights where the staff have seen us partake in a few beverages and then wanted us to go home. They have not been late nights, Bapak has locked and turned the beer fridge off promptly at 9.00 pm, so no point staying any longer. We thought if we got beer from the hotel tonight, we may get a reputation...well Ibu has been commenting on our drinking.

We needed beer. Hubby and I had decided, today when we got back to the village this afternoon, we needed to have a business meeting. After we had spent the morning running around Denpasar, paying car insurance (simple things like online insurance is not simple here, or online anything). Trying to find our cat in the house in the south, who thinks we have abandoned him for good, and a whole lot of staffing problems. It was decided, a company meeting needed to be called, between the two bosses, us. We conduct business meetings so much better on beer. We have had the best philosophical, game-changing team meetings on beer. Like a Chinese girlfriend once told me, you can't do business with someone until you have seen them completely drunk. I mean, how can you trust them until you have seen them in that state. I have seen Hubby, my business partner (well Boss, on paper) completely drunk, and so have a few other people. I trust him.

So, Hubby went down to the harbour and shared the love with a few little warungs (shops), buying a beer from a few old ladies (who had a few days prior mentioned they could provide cold beer). Well, he had to share the love as they only had one cold bottle each. His 'get a discount tactic' was, that his wife would be back tomorrow to check their weary knees. *This Doctor thing is ridiculous, good thing Immigration was not aware that the village calls me 'Doctor' (that's another story for later).*

Actually, late this afternoon, I was Dr Hewan, (the vet). It was rabies vaccination time in my gang. I vaccinated them all myself, so they would not get stressed. After my terrible experience, a few weeks ago, that I did not share on the day, as it was just too much, I wanted all vaccinated. I will share now, as I have gotten past it now. Well, I had a beer...

So, a few weeks ago, a boy was bitten by a dog near the school, and they killed the dog, and it tested positive for rabies. Oh boy, was my day hell, that day. They were darting dogs left, right and centre with me chasing them on my bicycle (them on motorbikes) to the next village to stop them. I had to explain that I had already vaccinated them all. Apart from some new-borns... I won't share any more than that.

So, back from the south, all dogs vaccinated, my dogs traumatised again by all the visiting dogs, all dogs fed and in a food coma, I now have a beer. Ok, two or three beers, and a promise that I will visit the old ladies tomorrow to check their sore knees.

Chapter 8 - The Busy Season

29 June 2018 - Ibu May Be Pissed Off Today.

The Governor of Bali is due here to have a BIG meeting at the hotel. Staff have been setting up for days. Agung decided to do its thing again yesterday and again last night. *I wonder if the Governor is still coming?*

I just checked the volcanic seismogram, it says Agung has stopped. *Maybe it is scared of Ibu?*

Hubby thought he'd better go to the office, just in case the Governor did show up. All the village heads were eagerly waiting, with their masks on. Staff and Ibu had their masks on. Hubby did not have the heart to tell Ibu that he did not think the Governor would show. He may be a little busy; mind you the election was two days ago, he's out, so he may not be that busy. The village head announced to Hubby that due to the extra 500 people in the village right now, from yesterday and today's ceremonies, they have handed out all our masks and run out. The village head was a little panicky that they did not have them for the Government staff coming. Hubby thought it best not to tell them the Governor would probably have his own mask if he's coming.

So, Hubby just called me to say he is off to Ubud to buy more masks, since the Governor is thirty minutes late. *He should be fine to do the two-hour drive and make it there and back, in Bali rubber-time.*

10 July 2018 - Let's Have A Meeting

It currently 3.00 pm. We came to the hotel on our day off to have a meeting with Ibu and Bapak, arranged for 1.00 pm. Hubby tried yesterday, but they were too busy. We have had to wait one week for a ceremony to be over, for this meeting, so here we are.

We arrived at 12.50 pm, to find Ibu asleep on the daybed in Bapak's office, and Bapak dressed to go to the city. *I know his city outfit, he's off to Bangli city. So, this meeting is obviously not happening.*

I decided Bapak could do my banking while he was in Bangli. It is the first time I have tried this move on Bapak, Ibu has done it with us forever. I felt a little guilty making him wait while I got out the account numbers and the cash. Bapak waited patiently, however, I did have to eventually chase him to the car with the cash.

I came back to find Ibu had put a blanket over herself, this is her 'leave me alone' move. I snuck up very quietly to put back the pen I had borrowed from Bapak's desk, and I saw her peak out of one eye – that Spy move.

So, Hubby and I went to the hotel reception, to discuss the meeting that never happened and then we saw the Bupati (the Regional Mayor) arriving. This was obviously not a planned visit, he had stopped in for lunch, with his entourage. *Boy, Bapak better get back soon.*

We commented Ibu would be up now. Hubby went to check it out and chat with the Bupati. He was gone for a while, so I thought I better go check if Ibu got up and if she was aware the Bupati was there.

I walked into Bapak's office, and the daybed was empty. Hubby was sitting on one of the guest chairs. Ibu walked out of the kitchen, and Hubby said, "What's up, Ibu?"

Ibu's reply was one exceptionally long, loud burp, then she turned around and went back into the kitchen and closed the door behind her. *I guess we are going home.*

Update: 4.00 pm, Hubby is still trying to talk to Ibu and Bapak. Bapak came back and gave him our bank receipts, then got back in the car and drove off. Ibu is now showing photos to Hubby of her Great Grandchild. It looks like hubby will just sit there out of protest.

Update: 5.00 pm. Ibu has now grabbed a towel and said she is going to have a shower. Bapak is back and suggests we try again tomorrow.

18 July 2018 - Ibu Update

We have a new staff member; he will be our new manager as our Nengah (not Ibu's Nengah) decided to leave after ten years to go and start a pig farm. *I guess tourism is too stressful.*

So, I am spending a lot of time training him. His name is Wayan. Of course, it is.

Ibu is fine, same as usual. I only saw her twice yesterday; she rang me to come down urgently and help her find out what bookings she had. Not sure who worked out her staff roster, but she did not have one staff member working that knew how to check bookings, let alone turn on a computer. I went down, and she was walking around the hotel with her hair dye in her hair. So, just a normal day.

Then I saw her at dinner last night, and she was watching her Indian soap opera and only stopped to ask me if I get itchy boobs. I told her she was scratching her boobs like a monkey. It is not something you say to a

Balinese, calling them a monkey is a huge insult, but she understood she looked just like a monkey and laughed when I told her so.

When Hubby came in, and Ibu complained to him that her boobs were itchy, we knew it was time to go home. So, Ibu is still Ibu.

19 July 2018 - New Rental Office

A few weeks ago, we signed a lease on a new location to store all our equipment; tour guests can collect their equipment there, or even rent the equipment. We were happy to finally have somewhere out of the hotel, as our staff have been caught out a few times, coming to work to find a huge government meeting and the carpark full. The staff could not get in or out.

The lease starts on 1 August 2018, and there is lots of preparation to do before that date. It is a great location, it has a good size building, set back, and lots of empty land frontage, which we can concrete for our carpark and for staff to put bikes out, and they can make a washing area for the canoes there.

I sent Wayan to go get the concreters to meet him, to get it done as soon as possible. We had permission to do this two weeks before moving, so the concrete could cure.

He just came back and said, "You can't use the office anymore."

I was like, "What the?"

We just paid five-years rent, what the hell is happening now?

I have been here a while, so I thought best to clarify: "Wayan, what exactly do you mean by we cannot use the office anymore?"

"Oh, they have started building the cremation tower, and they have moved to the front of the office, as the lake water level was rising."

"How close to the front of the office?"

"Where you want to concrete."

"And how long will it be there?"

"Until we take the tower to the cemetery on the day of the cremation."

"Okay Wayan, how about then you go get the steel guy to come and measure for the canoe racks inside, so we at least have one thing done."

"Not possible, they have blocked the front door, we must wait."

The cremation is on the 2 August 2018. *Sabar, sabar.*

23 July 2018 - Not The Pie Warmer

OMG, the pie warmer was out again today! I had literally just finished a meeting, and there was Ibu, standing behind me with her, 'great idea'. "Chul, Chul (her latest version of my name), please write in English, Please Take One."

Ibu wanted to put toast and scrambled eggs, pre-cooked in the pie warmer for people to take one for breakfast. Here we go again, she will not listen to me, I need back up.

So, I approached one of her guests staying there for some assistance. I explained to the guest what Ibu's idea was, and the French guest shook her head, NO, and screwed up her face. *No need for a translation with that face.*

Ibu thanked her, and the pie warmer was taken away... probably for another day.

Note to self: always get back up from strangers when arguing with Ibu.

26 July 2018 - Hot Jam Anyone?

She went and did it! I just arrived at work to find the pie warmer out, and full of plates of bread! It is nicely drying out in there, it has not been toasted, just put in the pie warmer. I am presuming Ibu has thought, 'Well, she said I could not put toast in there, she did not say I could not put bread.' Oh, and the single-serve packets of jam are inside the hot pie warmer on a plate.

Update: One hour later: I have just asked one of Ibu's staff to take the jam out. It was swelling and about to explode.

Update: Five hours later: When I left work today, I went to say goodbye to Ibu. Ibu had a headache. *I wonder if that was from the amount of bread, she had to throw out today?*

28 July 2018 - Toast

Ibu is a stubborn B@#$. I just had an argument with her about the bread in the warmer. Ibu said there was no waste the other day. *Yeah, right.*

I had just overheard one of her guests ask the waiter for 'Toast, without the butter already on it, and toasted properly please.'

Ibu won't talk to me now. *I give up.*

30 July 2018 - Number Plates

Pre-the Governor and Mt Agung ash visits, we had to go to Bangli city, to get new number plates. In Bali, every five years you get new plates, you put them on yourself, you even have to buy the bolts to attach them to the vehicle.

It was an interesting visit. I had to go, as I am the signatory on the company vehicle. In we walked to the large police station, a few stares, and a Police Officer a little shocked when we greeted him in Balinese. He asked us if we need help/directions anywhere. We explained we need to pay for our car registration and get new number plates. Well, then it turned into a circus, everyone coming over to get selfies with us. I commented that they mustn't get many Bules in here, and they said, "No, and especially ones that speak Balinese."

So, Facebook photoshoot over and back to business. The process is like everything else in Bali; take this to that office, then come back, then go up to that place and pay. Then come back with your receipt and go over there and get your car inspected, then come back here with your inspection report, then go get your plates made, and then come back here.

For obtaining a driver's licence in Bali, I once wrote down the instructions to help other Expats. This felt very similar, so much so, I decided I did not need to make the long walk in high heels to the bank. Hubby could do that, so I stayed behind.

While I was waiting in the carpark, checking out Agung's activity on my phone, a Police Officer entered the carpark and walked past yelling out in Balinese to his colleague about me. I laughed my head off, and he went bright red, as his colleague yelled back across the car park, that I understood everything he said.

The car inspection Police Officer was entertaining, I will refer to him as Mr Polisi. Hubby had to drive the van over an inspection pit for Mr Polisi to look under the car. Mr Polisi exclaimed, "Don't drive into the pit!"

Hubby asked him if people had done that. He said, "Oh yes, slows things down a bit, as it takes a while for everyone to help pull it out."

When Mr Polisi went to inspect the van underneath, he asked Hubby to reverse a bit, he said he was too fat to get in the gap left to the pit. Hubby offered to go in, as he is skinny, but Mr Polisi thought it best not to do so. I asked Mr Polisi if he could clean under the car while he was down there. He laughed and said he did not have the time.

Back in his little office Mr Polisi kept chatting away about everything, besides the vehicle registration. Then he commented on how everything was done manually, while he filled out all the paperwork. No computers there, and when he meant manual, he meant manual. It was quite fascinating watching the plates being made in the next room on a vintage press machine, that I am sure I saw in a museum when I was a kid.

Chapter 9 - Staff

31 July 2018 - Human Resources In Bali

I decided to stay up in the village, but kept out of the office, to do some administration. Hubby was in the south, no tour guests booked, rental office closed for the day, as all the staff had ceremony obligations. Well, we knew two staff members had the day off and Wayan is only new. When Wayan started he told us he could not work on the Friday, we said that was fine, even though our other staff member had Friday off as well (the same ceremony). Still, when our driver did not arrive on Thursday afternoon, to take our tour guests back to Kuta, we realised he may also be having the day off. We realised that, when we called him, five minutes after he was due. So, we decided at that moment the office would be closed Friday.

On Friday, I got a call from Hubby, saying Ibu's staff had rung him, and some people wanted to rent some bikes. So, I rang the staff member of Ibu's straight back and was about to explain we were closed. He told me those people had already left. Apparently, five minutes was too long to wait... *they obviously have not been in Bali very long.*

So, I arrived at work on Saturday, after my day off, of sorts. It was very hard to concentrate with the prayer over the loudspeaker going all day and still going, my brain does not cope well with any distractions. *However, I could recite this chanting I can hear from the loudspeaker right now, as the Priest is repeating himself. He may be drunk.*

Ibu's first words when I arrived on Saturday morning were, "Five of my hotel guests wanted to rent bikes, but you were closed, where were you, where was everyone?" Blah, blah, blah.

I zoned out, and just did the normal Bali thing, and replied, "Not a problem, everyone had a day off for the ceremony." *She can't really argue with that...but she did...apparently, I cannot have a day off...not that I was.*

So, I decided to change the subject to the pie warmer, and how I had noticed on Thursday all the bread wasted again... well, anyway, we all know how that went...

Ibu did not talk to me for most of the morning, she had my guests' offering making class and was getting angry that Wayan was still out on the lake canoeing with the guests. Even though her class time was not due yet.

So, I just ignored her. Then I heard her yelling out for Hubby. I went in and saw an official-looking man standing there. I told Ibu, "Stop shouting, Hubby can't hear you, as he is not here today, he is in the south."

Well, that was just not good enough, and he had to be here right this minute! Ibu has unrealistic ideas of travel time when it comes to us, but the opposite when it comes to everyone else.

I assured her he was due later this morning.

Apparently, the Bupati of Bangli had shown up at the Bali Banjar, and no one official was there to greet him. I felt like saying, well if he'd made an appointment... as I have never known the Government to make appointments... best I say nothing.

Hubby finally arrived, and Ibu demanded he put on his Adat gear, and get down to the Bali Banjar to greet the Bupati. As Ibu had yelled at him, Hubby went into 'stubborn mode'. Hubby took his time, Kopi Dulu, Makan Dulu.

Finally, when our guests were due to go into the village, Hubby went with them and then excused himself and went to the Bali Banjar. The village head and deputy head were not around, so Hubby had to have lunch with the Bupati and be the village host until they arrived. *That would have looked funny on Bali TV, the Bupati always has a press entourage. White Village Head???*

So, of course, with Hubby saving the day, Ibu started talking to me again. She did throw in a quick, 'Did Hubby go to Lottemart for her?' but she let me off when I said he had not bought her coffee as she wanted him here so quickly.

Later that day, one of Ibu's drivers was supposed to be driving our guests back to Kuta (as ours was busy with the ceremony). Ibu made a big deal about ensuring that he would be there, she would make sure personally. He did not show up. Our new staff member Wayan was not answering his phone. I had to ride my bike around the village until I found a random driver.

The next morning, none of our staff showed up, Hubby rang Wayan, and Wayan made some comment about Gamelan. Later, when I told Ibu, she said, "He was probably just drunk."

Wayan was supposed to be taking the guests canoeing. Hubby had to go out with them instead. Not that Hubby does much when he goes out. He took a rope, so I am sure he just tied himself onto a pole and sent them on their way, so he could catch up on some *zzzzz*'s. I was standing at the end of the hotel driveway, watching the canoes on the lake head out, and a village head approached me, and asked who was going out with the guests. I told him Hubby was. He asked, "Does he know how to canoe?"

I giggled and said, "Yes. He had to go, as Wayan has not shown up."

He said, "He was probably just drunk."

Oh, great, who have we hired?

Wayan was also supposed to be taking our guests on a tour of the village, as our other Wayan (part-time Guide) was busy with the ceremony. I ended up escorting the guests alone in the afternoon around the village. I took them in to see the cremation preparations (which was the ceremony everyone was busy with) and checked out the Gamelan music tent. Although all the Gamelan players were all dressed the same, all with their matching tough guy dark sunglasses on, I gave them a real look over, to see if our new staff member, Wayan was there. There was no Wayan, well no one small enough to be Wayan... but our driver, Wayan and our part-time Guide Wayan (yes, same names) were both happily smiling at us from the donation tent.

Today Hubby saw all the Wayans walking in the procession, so we know they were busy today. *It will just be a surprise to see if anyone shows up to work tomorrow.*

Now, having a Degree in Human Resources, you may think this type of thing may frustrate me. In the beginning, of course, it did, but after many years you learn that frustration comes from yourself, and how you see things.

You must look at the Employment Act of Indonesia if you want to hire staff in Indonesia, it reads under Chapter IV Work Culture in Indonesia:

As a form of employment practice based on the values contained in Pancasila, the Indonesian workers always give priority to interaction with the One Almighty God. In addition to it, the employment relationship between corporate leaders (employers) and workers should always be linked with the aspect of togetherness/partnership.

1 August 2018 - My Wisely Advice

'When you don't have high expectations, you don't set yourself up for disappointment'.

Instead, you get a wonderful surprise when you get to work, to find your staff have shown up, and Ibu is not using the Pie Warmer.

5 August 2018 - Online Shopping

We decided to go to the hotel for the buffet for dinner, just a quick bite (well, hubby has three or four plates, but I have a quick bite), before heading home.

We walked in, to find Ibu wearing a Ushanka (Russian fur hat). I quite liked the hat and thought that would have worked well on the ride over, as I needed to stand over the pots cooking in the kitchen to warm up my ears. I explained to Ibu, it was a Russian hat, then she decided she did not want to wear it anymore. *Where the hell she got it from, I have no idea.*

Ibu asked, if any friends coming from Australia could bring her a warm hat for a big head. Apparently, Ibu has a very big head, so she told me, a few times. So, I said we could look on the internet at pictures and then send one to a friend to bring over. *So, stupid of me.*

Somehow this turned into some funny video calls to a girlfriend in Australia, Ibu waving at her on the phone saying, "BIG Kepala, BIG HEAD."

My poor girlfriend kept getting late night calls about this damn hat. Ibu found the one she wanted and demanded I call my girlfriend back to show her. My girlfriend decided it would be a good idea to measure Ibu's head, so we managed to do that. Ibu had a staff member put a rope around her head and then lay it down on the floor tiles, Ibu announced her head was 70cm, "Quick call back your friend."

The hat Ibu wanted, turned out to be pretty much what I was wearing on my head at the time, but Ibu said it was too small, I told her it stretched. So, Ibu pulled it down over my entire face, just to check it stretched and said: "No, I want a wool one, that one is not wool!"

So, hat sorted, Ibu went on to sandals. Ibu wants real Birkenstocks. Personally, I am not a Birkenstock wearer, but I know they are of good quality. Ibu had a fake pair she bought in Bali, and boy are they fake. I called back my friend, and we both agreed to tell a white lie, and say to Ibu that they were not available in Australia. *Well, we just agreed they were ugly, no need for other words, apologies to anyone who wears them.*

Next; she wanted my friend to bring her a real Indian Sari. Not sure why Ibu thinks Australia is the best place to shop for Indian Saris?

I explained that maybe Malaysia might be a better place, or God forbid, even India. Still, Ibu was not getting on a plane anytime soon, actually, never.

So, I googled it... well, apparently, there is a shop in Jakarta that sells Indian clothes online... boy, that was it. Rather than using a girlfriend as a phone shopping resource, we had our own right there at our fingertips, well my fingertips. No matter how much I tried to get Ibu to use the mouse, it was like kryptonite - others must move the mouse for her.

Ibu got very excited about online shopping and started some funny clicking sounds and she got even louder than usual. I wish I could have captured those Tick, Tick, Ticks on camera. Ibu got so excited that I am sure the guests in the restaurant enjoying the buffet, were wondering what the hell was going on. *I have only just realised while writing this that she was mimicking the sound of the mouse-clicking! Geez I'm slow sometimes.*

So, my night ended up, with Ibu getting very excited, and me clicking and clicking the mouse, and Ibu clicking and clicking her mouth. *I presume Ibu thinks if she makes the noise of a mouse click, then she is contributing in some way.*

After rolling that mouse so much, my wrist hurt. I set Ibu up an online shopping account. When I suggested Bapak could just pay online, Ibu said no, Bapak would have no idea what to do, so I was to order them using my bank account, and she would give me the cash. Ibu's shopping bill came to about IDR 3.8 million in Saris. She will leave the money at my office tomorrow. Ibu does not care how much they cost, as she is so excited that she will be the only one in the village with these Saris. *So much for we are not supposed to be individuals in the village...Ibu is such a rebel.*

I will not be telling Ibu that online shopping has other items, besides Saris. Or she will be addicted like Bapak is after I introduced him to Facebook, one of my big regrets. We were finally able to go home.

So much for a quick dinner and home early.

7 August 2018 - Training Ibu Style

Ibu must have some new kitchen staff again. Not that I have been told that or met them yet. How do I know? Let's put it this way, it involves furniture moving, no matter what position you applied for in the hotel. She asked me how the new set up in the kitchen was looking. I answered, "Well, it's the same as you had it last year before training staff moved it all."

Ibu changed the subject, "Have you ordered my Saris yet?"

10 August 2018 - Aduh

Trying to have a meeting with Ibu and Bapak is always a challenge. Meeting on hold - Ibu needed to fart... Bapak tried pushing it out, by massaging Ibu's stomach. I suggested we all put on masks.

Ibu still needs to fart... Bapak is still trying to push it out... meeting is still on hold.

Sabar Sabar.

11 August 2018 - All Ideas And No Action

Today we were striving to get our rental office organised/renovated. (It is where all the equipment will be stored, and guests can rent the equipment from there; it is great for launching a canoe right out the front of the office). There is a lot to do. We, of course, had to wait until the cremation preparations, actual cremation and then after ceremonies had all finished...*and then for everyone to be sober again.*

So, although our lease started on 2 August, we are not in yet. Sabar Sabar.

Today we finally had the steel racking guy out to measure for the canoe racks. It really isn't a simple task to do anything here. Our Mangku had to get in his two bits worth, he had all his own ideas. This was not anything to do with religious beliefs, feng shui or any of that stuff. This was just him walking around in his flowing white robes, cigarette hanging out of his mouth, telling us his ideas for our office layout. He also had his own ideas about where the canoes could go, etc. *Thanks, Mangku but we have an actual draftsman plan for everything.*

I know once we finally get it all done, the Mangku will then delay us moving stuff over, as he must bless the building first, but a simple measurement took so long today.

I also wanted my manager Wayan to go and get some quotes for our window signage. Wayan is training to be a manager, he has never worked in an office environment before, so he needs to start from the ground up. Wayan also had some of his own ideas about the signage. It is great he has ideas, but in the end, I had to put my foot down and say, "Please just go to the printer and get a quote on the signs, as I asked you."

Visually he does not think like me, well he is a man. He kept throwing ideas at me, such as, 'Why not use Perspex or a wood frame and a big banner on the roof?' when I just wanted a quote for a sticker sign for the glass frontage.

Wayan had to go have lunch first, and a few cigarettes first, and then returned 1.5 hours later, and then sat down for another cigarette with the Mangku. I asked him calmly again, to go to the printer, as it would be closed soon. He just sat with the Mangku with his cigarette in his mouth, in our Bale (little Balinese hut) and started spouting off his ideas again.

I finally had to take his arm. *Ibu taught me this one.*

I escorted him (okay, pulled him, Ibu style) to his motorbike. I gave him a note for the printer. Like a child, I told him to go straight there. Do not pass go and do not collect $200. *Well, don't go to the cockfight on the way.* I told him he could get quotes on all his ideas as well, I just needed him to get a quote for me, and to go, as he really had not done anything all day.

As he got on his bike, he was still asking non-logical (to me, not to Balinese) questions, such as, 'Was he to order the sign while he was there?' *How could he order anything, as I had not even given him a file with the design for the sign, just a little hand-drawn sketch, and I am not an artist by any means?*

I had three simple questions written down for the Printer: 1. What file format does the Printer need? 2. How long will it take? 3. What is the price per square metre?

I've gone home.

15 August 2018 - Saris

Just had a meeting with Ibu and she jumped on the Sari thing again,

mid-meeting. She wanted to show me the one she wants on her favourite
Indian Soap. I had to put my foot down and say my wrist hurt too much.

15 August 2018 - Graffiti

So, Wayan's job, is to get the rental office ready. He did a great job of
organising the partition walls. The same person that made the walls made a
very large reception desk. The reception desk was to be painted black,
Wayan said he could do that. So fine, I said he could go ahead, and be
careful not to get the black paint on anything else. The partition walls
behind the reception desk will to be painted yellow, the next one red, the
next one blue, like our main office, and the theme of our corporate
colours. All the rest of the inner building walls will need to be painted
white, as it is a little dark in there.

I just came back to find the reception desk has been spray-painted
black, which is great. But Wayan had used the spray can, and written C
BALI graffiti-style on the new partition wall. The wall that faces the front
door, the wall that is supposed to be yellow, or maybe white. I nicely asked
Wayan, "What the F did you do that for?"

He replied, "It's okay, we just paint all the walls black."

Aduh.

17 August 2018 - Amor Ring Acintya (RIP)

I lost one of my dear ladies in the village last night, she was a diabetic,
and I checked her blood sugar every day I could. She passed away in her
sleep. I also lost my mobile phone, I found it later at the new office
building site covered in dust. I also lost my purse and looked everywhere;
no one had seen it. I was even sending Hubby messages to look for it at
home. I found it later, Ibu was sitting on it.

I was the only one crying when I went to the family compound, to put
rice on her deceased body today. Her son left me alone with her, telling
me I should have some private time with her, and tell her off for not taking
her medication. *Get her husband in here, he's the one that kept forgetting
to buy it.*

When we took her body to the cemetery, most of the old ladies were
gossiping about who could buy her land now. I just held her husband's
hand. *I guess I am still a Bule inside.*

20 August 2018 - Panda

Panda is my best worker; she never gets anything wrong. She does not
sit around smoking all day. She does not graffiti walls. She does not blurt
out 100 ideas, none of which make any sense, while sitting down and doing
nothing that I ask. She does not cut up the new laminate flooring that was

delivered, when told not to touch it. She does not take odd pieces of laminate and tape them to the black and white checkered flooring, to make uneven patterns at all strange angles, that are dangerous as a guest may trip over the tape. She does not get blue paint all over the new laminate, even though I gave her drop sheets to use. She does not destroy new laminate flooring by not rolling it up and moving it before the racking is installed like she was asked. She does not have me lose my cool and storm off, as the installer has destroyed rolled up laminate by just stepping on it while rolled up.

Panda also comes and knocks on the bedroom door 30 seconds before an earthquake and gets me up and dressed, just in time before the quake hits. Hubby, on the other hand, sleeps like a baby and does not hear the knocking, so while all of us were outside in the cold last night waiting for the quake to stop, he had to wait naked.

I think I will give Panda a raise, she is having a nap right now, she deserves it, we are all a bit tired. Panda is such a good dog; she will be seven years old this month.

2 September 2018 - Saris, Again

Ibu had family arrive from Denpasar, while I was trying to have a quick drop in to see her.

She got them all involved in Sari online shopping. Ibu demanded I show the family the online Sari shop. I told one of the ladies my wrist hurt from Ibu's Sari addiction, so could not continue. She laughed, and then started massaging my hand, so I could continue...

I eventually escaped. For a moment, I thought I was trapped in online shopping hell when the skies opened, but I managed to borrow an umbrella and ride my bicycle home true Bali style.

Chapter 10 - T.I.B. (This is Bali)

3 September 2018 - Um, Where's The Roof?

When Ibu gets an idea in her head but does not tell anyone else.

I have just arrived at work and was a bit startled to walk in and find the whole roof to the kitchen, and to Bapak's and my office, is gone!

The problem is that the demolishing started, but nothing was covered, including computers, etc. I have finally got staff here cleaning up and moving stuff... they were not aware the roof was going anywhere either.

And the temporary cooking area looks like we have gone back 100 years.

6 September 2018 - Re-gifting A Gift

Now, we have all done it. You get a gift that you have absolutely no use for, or already have two of. Even worse, you do not like it, and you keep it to give to someone else. There is a bit of planning involved, ensuring that the giver does not know the receiver. Maybe a quick check of Facebook to check their friends of friends, and you are good to go. Ibu does not get that concept.

Many years ago, I lent, LENT, no miscommunication, Ibu 'borrowed' my scarf. It was a special scarf, as it belonged to my deceased grandfather, it was grey cashmere wool. I loved that scarf. Ibu borrowed it one cold night, to pop up to the Temple.

The next day I asked and asked about the scarf, and she could not remember where she put it.

Then one day, her mother, the grumpy 93-year-old thing she was, showed up wearing the scarf. I asked her for my scarf, and she snarled at me and told me her daughter had bought it for her. *Not sure how Ibu bought a fifty-year-old Scarf with a David Jones (old retail department store in Adelaide, Australia) label on it.*

I pestered Ibu a few more times about the scarf. Then her mother went and died. *Well, at least I can get the scarf back.*

Wrong. Turned out they buried her, wearing it!

So, I now know not to lend things to Ibu that have significant sentimental value. Ibu now knows I will not lend her things, in case retrieving them involves a midnight dig at the cemetery.

Ibu wants the Sari I bought in India. It is just a souvenir to me. I will never wear it, but it reminds me of my time in India. Which, although I did not enjoy, it changed me, hopefully for the better... she isn't getting my Sari, and she has been told numerous times.

So, the other day, a very kind person who had done our tour, came back to do another tour and brought me a warm cardigan, and Ibu and some village ladies, bras. Now, this was no ordinary cardigan, this was Marino wool, gorgeous wrap-around, flowing, very stylish. Ibu pounced! I explained it was for me. That did not work, Ibu tried it on, parading around. I said it was not from India. That did not work. I said it made her bum look fat. That did not work. Ibu claimed the cardigan, and I went home empty-handed, defeated in my battle.

Yesterday, I was in the lobby at work talking to one of the guests, and I was distracted to see Ibu's seventeen-year-old granddaughter walking past in said cardigan. I rudely interrupted the guest, luckily a reader of the Ibu Chronicles and raced out to confront the grandchild. "That is my Cardigan!" Hands on hips, ready for battle this time. She was quite shocked, saying Ibu had bought it in Denpasar for her.

I let her have it, apologising for my mistake. I can't crush a 17-year-old, they have fragile emotions at that age.

Having said that, I did feel the Granddaughter did not need to flip the cardigan so stylishly over her shoulder, like a cat-walk model as she walked off.

9 Sep 2018 - Death & Taxes

Benjamin Franklin said, 'there were only two things certain in life: Death and Taxes.' He certainly didn't live in Bali. In Bali, it is Death and Ceremonies.

We have had a few deaths in the village in the past month, poor timing really, having just cremated forty people to empty the cemetery... we had an impromptu cremation as the lake level had risen dangerously close to the cemetery. So close, in fact, there was a fear of one big rain, and everyone would be floating around in the lake. *Not a good look.*

Now it seems we are filling up the plots with people again. *Hope they have their floaties on.*

Wayan, our Guide, has also had to leave work a lot this week as his Aunt passed away. With these deaths in the past month, not much work gets done. Wayan has had to leave work for all of them, but then again, so have I. Our villagers working in the south of Bali, have had to leave work or close their businesses to come up to the village every time someone has died.

Now, in a Western world, you give people time off for compassionate leave for family members of course. In a traditional Bali world, that we live and work in, we need to understand that 25% of the village is related to our staff members. Their wife may be related to another 25%. We consider everyone family, the neighbours we treat like family, our staff etc., so then you may as well make it 100%. It may be different in some villages, where there is a mix of other people living in the village. Still, in our village, we are the only foreigners, be that from overseas, or even another Island. Two other non-Balinese work in the village part-time, both Indonesians (but still not village descendants, so foreign). One being Hubby's Aunt, the other her business partner. So, the whole village is like one big family. So, if your staff use up their compassionate leave on their father dying, then come to you three months later and say their father died, you can't exactly deny them the leave by saying, 'Oh HR has it recorded your father already died.'

If a Balinese considers this man his father, it was most likely an Uncle he was raised with in the same compound. This time off is not time off for grieving, it is time off to pay respects, visit the home, see the body, maybe be part of washing the body. Then there is taking the body to the cemetery to bury, until our cremation held every five years. (Or, two years when your lake rises and gets too close to the cemetery). They may be needed to take turns digging a hole. Then there may be the case that it was not the best day to bury someone, but you can't have them sitting in your house for days...A friend in Denpasar gets hold of formaldehyde and other chemicals (the things you can get over the counter in Bali) and keeps their loved one for up to a week, on the kitchen table. Another friend in Ubud puts their loved ones on dry ice. The villagers here do not have access to any means of preservation. So, if it is not a 'good day' to bury in the calendar, they just bury them the day they die, then dig them back up on the day when it is a 'good day'. They will just clean them up, invite their soul back to the home, so everyone can pay respects. Then wrap them back up again, go to the cemetery and put them back in.

Now, the first time we were part of this process, and they told us they were bringing the deceased back to the home, we were not too keen to visit. Hubby and I walked in the procession down to the cemetery, hid behind a tree, waited for them to come back past, and re-joined at the very back of the procession, hoping there was no room at the house for us to pop in and give our respects. I mean, they had not really explained it properly, and I had that vision I get of Weekend at Bernie's, and I was going in to shake the hand of a deceased person wearing cool sunnies. Sometimes they do bring the body back, depending on how long it has been in the ground, but generally, they just bring the soul back...I am always hesitant about that visit, I have a weak stomach for seeing dead people. So, when they are ushering me into a room to talk to the deceased, I have one eye closed, hoping it is just a photo and a symbol of the person.

Hubby was once asked to scrub a young girl that died. They scrub the body with rice, and he found it extremely uncomfortable, the idea of scrubbing a naked girl that he worked with, and he declined.

Everywhere around the world has different customs when it comes to death. Even in Bali, different regions have quite different customs to funerals/cremations, etc.

So, having a traditional Balinese staff member, can mean that you pay staff for days that they are not there.

Now, there are employment laws, I have shared in a previous post that God comes above employment. However, in more detail, employees have paid time off for death, but they also have time off for religious obligations. So, there is a BIG Ceremony tomorrow! Well, that's what one of the ladies down at the harbour told Hubby this morning, as he went down to buy rice for the dogs. Now, I know it is big enough for Wayan to send me a message last night saying he cannot come to work today, as he must build a stage/tower for a ceremony. But, just how BIG is this ceremony? We hadn't heard anything about it, and haven't we just had over one month of a BIG ceremony? Usually, the BIG ones Wayan knows of in advance, at least a few days.

So, Hubby had to go and see Ibu to find out the Ibu scale of Big ceremony. Yep, it's big, the whole village is visiting two main Temples in Bali. *Okay, guess no one will be at work tomorrow then.*

The month before, we had thirty days of cremation preparations and the staff could only be at work half of that time. I can imagine some foreign business owners would find this difficult to manage. Or even get their head around. They may even think the staff are pulling their leg to get a day off. However, as we are generally in the village when someone dies, or go to the village when someone dies, we know our staff are genuine. We can't put a monetary value on one life over another, so we just pay for compassionate leave every time. We know Wayan has religious obligations to the village and so he needs to be there rather than at work. We can't put a monetary value on those obligations either. We chose to set up a business in a very traditional area. Our business motto is: 'We believe responsible and Sustainable Tourism is when Tourists adapt to the place they are visiting, and do not expect the place to adapt to them'. We must practice what we preach.

Our driver, also called Wayan, is a Mangku (village Priest), and he has many religious obligations. Our other driver Gede, also a Mangku, was very late the first day he drove for us. I kept ringing him, and he kept saying he was on the way. Well, he was on his way, he just had to stop to bless the oranges first. *You can't really argue with that.*

Anyone deciding to run a business in Bali really needs to take away their Western ideas and just go with the flow here. Whether your staff are traditional or not, there will always be Death and Ceremonies.

10 September 2018 - The Village Healer

Now, I know some book that became a movie had tourists excited that every Balinese village has some Mystical Healing Man. Tourists try to find these 'Healing Men', to go and see, to fix an ailment, or even tell them their future. That book also brought a lot of thirty-something females to Ubud, searching for Brazilian lovers, wandering amorously through the streets of Ubud drinking Chai Lattes, carrying yoga mats and chanting 'Namaste.'

What tourists believe they are searching for, is a Balian, but true Balians generally are hard for a tourist to find. They do not generally speak English, and they do not advertise, they are not allowed to draw attention to themselves. They do not tell you your future, and really if you are not practising the Balinese religion and beliefs, I can't see how a Balian can help you, unless you have many visits to one, live in his village, etc. Even then, sometimes, things would get lost in translation. Locals will take a Balian a gift and leave a donation. The Balian cannot ask for money. The local may wait all day at the Balian's house for the Balian to be ready to see them.

Don't get me wrong, there are some great massage/reiki/something-'magic in their hands' healers in Bali, and you can find them on Facebook. They can really help with injuries, back pain, etc., but generally, they are not actually a Village Balian, as such.

Locals put 100% faith in the Balian's word. They usually go to see them when it is something unknown. So, not from an obvious injury, maybe a child is always crying, or a constant headache or ongoing stomach ache. A Balian will generally tell the person the reason behind the ailment. This could be that they are cursed, or they were born on a wrong day, or they are possessed, or they are greedy, etc. To fix this problem, can sometimes take extreme measures, which I am sure a tourist would most likely not always follow through. It could mean changing the whole design of your home, or some extreme change to something in their lives, changing their name or even sacrificing an animal. It really comes down to beliefs, and Balinese have a lot of beliefs. Balinese believe in black magic, ghosts, the spirit world, Demons, Gods, you could throw in the Easter Bunny, and they wouldn't even notice.

Now, I am not having a go at these beliefs in any way, but what I have learnt in Bali and what the very smart Balians know, is that a lot of illness comes from the mind. So, they give you a reason for your illness, help you remove that reason, that in turn will remove the illness—mind over matter. The mind is a very powerful thing, but you need to be prepared for it, as you may not like the message given, or the solution.

19 September 2018 - Still No Roof.

I arrived at work and there is still no roof.
I just asked Bapak, "What if it rains?"
He answered, "Everything will get wet."

20 September 2018 - Tiara

Last night I spoke to one of the committee members for my thirty-year High School Reunion, on messenger. I had not spoken to her in thirty years, we are not Facebook friends, etc. I apologised that I could not make it. I first suggested for classmates like myself living overseas, maybe we did a quick video to say Hi.

Then we discussed doing a video link-up, well, just a video call, when they were all pissed enough. I said, "Just let me know, and I will wash my hair that day."

I think she thought I was joking. Well, the reply was "Bahhaa, let me find my Tiara."

24 September 2018 - I Need to Know!

There is one major problem I have, being a Westerner. Yes, I am still a Westerner. I grew up in a Western World. I always need to know everything.

From the minute, I could speak, I was the 'Why child.' You know, the annoying child that asks 'Why?' all the bloody time. Probably because I am a Sagittarian. My mother, Ibu Dua, was a school teacher, so I was lucky that she was accustomed to young children asking questions and being downright annoying. Although I think she just zoned out and said "hmm, ah huh" a lot, as I certainly learnt that trait later when she would talk to me.

Having a primary school teacher as a mother meant I got to learn before the other children. Well, all those flashcards and stuff Ibu Dua was preparing, she'd just test them out on me. I was reading the newspaper at four years old and bored with everything by five years old. I must have been the most annoying child. Back in those days, there was no concern for the safety of your child, whatsoever. So, I could wander off and play with dangerous farm equipment, even things like old rabbit traps, etc. I could ride my bicycle to the next town. I basically kept myself amused in so many dangerous, quite tomboyish ways. I obviously survived, and with all body parts intact.

It is very much like the children here, there are whole days where you do not know where the kids are. If they did not come home to eat, no matter, someone would have fed them. They are out in the fields, no TV or computer games here, probably pulling legs off frogs, or getting up to some sort of mischief. Children at the age of three go to the shops for you or walk up to the school to see their older siblings or walk long distances to check out what their parents are doing at work. Wayan's son, Master Four, shows up at the office quite often. Well, when Wayan shows up for work.

Children here are encouraged to be independent and learn by doing and making mistakes. So, if you cut off a finger while playing with knives, well, you will not do that again, will you? A bit like the dogs you see that live on main roads with a long time, healed incorrectly, break on their legs. They are still alive, they have learnt to cross the road and look both ways now.

Balinese children are not 'Why' children, well, some are, they must be the Sagittarians. Still, it is discouraged, not because it is bloody annoying to the parents, but it is disrespectful. If your parent says it is so, then it is so. Do not question it. So, you could ask, "Why the Sky is Blue?" most likely, if your parent (in this village) does not know the answer, then they would tell you to go and find out, maybe listen more at school. Surely, that stuff is covered at school?

But if you are at/going to a ceremony and ask, "Why are we here?" or "Why do we have to wear this?" or "What is this ceremony for?" then you are being disrespectful. It is faith, it is your parent's role and your village mangkus' and village heads' roles, to know what is right for you, so you do not need to know why, you just need to do. Eventually, after many lifetimes you will have all the answers, you do not need to know them all in this lifetime.

Unless you are me, I need to know! And that is where I get it all wrong. And I know it is wrong, but I have not learnt to control that urge. And of course, Ibu and Bapak think I do not need to know, and they torture me. You would think I could control it, this urge to know, this urge to speak and ask, "What is this ceremony for?" but it still niggles away at me. I should have some control.

When I was very young staying with Romanian grandparents, I was told that if I spoke when adults spoke or questioned their instructions, I would have my tongue cut out. So, you would think I would have learnt to just shut up. It's funny, I remember when I was seventeen years old catching up with my Romanian family after a gap of over ten years. My Aunt commented that she could not believe how much I spoke. That, when I was young, they thought I could not speak and that I just hid. *Of course, I bloody hid Aunty, your father chased me around with a carving knife saying he'd cut my tongue out. Geez.*

It was also difficult in my family when no one spoke any English. No matter how many times they dressed me up in those silly costumes for Romanian dances and all the other traditional stuff, I didn't say much to them. Half the time, I did not understand them when they spoke so fast. It should have been good practice for now.

So, I got to work this morning to find Ibu preparing for a BIG ceremony. I knew it was big, as a lot of people arrived in the village the night before and every home had a Penjor (bamboo decorated pole). I presumed it was a BIG ceremony, as no staff of mine had arrived yet. In my mind, I needed to know what the ceremony was, so I would know when the staff were coming in. *Makes perfect sense to me.*

So, I tried to ask Ibu what the ceremony was for. Nope, she was not having a bar of it and started talking about preparing for Hubby's birthday party. I asked if it was for Purnama (full moon), she growled and said that is tomorrow, this is tonight. *Well, then, tell me what it is bloody for!*

I have my own Ceremony Importance Scale, and I am still Western. I still have so much to let go of - from my ingrained Western values. I gave up and thought I would go do some work.

I walked into our office to discover that the night before the builders had torn the office down. *Aduh.*

So, I soon realised that Bapak and I do not have an office or a desk. *I will go and use our tour desk in the lobby, not a problem.*

I discovered that our tour desk was being used as a printer desk. I could not really get in there without stepping over a mess of tangled cables. *This isn't going to work. Wayan would have done this, but he hasn't shown up for work yet. I will come back when he comes in.*

I sat down on one of the reception guest benches and opened my laptop (*well it is a lap-top*), to discover the mouse on my laptop was not working. *It must be a sign - I cannot work.*

So, first, I saved a bird that was flying around the lobby smashing into the windows. *I know how he feels.*

Then I went back to see where Bapak was working. He had managed to set up his make-shift workspace in the restaurant. The only electricity was near the fridge, so he had one chair as a table for his laptop and was tucked up next to the beer fridge. It stopped me from complaining about my lack of workspace, as I was going to him to complain. *Oops.*

I went back to Ibu to try one more time to find out what this ceremony was. That way, I may have been able to gauge how long the staff would be absent. Nope, she started going on, asking, "Will Bram have a Disco for his party?"

Huh?

Then she started on some village gossip. Arrghh.

I called Hubby and told him I was not getting anywhere today, and I asked him to buy a new computer mouse while he was in the south. I will just head home. *At least I can use this spare time to wash my hair.*

I got a bit held up, as there was a dying dog chained in the sun, poor darling, he's fine now, I went back and checked on him.

When I finally got home, after achieving nothing all morning (apart from two animal rescues), I found the water was turned off. It was either off, or it just was not reaching our place, as there were so many people here for this BIG ceremony, that I still did not know what it was for. I was contemplating going back to the hotel and washing my hair in the restaurant as Ibu does. Then I realised that she usually rinses in the kitchen sink and that has been demolished.

Hubby came back from the south and went and found Wayan's wife to ask if Wayan was coming to work. She indicated this month we have lots of ceremonies, so she was not sure. *We always have lots of ceremonies. What is she on about?*

So, I will stay home and try to fix my laptop, as now the Wi-Fi has stopped working on it. *I should listen to these signs not to work, but then...how will I write up the Ibu Chronicles?*

25 September 2018 - Another Day

Got up this morning to find no water still, but it finally came on at 7.00 am.

Then it stunk like sewerage, so by 1.00 pm today, after draining the hose for a while into the garden and only ten buckets (five saucepans on the stove), I have washed my hair.

I also managed to fix the Wi-Fi, so, a productive day so far. I can hear the Gamelan playing at the Pura Desa (Village Temple), the Mangkus are praying over the loudspeakers and there are people everywhere. I know today is Purnama (full moon), yet no one could tell me what last night's ceremony was for, apart from one lady in the street who said, "It's for God?!" (and was quite upset that I asked her.)

Oh well, at least I will have clean hair when I attend the ceremony later.

2 October 2018 - Party, Party

I wanted to talk to Ibu about Hubby's big birthday party on Saturday. She was dying her hair in the temporary kitchen sink, so perfect time to chat. Ibu tells me this renovation will be over by Saturday, if we want, we can use the space for a disco. *What's with this Disco thing?*

It looks to me like she's building an indoor basketball court. It has an extremely high new roof going on, finally, and there are no internal walls.

I did not get far with the party planning... Ibu is too busy bossing the builders around while waiting for her hair colour to set.

5 October 2018 - Architectural Planning

This morning I arrived at work, and Ibu wanted my opinion on where we should put the kitchen... and the doors... and our offices... and the cashier... and the windows. *Ummm...aren't they the type of things you plan before you build?*

This is one of Ibu's 'build as you think of something' kind of projects... The builders are all asleep over in the corner...*I guess they must wait till Ibu and I draw up some plans.*

5 October 2018 – Where the Sand Blows.

I just told Ibu that sand from the building site was blowing into the restaurant and all over the guests.

I went and made a quick sign that apologised for the renovations.

I came back to find Ibu hosing down all the sand, inside the new building, there is now at least one foot of water in there.

Well, it has stopped the sand blowing, I can't argue with that.

5 October 2018 - I Just Made Ibu's Day.

I said she could use the pie warmer tomorrow for the party.

10 October 2018 - Saved By The Doctor

The Beautiful Doctor has saved Ibu from dying. She came with her husband Santa, to attend Hubby's birthday bash, not to save Ibu. But, since she was already in the Hotel, it was very handy, as Ibu was dying.

Ibu was sick the day before. The whole family were summoned to come down to her bedside for her last dying moments.

She is okay now, Ibu told the family that the beautiful Doctor gave her pills, and now she will live. *I think it was paracetamol.*

The beautiful Doctor also has saved me from Sari shopping, as last night the Beautiful Doctor gave Ibu socks, a cap and a Pashmina.

Ibu is fine now.

24 October 2018 - Hubby's Birthday Party

So, I forgot to let you know how Hubby's birthday party went. He had the Big FOUR O. *Yes, I am a Cougar.*

We have always celebrated his birthday at our home in the south, a joint 'Birthday/end of the busy season/apologises for not catching up with friends for the past months' type of event.

This year we were still up in the village, so I had not thought to throw a party. Well, apparently, I had thought to throw a party in some drunken state, as friends from overseas sent me a message asking what date Hubby's actual birthday party was, and that they had booked flights.... *oops*.

So, a party we were having, and this time everyone would just have to travel up to us. Now, usually, I am the Hostess with the Mostess and go to a lot of effort with days of cooking, but I did not have my kitchen, nor did I have the time. So, a party at Ibu's Hotel, where all his guests would stay was the plan. I gave Ibu plenty of notice, but when the kitchen was torn down, I started to worry. When Ibu asked if we wanted to use the open space as a Disco, I started to worry. In the end, she pulled it off, a buffet lunch and a buffet dinner, but of course with Ibu, there is always some sort of drama.

Ibu was very calm about the whole thing, up until the day of the party. It was 10.00 am, and lunch would be served from 12 noon, so our guests could eat as soon as everyone had arrived and checked in. I went to the hotel to double-check the setup, and I was counting again how many guests were coming. I was counting out loud, saying the names, just to make sure we had numbers correct. Oh Boy! Ibu heard one of my girlfriend's names, told me to back up a bit, and say that again, and then she flipped out. I forgot one of my girlfriends is a High Caste (Brahman) and boy was I in the poo with Ibu. Ibu is old school, stuck in an old village, in a time warp basically. She still follows the old ways, and the old ways are strict when it comes to the Caste system.

So, our plan of using bamboo plates with paper as there was no kitchen, to save the staff doing dishes in buckets out the back, was immediately dismissed. Ibu was screaming at the top of her lungs, "Where is the crockery for Brahmans?" (highest Caste.)

Ibu had staff going to her house looking for 'The special plates', going to her son's place of business, turning the hotel upside down.

You see, there is a hierarchy for plates, glasses, utensils. Certain Castes can use certain ones, and then they cannot be used by a lower caste. It is obviously fine for me and all of Hubby's friends to eat off paper and bamboo, but not for a High Caste. And I should have told Ibu this information weeks ago, and now she must go and get the best silverware and the best warmers. No, not the 'Pie Warmer', that is only good enough for a commoner like me. Ibu needed the silver serving trays with their individual warmers for this special guest! Boy, was she pissed off.

Now, this turned into a 'Nothing I could do right moment', and she turned the subject to what I was currently wearing. I must admit I had forgotten about something to wear for the party. I was at that time wearing my usual village attire, a t-shirt, a sarong and thongs. Ibu turned on her heel and started yelling at me about what I was wearing. "You can't wear that! Did you buy a special outfit to wear? Did you buy Bram a special outfit to wear? Will you put on makeup? Will you do your hair at least?!"

Luckily, our overseas guests arrived, and I had to go and greet them. I walked off with Ibu following me and yelling at me that I should not greet them dressed like that. She stopped once she got in hearing distance of our guests, and was the sickly sweet Ibu again, greeting and welcoming them, while turning to me and screwing up her nose with that snarl she gives me. I explained to our guests that Ibu said I had to go home and change, and that I had not really thought about what I should wear. They know Ibu, so we had a laugh and off I went home to change my clothes while they checked into their rooms.

Once I arrived home, Hubby seemed to have worked out on his own what he would wear. I told him what Ibu had said, and he replied, "If Ibu is not happy with what I am wearing, she can shove it", and he headed off to the hotel to greet his guests.

I pondered and pondered, I looked through our very small wardrobe. *If it is not a sarong and does not show boob, I should be fine.*

I have not purchased many clothes in the past twelve years. Okay, I admit it, I have only been shopping for clothes twice.

Even if someone brings me something new to wear as a gift, generally Ibu takes it, or our girls, or anyone in the village.

I even attempted some makeup, not that I really own any, apart from tinted moisturiser and mascara. Still, I put on some bronzing powder I found in the back of the cupboard. I think it belongs to one of our girls as it was quite dark. I did my mascara thicker than usual and headed off with my chosen outfit. I even pulled out the high heeled rubber thongs for a bit of glamour. Now, since I was riding a bicycle to the hotel, it had to be a practical outfit. I did not really have much to choose from, it was either a skirt or pants, and the only clean t-shirt that I had was a simple tight, off the shoulder number. I went with choice Number Two, some cotton flare pants. Look, I know what you are thinking, but there are no Fashion Police in the kampung. As far as I know, they could be back in fashion, fashions have always made a comeback. I am sure if I opened a fashion magazine, if I ever bought a magazine, there would be flares, well maybe. So, I got a rubber band to lift one pant leg and rode off on my bike.

Note to self: to remember that rubber band later, or I could have a nasty accident riding home.

It is funny, the stares the Dadongs give you when you are not dressed the same as every other Dadong in the village. One old Dadong walking in front of me on the way to the hotel could have been me. I am sure we have the same sarong, thongs and even the same cardigan. However, I still have not started wearing the towel on the head in public.

Note to self, leave the village immediately, if you ever wear a towel on your head down the street.

Upon arriving at the hotel, Hubby and his friends had started on the beers, but I knew what I needed to do first. I went around to the kitchen/building site and saw Ibu perusing her project, and I got a smile. *That smile is the signal that I can get closer.*

As I approached, her smile got bigger. Then as I was just in front of her, standing in the middle of the building project surrounded by workers, she grabbed both my boobs and asked if I was wearing a bra! The poor workers from Sulawesi are probably not used to Balinese woman and their boob handling. Ibu was impressed I had on a bra. *I am not sure why? I have always worn one, I do not like the National Geographic look some of the other women my age in the Village go for.*

But Ibu was not so impressed with my pants. She asked why I did not have on a nice dress, but the pants would have to do, at least they were clean she said. She spun me around, impressed they were tight in the bum and slapped my bum and said it was sexy, so that was good. *Those poor workers.*

Ibu then proceeded to ask why I did not have lipstick on. I explained that I have never owned or worn lipstick in my life and that this was all she was going to get. She was surprised she did not know that and gave me a pass. I was now allowed to go to the party. *Thank God, as I need a beer.*

The Morning After

Now, a little follow-up, the next day. The next day we went back to the hotel to check on our guests. No memory of going home, but we did not have a scratch on us. Good effort, since we were on bicycles with no lights and no street lighting. *I must have remembered my rubber band.*

We all had hangovers, but we managed to get through breakfast of coffee and leftover birthday cakes, yes cakes, plural. This always happens with our friends, somehow on my 40th, I had five birthday cakes. Hubby only had three, but still, it seems the norm for us.

After coffee and cake, we all decided the only way to get through this, was to have a beer, as you do.

Now, a few things had gone missing, such as a kid's shoe, a ball, a stubby holder, so we had all the kids looking for them, while we drank. The shoe and the balls showed up. Some kids toys that we did not know were missing appeared. Still, the stubby holder, with sentimental value, did not (it belonged to the brother of one of our guests, one of our dearest friends who had recently died).

So, after me going for a look around the back of the hotel where the empty bottles go, then asking all the staff, Hubby suggested my girlfriend use her 'Caste powers' and go and ask Ibu.

I took my girlfriend round to ask Ibu, and Ibu profusely apologised that it was missing, said they would find it and give it to me. Some small chat about who knows who (turns out Bapak went to school with my girlfriend's uncle, small Island, everyone related, etc.), we headed back to join the others.

I had not clicked; my girlfriend was talking to Ibu and Bapak at 10.00 am with a beer in her hand. Swigging away, puffing on a cigarette as if her life depended on it.   I had clicked that Ibu was staring questioningly, but thought she was star-struck by the whole Brahman thing.

The next day some of the younger staff were asking me questions, such as, 'How many beers did I drink? Did I drink at 10.00 am every day? Would I have a beer today?' *Yeah guys, right here at work.*

It then dawned on me, a Balinese female drinking and smoking, and she was a Brahman. Their little world had just opened a little bigger. *Imagine when they get smartphones.*

Chapter 11 - Back to the South

3 November 2018 - Ibu's Celebrity Status

Ibu does not know about the Ibu Chronicles, by now readers would realise that if she did, she would surely find some way to make money from it... *Well, she is smart.*

However, sometimes Ibu just acts like she is a Celebrity.

Yesterday I was up in the village. We have been living back down in the south for a few weeks now. Our time in the south has been spent connecting water pipes and moving water tanks around our house. It has been five years since we started building, and in true Balinese style, we are doing it slowly, pelan-pelan (slowly).

The neighbour gave us some water from his tank yesterday, he was very generous and then encouraged me to wash my hair now... That is my big plan for today, just waiting for the hot water to be connected... sabar sabar.

So, back to Ibu, I was not sure if Ibu's renovations were still in full swing, as I had rung the hotel from home. The number was disconnected...*hmmm, that could be all those tangled cables in the hotel lobby.*

I tried Ibu's new mobile, but no answer...That could be because the staff just think it's a cat in the roof, as Ibu's ringtone is a cat crying, bloody grandkids.

So, I thought it best to drop in when I was in the village yesterday, before going home. Just to see if Ibu still needed us to bring our guests to her, for her up and coming Offering Making Classes they are booked in for, or could she come to us now. I was prepared to receive a lecture about how dirty I was. We had been in the lake cleaning up rubbish left by some lovely builders, who came, built, dumped and left. They have built a two metre x two metre concrete structure, with a gate on it, for unknown purposes, at our launch point on the current lake's edge. Maybe unknown to them it is below the wet season water level. Maybe Wayan can use it in a few months to tie his canoes onto and have the guests launch from there, not even Wayan knows what it is for.

127

I walked past the restaurant to the gardens of the hotel to find Ibu sitting down in a chair placed in the middle of the garden path, facing all her builders, Bapak, and all the staff. Everyone was busy working on Ibu's kitchen, and Ibu had managed to find a prime viewing position to yell out her orders. She really needed DIRECTOR written on the back of her chair. As I approached, always a little wary of the response I would receive, Ibu asked me how I was. *Phew, that is a sign I have permission to approach.*

So, I sat down next to her, in her Assistant Director Chair, she had placed next to her. Then she started, "Why haven't we seen you in so long?" Blah, blah.

Nag over, apologies, etc., I asked her, okay reminded her, that she had an Offering Making Class for six people on Sunday, and did she want the guests to be brought here, as I knew she was busy. Or could she come over to our office, to the warung? Ibu pondered the question, and then said, well screamed: "WHY IS KOMANG NOT DOING THE CLASS?"

I explained calmly that Komang was not working that day, and that was why I needed Ibu, and that Ibu had already confirmed that she would take the classes on Sundays. Then in that 'I don't get out of bed for less than $10,000' look, Ibu screamed, "I AM TOO BUSY, GET *NI WAYAN TO DO IT, SHE MAKES OFFERINGS ALL THE TIME."

Now, that's a silly statement, not that I was telling Ibu that. Every one of the women in the village makes offerings all the time, a teacher it does not make them. Also, Ni Wayan was a bit busy that day, I already had given her a list a mile long. So, I approached the topic again, saying, "But Ibu, people come to do your class, as you are entertaining. Komang is a great teacher, but she doesn't make people laugh as you do."

Ahh, the suck-up treatment, I think I have her...or maybe not.

Ibu calmly explained there was a BIG meeting at the hotel, and she could not make it. I know not to push these things, even though the class date was on the wall schedule for over a month. You know celebrities.

I calmly mentioned the meeting was Monday, and her class was Sunday. She screamed for her Assistant. Okay, not Assistant, just Jero, the old guy that says "Yeah, Yeah, Yeah", all the time, to double-check her schedule.

There was not much point for me to pursue this, especially if she was relying on Jero, as he would take a few hours to look that up. So, I thanked her, went to our tour desk, and told Ni Wayan she was doing the class, to which she just stared at me with that, 'Understudy that has not rehearsed' look.

It is so hard working with Celebrities.

---

*Ni in front of a name means girl, I in front of a name means boy, so we have I Wayan and Ni Wayan, easier for staff to just say Wayan and Ni Wayan.

5 November 2018 - Who needs Ibu.

So, you probably want an update on how Ni Wayan went with her first Balinese Offering Making Class. Things never work out the way you plan in Bali. Tours are now being held at our new rental office, in the warung attached, so we do not go to Ibu & Bapak's hotel anymore. Two out of three staff were already at work when we arrived, this was a great sign, one was not due yet.

So, when Hubby came down for a coffee and started panicking that Wayan was not there, I had to remind him he did not start till 9.00 am. At 9.01 am, Wayan arrived. *This is going to be a great day, beautiful weather, all staff here, I just get to hang out, Happy Dance.*

I went into the kitchen to get my coffee. I reminded Ni Wayan that she was doing the offering making class today. She sheepishly told me Ni Nengah was doing it. *That's fine with me, Ni Wayan is very young, and this is her first job, so I am glad she has at least found a replacement.*

Ni Wayan has improved in leaps and bounds in only a few months, she went to a Hospitality School, and we have had to re-train her on so many things. *I want to go down to that school and shake them, it is like trying to train Ibu's staff if they work for us, we must re-train them.*

Well, with Ibu's staff, we first must explain there will not be a lot of furniture moving in this job, then we must explain to them not to yell across the road if you see a tourist, and then we must teach them how to smile.

Wayan took the guests canoeing, and I took the time to go through some donations and medical supplies, and have a coffee, etc. *Ahh, a peaceful day in the village.*

One of our foster girls' grandfathers walked past, so I waved and went out to say Hello. He asked when I had arrived, and told me to wait, as his wife would catch up soon. These two always walk everywhere, Grandma is a little slower, but only because I think she stops to gossip more. Grandma approached, I had my arms open for my wonderful hug she gives, and BAM. "Where is my Oleh Oleh?"

Oh, dear. In Grandma's mind, as I'd been 'away' for two weeks, on what she referred to as 'a holiday', I should have brought her a souvenir from the south. An Oleh Oleh (like a souvenir) is expected when you go away, it's an Asian thing. With our Balinese old dears, they get even more excited, as Denpasar is so far away, and such a land of mystery. It is only 60kms away.

Boy, did I get an earful, Grandpa finally changed the subject and asked how many guests we had, and would we be coming over for afternoon tea later. *Yee Ha, Grandpa, love that man. Although, he does have a habit of telling our guests, that God hates me because I never gave birth to children of my own, apart from that, I love him.*

Any guests we have on our tours automatically become guests of our family. So, if Grandpa sees any guests, it is expected they visit Grandma and Grandpa. Whether we have time or not, we better bloody go, or I am in the poo.

As we were chatting, some of our guests were coming back carrying their canoes. Grandpa greeted them in English, did the usual, 'Where are you from, first time to Bali, etc.? Okay, see you later,' and off he went.

He had to catch up with sulking Grandma, who had walked off mumbling under her breath how I had forgotten to get her a souvenir. Now, I was in the poo so much with Grandma, that I explained to the guests the situation. We all went scrambling around trying to find something that looked like I had bought it for her. I even got desperate and considered a foam pool noodle. I finally found some shampoo and conditioner someone had donated from their hotel toiletries...*Geez, I'm cheap.*

So, souvenir sorted, the guests could have their offering making class. Ni Nengah did a great job. I came to find the guests were timing her after their class, to see how fast she could make an offering (Canang Sari) from start to finish. The guests have thirty minutes to make one. Ni Nengah made one in two minutes and two seconds. *I thought she would have done it faster, but that's a bloody good effort.*

Then someone went and bloody died! Always the way, you have a great plan, everything seems to be going smoothly and then someone in the village dies. So, Wayan had to go.

It turned out it was the Klian's father (like a Deputy Mayor), so Wayan left, and I went to break the news to Hubby. Hubby headed off to find our backup drivers for later, just in case, always good to have a spare.

So, I had to take the guests into the old village, so they could walk around, and on the way, we could go for afternoon tea at Grandma and Grandpa's house.

I was chatting with the guests in one of the small gangs and another one of our kids' Grandmas was approaching. This Grandma has always been a bit of a bitch, but has slightly mellowed since someone ran her over with a car at the Gianyar market. Today, she was not so mellow, she was trying to catch up with her grandson. He's four, she has a pin in her leg, and he has the patience and energy of a four-year-old. I blocked him to stop him, told him to slow down and wait for Grandma. He was not impressed; he wouldn't talk to me and gave me that look. You know that death stare children at four perfect. And then BAM, Grandma had caught up, and she started to slap my arm and yell at me to let him pass and that he was not happy, and that was my fault. Also, it was my fault that her granddaughter had not come to visit her up from Denpasar with me today, as today was Sunday, and she did not have school today. That I put these stupid ideas in her granddaughter's head about going to school instead of getting married at fourteen. That we should still be up here living in the village, and that she cannot keep up with a four-year-old. It is all my fault, and it is too far to walk to visit the dead guy, and that's all my fault.

I presume she did not mean his death was my fault, but if she could maybe pause in the conversation, she may also get her breath back. Off she went muttering under her breath having a go at me. I am still not sure what I did. I did not dump her with a four-year-old.

After our guests got over the fact that Balinese old women can get quite heated, and yell, and slap, we continued, as we would be late to visit the other Grandma and Grandpa's home. We headed off, me assuring the guests, that these Grandparents would be much nicer.

We had one slight problem. One of the guests was petrified of dogs. That's not a great thing when you are around me, as every dog in the neighbourhood will come up to me... and one of ours decided she wanted to come with us. She could not understand why she was not allowed, so she kept sneaking back to me. It took a bit longer than expected to see the village.

Eventually, we were nearly at Grandma and Grandpa's house, we were about one hour behind schedule, but we still stopped for some photos in the town square... You cannot expect people to walk around this village and not want to photograph absolutely everything, there really isn't another place like it.

While the guests were taking photos, along came the village head's mother. I love her, she is the tiniest, crinkliest thing. She is probably seventy years old, but with her wrinkles etched from working all her life, looks one hundred and fifty. I waved at her and smiled, ready to give her a big hug and, BAM, she started lecturing me that Grandma has been waiting for me to bring guests, etc. Now, she speaks very old Balinese, which I do not, so half the time I miss what she is saying, but just like the guests, who do not speak any Balinese, we got the gist of it all.

When we started heading off, and she started demanding we take that small gang right there as it is a short cut, I realised she meant business. She even stood and watched to make sure we were headed to Grandma's house without detouring.

So, I really do not need to see Ibu at all, I did not see her at all yesterday, I can get yelled at by an array of women in the village.

8 November 2018 - Staff Retention

Now, running a business in Bali is not all it is cracked up to be. Some people just get lucky and get a group of staff that run their business, and they never have to be there to check up on things. I have not personally met those people.

Ibu and Bapak never take a day off, they sleep in the hotel, so they are there 24/7. Okay, they take a lot of days off for ceremonies, but they practically live in the hotel, so their whole life is the business. It is sad, as Bapak is now seventy-six, and he is looking really tired lately. It also probably explains why Ibu and Bapak treat it like their home and do their hair or shave in the restaurant washbasin.

Some of their staff have been there a long time. So long, they died at work. Well, the Chef did. He also lived at the hotel, and only had times off for ceremonies. RIP Doyok.

The Sous Chef also lives at the hotel, Nengah, she has been there since she was twelve years old, that's twenty-seven years. The Security Guard lives at the hotel, he's been there quite a while. One of the newer staff lives at the hotel.

We also once lived in the hotel, up until about nine years ago. After nearly two years, we could not do it anymore and had to move out. Okay, I lie, Bapak kicked us out for having two dogs in our room and six rescue cats that we fed under the table in the restaurant, but we wanted to move out anyway.

Ibu insists she and Bapak must live in the hotel, or the staff will not show up to work, or they leave. Is that the secret of staff retention? I hope not.

Now, we have not lost any staff, and none have died on the job either, so win-win. As you know, I get very excited when our staff come to work, especially when Wayan does, as he has the most excuses, or is related to the most people that die during his working hours.

Hubby went today, just to drop in and check on everything. Wayan was there. The girls were not, everything was locked up, so our guests could not even pee, as the girls have the keys to the back, where the toilet is. Hubby rang the mobile phone, the one we bought to use to leave messages for the next day's roster. The mobile phone that Wayan had texted the girls at 4.00 pm yesterday to confirm how many guests he had today. Ibu answered it.

Turned out that at 3.00 pm yesterday, Ibu 'borrowed' the girls for her restaurant, she also 'borrowed' the mobile phone.

So, Hubby drove the guests up to Ibu's restaurant for breakfast and then took them back to Wayan, so they could go canoeing. When Hubby questioned Ibu about 'borrowing' our mobile phone, Ibu could see no problem with that, if we lived on-site, we would have known that, so it was our fault.

24 November 2018 - Bali Moment

Just had one of those Bali moments, where you just let them do their thing. The girl at the local supermarket checkout just kept packing my groceries into a plastic bag... I made numerous attempts to explain no plastic, but the green bag meant nothing to her.

She was very sweet, though, when she finally realised I wanted to use my green bag, she carefully placed my plastic bagged shopping inside my green bag.

2 December 2018 - Bali OHS

Went to see Ibu yesterday. Ibu could not understand why I wanted to film one of her staff welding, using sunglasses as eye protection. Typical Bali OHS (Occupational Health & Safety) moment.

20 December 2018 - I Miss Ibu?

I have only seen Ibu a few times in the past couple of months, as we are down in the south and it has been very quiet, so the staff are handling it.

The first day we arrived back in the south, Hubby went to the local warung in the next street. He was hit with six months of gossip on who had divorced, remarried, moved in, renting out their place, whose dog bit who, and what's going on with the garbage collection, the new Banjar, who built the funny looking Joglo down the street, etc. So, all caught up.

So, after catching up on the gossip, I spent the next few days going to see all the neighbours in the village to say Hi. And then, *I admit I missed Ibu, just a bit...*

I rang to see how Ibu was. I also wanted to ask if the renovations were finished. I asked four times in the conversation I had with her. Mind you, the conversation I had with her, was not actually with Ibu personally. *It is that celebrity thing again.*

I rang Ibu's new mobile number, one of her staff answered, so I did not actually speak to Ibu, but could hear her yelling her replies in the background. Halfway through the conversation, Ibu apparently walked off, even though I had more questions to ask her. So, the staff said they would have her call back.

Instead of Ibu calling me back, one of her staff rang me back, twice, to relay the answers from Ibu.

By the end of the day, I had a lovely catch up with Ibu and found out they had some BIG groups coming, and there was a BIG ceremony.

Not, that I spoke to Ibu personally, it was nice to hear she had been busy.

22 December 2018 - Catching Up

The very first time I went up to the village after a break of three weeks, I thought I better go and see Ibu and Bapak. Okay, I lie. I had been in the village once before that. I had the greatest of intentions of visiting Ibu and

Bapak, it just did not happen. They do not need to know that.

I did plan to visit them that prior time. When I arrived in the village, I went straight to our new location. All three staff were there, so that was a pleasant surprise. When I arrived, Ni Wayan (female staff member) asked me if I knew if Ibu was doing the Offering Class. I said, "Yes, when I was speaking to her the other day (well, one of the staff), I was told the 'Program is Back to Normal', and someone will bring Ibu down here for the class."

I told Ni Wayan I could go down and see Ibu and Bapak, and while I was there, I could confirm. Ni Wayan declared it was better that she rang Ibu and ask about the class. Ni Wayan knows Ibu so well now that I got the feeling Ni Wayan was trying to protect me from having to talk to Ibu. *Maybe Ibu is in a mood?*

I came back later to find Ni Nengah would be taking the Offering Making Class. *Best not to ask any questions.*

I kept meaning to just go down to the hotel and say Hi to Ibu (it's only 700 metres away). Still, as I could not walk more than 100 metres without getting nagged by so many other old ladies, I really did not need to go see Ibu that day.

The second time I did see Ibu, and I was wearing a new kebaya. After the initial greetings, Ibu was pulling at the neckline of my new kebaya and saying it was wrong, that in Bali, they make them like this and that. A Balinese had made it, copying the exact one Ibu had bought me years ago, but I just let Ibu stretch out my new kebaya and have her little rant. *It is not worth saying anything.*

Ten minutes later her eldest daughter arrived and said she wanted to order a kebaya exactly the same as mine.

The third time I visited, I saw Ibu, and she asked the strangest questions, with a very suspicious look on her face.

Then, when I went to say hello to Bapak, she followed me like a puppy, and Bapak asked the same strange question, "Had we been staying in our new rental house?"

I answered that we had been staying in our house in the south. It is not a rental, and they know the house. Bapak said, "No, someone told us you rented a house near the Bamboo Forest."

This turned into a crazy discussion about us living somewhere we were not, and that I had been avoiding Ibu. I had to go and get Hubby for backup on this one. Ibu had a look of suspicion and disappointment, like we have gone and found a new Balinese family to look after us, or something to that effect.

So, the story was, that when someone died the other day in the village, some of the villagers that live in Denpasar for work had to come back. They told Bapak, while they were walking the dead person to the cemetery (it's a long walk, a good time for gossip), that they heard from someone who heard from someone, that the reason we were not there, in the village, was that we had rented a house thirty minutes away in the Bamboo Forest. *Where do they come up with this stuff?*

We managed to calm Ibu down, and eventually had her back to her normal self. *The good normal self, not the evil one.*

We spent the rest of the day in the restaurant, trying to keep Ibu and Bapak away from the final renovations. They could not understand our concern for the cocktail of enamel spray paint, tile glue and welding fumes.

Speaking of cocktails; Ibu announced she is going to start selling spirits, Johnny Walker Black Label, Absolut Vodka, etc., this was a bit out of the blue. *Who put this idea in her head? Maybe the guys with the fuel on the side of the road needed some new bottles?*

I asked if it was for locals or Bules. Ibu said, "For Bules."

I said, "You know you will need ice, Bules only have their spirits with ice and most with a soft drink mix."

Unlike the locals, who used to come to the hotel years ago, for an Arak with lemon and honey. Ibu stopped serving that after two brothers died in the village of methanol poisoning at a ceremony.

Ibu pondered the ice remark, and then said, "We will make ice."

Hubby quickly pointed out that it had to be clean ice made from Aqua.

"Not a problem," Ibu stated.

This was one of those 'Out of the box, I know Ibu did not come up with this idea herself, I know Ibu hasn't thought this through, I know this will fail when she works out the costs. One of those ideas.' *Did a travelling salesman come to sell Ibu top-shelf spirits? Did someone from Denpasar chat to Ibu, while walking the dead man to the cemetery?*

The answer may have been revealed to me later that day. We had some guests that day, that visited the Hot Springs, and I spoke to them after their visit to see how it was.... One of them commented she didn't expect to be able to get a cocktail at the Hot Springs. I was a bit shocked, especially when she said they had a special on Cosmopolitans. She said that although they didn't have the colour or the taste of a Cosmopolitan, after a few beers and a bit of sun and Hot Springs, they went down a treat. So, after checking her pupils and realising, she was still standing, albeit a little bubbly, I was fairly confident she was not about to cark it on my watch. I did mention that she was living on the edge a bit, and maybe not to push her luck and not try twice in her Bali holiday a cheap cocktail.

24 December 2018 - Man Cave

We went up to see Ibu and Bapak, the renovations were finished. *Halleluiah!*

The only slight problem is that there does not seem to be an office for me... or even a space for my desk... there is a lovely, what we thought was our office all along, bedroom set up for Ibu and Bapak.

There is a lot of space in Bapak's new office, but he has filled it with some new black vinyl couches. It looks very like something from the 1970s, the dark fake wood panelling walls, the mirrors on the wall, the black low vinyl couches, it just needs a lava lamp, and bar in the corner...*Ahh, this might be where Ibu will serve spirits.*

It is certainly not an office space that I want to share. Bapak has his huge CCTV monitor setup strategically, and he has tinted windows, so he can see out to the restaurant, but no one can see in. *Spy Control Centre/Mancave.*

I thought best just to praise Ibu on the completion of her renovations. Let her go on and on about it, and brag about how much it cost. Especially since she had a headache, a backache, and a stomach ache. *No wonder, with the amount it cost. I was thinking of hitting her up for a loan, but not today, not with the headache.*

So, Ibu is still Ibu, Bapak has a Mancave, and I will not see them until after Galungan.

We are not doing Christmas again this year. The family all have Galungan on the 26th, which is just like Christmas anyway. I mean you decorate everything, cook for days, wear a new outfit, get together with all your family members, in this case, dead and alive. Eat too much food, drink too much alcohol early in the day, pass out a few times, wake up just to eat and drink more, pass out again. Except this is held twice a year, the Balinese really know how to rock a religious holiday.

Merry Christmas and Happy Galungan to everyone, whatever you celebrate, or do not celebrate, just be safe.

30 December 2018 - Golden 50th

Today is Ibu and Bapak's 50th wedding anniversary. They married when Bapak was 24 and Ibu was 14. This may seem strange to outsiders, but they married for love, and they have been in love ever since.

As Ibu says, if you don't marry for love and you marry for money, how can you be truly happy, like she and Bapak are.

30 December 2018 - Lost In Translation.

So, I thought it was cute when I started getting text messages from locals, to 'Marry Christmas' and to 'Marry' someone called 'Xmas'. Just had one better, we bumped into our neighbour just now, as we were coming back from walking the dogs. He was washing his car, and we chatted in Indonesian about their plans and ours for New Year's Eve. Just as we were going inside, he yelled out in English "Ok, Have a Happy Ending!"

Chapter 12 - Celebrity Status

12 January 2019 - The Bitch Ladies

We had an *Ibu Chronicles* Reader book for our Kuningan Tour on 5 January, who sent a message saying, 'So, I can meet you.'

Now, that's a lot of pressure, especially when you meet them in person, and they say they love the *Ibu Chronicles*, and you're so funny. Now, I am not funny in real life, I did not really think I was that funny in my writing. I am just writing down life as it happens, life is funny, but not me. I did mention to them that I could possibly be funny if they gave me beer.

So, pressure on, they came on our tour. Ibu had the tour written down in her schedule for quite some time. I reminded her, I checked with her, and she assured me she would be doing the guests' Balinese Offering Making Class in the morning. We just needed to have them brought to her hotel, not a problem.

Guests all arrived, no Ibu. That's fine, I can entertain them with my wit, until Ibu is available to take the class.

Our Ibu Chronicles Reader and her husband were from Australia, our other guests were from America. I had been talking with the Australian guests about the beach vendors at Legian Beach. How they had befriended one lady, and that maybe she was actually from our village. I explained there was a high chance that she was from our village, as 50% of the beach vendors from The Turtle Statue on Kuta Beach up to Seminyak, are from our village. You know the annoying ones, 'You want massage, paint nails', etc., etc...

We also discussed the perception people have that the ladies on the beach are extremely poor, and how I know who to go to if I need a loan. I mentioned they may see the Jeep Wranglers and Hummers later in the village today and would know which cars belong to beach vendors. Mind you, they would have them on finance, probably not the best idea when tourism is so fickle.

So, we met the rest of our guests, and while they got changed into their Balinese attire, Komang rang Ibu. It was decided I would take the guests into the village for their walk, and we would come back later for their class. Komang was working alone, so could not do the class herself, although I heard Ibu screaming on the phone for her to take the class, poor kid.

So, with our guests looking beautiful, all dressed up in their Balinese Adat clothes, we headed off to the village.

Everyone was buzzing around for the final day of the Kuningan ceremony, and the village was decorated looking amazing. I explained to our guests that if you have someone confidently approach you and say in English, "Hello, where you from?" I guarantee they are beach vendors, up in the village for this ten-day ceremony. Everyone else that lives in the village full time will not approach you first, and does not speak English. I also knew, that if a local from the beach did not know me, after we heard the war cry of, 'Where you from?' It would be followed by, 'What's your name? My name is [insert Western name such a Suzy or a Helen], I work on the bitch.'

It is amazing how the 'Bitch Ladies' flock to Australians like flies. The Americans did not get past 'Where you from?' apart from one beach bar vendor who did say 'Donald Trump.'

With the Australians, well, it is like the 'Bitch Ladies' can smell them a mile away, and they come buzzing. Luckily, I know most of them, so they do not do the hard sell on anyone I am with; otherwise, it will be, 'Come visit me on the bitch, I do massage,' etc., etc. However, today one bitch lady just zoned in on the Australians, and she was relentless. I have never seen her before, she did not know me either. So, when she did ask me first, where I was from, I answered, 'Australia', she went in for the kill on me, with her 'I work on the bitch' spiel. Only to have me get out my local talk repellent and repel her off me. She was a tough 'Bitch Lady'. In one swift move, she was straight on to the Australian couple. Explaining she had a deep massage, doing the 'touch the shoulder and start massaging' thing before I could divert her. I gave it thirty seconds, and then I got out the repellent again and shot her down with a: 'We need to go pray now.'

The 'I need to pray,' move is a handy one in Bali, it works for all sorts of occasions. You can use it when you are late for a meeting, or you do not want to go to a meeting, or you are late for work or do not want to go to work. You can use it if you can't be bothered talking to someone, or if someone is trying to sell you something. It took me a while to learn that one here. The Americans were completely ignored by the bitch lady, we may have found another way to repel the bitch ladies when you are on the beach. We only spotted two other Westerners all day, some Dutch, also dressed in Adat clothing, as a guest of a local. I am sure being Dutch, they were left alone as well. I mean they did not say 'Hello,' when I said it to them, and everyone knows the Dutch are tight with their money.

So, if you do not want to be hassled 'on the bitch', maybe try saying you are American or Dutch, or you need to pray.

Now, when we got back for the class, Ibu was in Bapak's office yelling, well, talking loud, to her builder, and Komang was still working alone. *Oh no, no class.*

Then one of my staff Ni Nengah, popped her head around the corner. Ibu must have had Komang ring and demand she came in for the class, on her day off.

After the class and lunch, we went to the carpark to do goodbyes, etc. *I should at least introduce my 'Ibu Chronicles' fan to Ibu, I mean, I think she dragged her Hubby all the way up here just to meet Ibu.*

Before they left, I took our Ibu fan around the back to meet Ibu. Ibu was peeling beans and looking the ever-angelic traditional Balinese woman. I introduced our guest, and said to Ibu, that my friend had seen a photo of my Balinese mother on my Facebook page and wanted to meet her. *Little white lie on the facts there.*

Ibu seemed a little puzzled and a little suspicious at first. She did the whole 'Happy Kuningan, Happy New Year, thank you for coming, lovely to meet you, Rach is my Australian child, safe travels'. Mind you said all in Bahasa Indonesian, so the guest just smiled and nodded, having no idea what Ibu was saying. And then Ibu hit me with it, "Rasch, you have photos of Bapak and my wedding anniversary on Facebook!"

I can only imagine the look that must have been on my face. I have one of those faces that does not hold back with expressions, if I am caught out lying, or just trying hard to bullshit, it is all there on my face. A poker player I could not be. I only have photos on the Ibu Chronicles, which I thought Ibu did not know about... Ibu may know more than she is letting on...*I have some investigating to do.*

13 January 2019 - The Lasers

Don't you just love the way Balinese and Indonesians in general, just say what they think? I love it, no PC Bullshit here. I only learnt the term 'PC' (Politically Correct) recently. I am not PC in any way, but hey, I live in Indonesia.

I also only learnt last year that a tablet was not drugs but a gadget, so I am a bit behind in the Western World of Technology and Bullshit...

A neighbour was just at our front door asking for medicine for his dog, and he started commenting on our house. We explained that it was not finished, and what it should look like, as opposed to the bare concrete and exposed pipes look it has at present. After describing what the finished result would look like, he said, "Oh, yeah, not my style."

Then we got to talking about a few more things about dogs and his beliefs about raising dogs. Very different ideas. It made me remember that I had recently found in the notes section of my personal Facebook page, something I wrote a few years back. When I stumbled across it, I thought I would cut and paste it here, but I forgot to. *I can walk into a room and forget why I am there, so it was a good thing he visited.*

OBSERVATIONS LIVING IN BALI, INDONESIA

Living in Bali is, of course, living in a different culture, although some Australians think it is the same as Australia, it is most certainly not.

WHO ARE WE TO ARGUE?

Masuk Angin - (wind enters), the wind gets inside you and makes you sick. Getting it out again involves someone giving you tiger stripes by scraping it out with a coin, or an edge of a spoon, or lid of a bottle, which is rubbed vigorously and repeatedly, stroking down in a linear pattern on a person's back.

Panas Dalam - (means hot inside) – again if you are sick. If I am feeling cold on the inside and hot on the outside people here will say still Panas Dalem.

Vagina Spas - done at a spa, it is smoke from something burning in a large ceramic pot that you sit above to tighten the vagina, and it gets rid of the smell (hmmm??)

IN TRAFFIC

On a roundabout - people give way to traffic entering the roundabout, as it is 'give way to the left' here. You can just go around again if no one is letting you off.

Indicating - instead of using an indicator light on a motorbike, people wave. They stick their hand out (like signalling on a bicycle) and flap their hand up and down, and the hand gets faster, and in more of a panic if they realise you are not letting them in.

Large buses – buses will have someone in the passenger seat to wave to indicate they are turning, instead of using that little switch that turns on the indicator light. Amazing how the rest of the world just depends on one little blinking light. This same waving action can be used by a pedestrian for crossing a major highway with speeding traffic if you are game, and a lot are.

Right of way - Pulling out onto the main highway from the left on a motorbike is the norm, as the law states: 'you must give way to the left and to smaller vehicles'. That section of the law hasn't changed in the Act since written in 1965. *Wasn't it horse and cart here then?*

Never check the blind spot - I believe it may be physically impossible for people here to turn their head while on a motorbike.

You cannot walk - it seems that in the south of Bali you must use a motorbike to go to the shop, no more than fifty metres away. I have yet to work out why walking is not possible.

OTHER CULTURAL DIFFERENCES/HABITS

Burping - is considered a sign of appreciation for a meal. Hubby has this one perfected, tick.

Confrontation - Indonesians do not like confrontation, public displays of anger are frowned upon, even considered uncouth. Tourists complaining have not quite worked that one out yet.

Apologising- Indonesians rarely apologise if they stuff up, they will just make an excuse, or not admit guilt at all.

Honesty - they are bluntly honest when discussing personal topics, such as 'you look fat today.'

Public Displays of Affection - Public displays of affection are not allowed here between the opposite genders; however, men will hold hands, arms around each other while walking. Hubby gets a good thigh rubbing at government meetings.

Status - Some men have very long thumbnails or the smallest fingernail (so gross), it is a sign that he does not do manual labour so a status thing. It is still gross, as they often clean their ear with it. I guess it saves on cotton bud rubbish.

Plucking - Men plucking chin hairs with tweezers – they have so little hair that they can just pluck, this is a very common thing to do while stuck in traffic jams.

Privacy - there is none, Indonesians are rarely alone, so do not understand this concept.

Gossip - and curiosity are rampant, and people will ask you a wide range of personal questions without batting an eye. Then tell another person without it being seen as a problem at all.

Jealously - if someone says something bad about you, it is always considered jealousy. So, if someone calls you lazy, even if it is true, they are just jealous that you can afford to be lazy. Or they say to someone 'her husband is fat and ugly', that is not an insult, as they are just jealous and want your fat and ugly husband.

Spitting - whenever and wherever you want.

Blowing your nose - without a tissue, just one finger on one side and snort it out to the street. Or, in the bank, just yesterday.

Head checking - you always see women sitting down checking for nits in their children or co-worker's hair. It seems like a bonding thing, as our girls did it to me when they were young, no matter how much I explained I did not have any nits.

Toilet paper - goes in the trash bin, not the toilet – due to bad plumbing of the past. Now, even with the best plumbing, you will still see a sign that toilet paper cannot go down the toilet.

COMMON IN THE WORK ENVIRONMENT

All large business meetings/conferences have a prayer (sometimes more than once).

Government departments, including schools, police stations, mayor's office line up for Attention and uniform inspection in the morning.

All employers must understand God is a priority to their employees - that is in the Employment Act of Indonesia.

Common attitudes:

Not showing up to work (no phone call), does not mean you will be fired.

Not showing up to work (no phone call) for two weeks, and then coming in to get your pay owed without blinking an eye.

Not showing up to work the day after payday.

Quitting your job, without notice or even a phone call.

Expecting a major pay rise two weeks after starting, even when hopeless at the job and have not been on time or some days have not shown up.

Leaving family for six months at a time, to work on another Island. (Very common for men to come to Bali to work on building projects, but also some mothers leave their children with relatives for years, to go and work caring for other people's children).

Not giving references, just saying worked here, worked here (A lot of the time they will say no one works there now, that was there when they were there, so no one to call).

It is a good idea to check the legs of any prospective hire if you do not know them already. Police shoot people in the leg here for muggings or resisting arrest, etc.

HEY, IT CAN'T ALL BE PARADISE IN BALI, SOME ANNOYANCES

Burning plastic/toxic rubbish – and those burning will stand next to it having a chat, feeding their baby.

Dumping - their rubbish in river beds (which lead to the ocean).

Throwing - rubbish from the car/bus/truck window.

Cutting in - on you, when you have been lining up at the supermarket or minimart. (Not nearly as bad as the Chinese though.) Although this can also be blamed on the cashier. They will open a new cash register and tell the person at the back of your line, that you have been waiting in for twenty minutes, to come through.

Overtaking - up a hill, flashing their lights at you that they are coming through. (Although they are now in your lane, and you must slam on your brakes to avoid hitting them head-on.)

The most common question - asked here by a stranger: "Do you have children?" And often asked of Hubby, after that: "If you do not have children of your own, why don't you get a better wife?"

THINGS PEOPLE SAY/BELIEVE

Sprite aborts babies - I am pretty sure there was some clever Marketer at Coca Cola who came up with this one. How else do you get 270 million people to believe this? Helps when it is a country where either contraception is taboo or expensive.

Bathing in rainwater makes you sick - We had a civil engineer when building our house that refused to put in a rainwater system. He refused to have his plumbers attach pipes from the roof to the tanks, although we have no mains water. He came up with the excuse that we would get sick and then said we would get mosquitos. In the end, he agreed to leave a pipe hanging from the roof, and Hubby connected it to the tank.

OR: Rainwater makes skin soft - so you are not getting clean. The neighbour buys every week, 5000 litres of quite dirty 'hard water', and Hubby diverted her roof gutter into our tanks, as she did not want it. She thinks we are dirty as we bath in rainwater.

Bathing in Hot Water - is only for old people and children. This is what many of the older generations believe, so when I mentioned to the old neighbour across the road in the village that I was going up to the hotel to have a hot shower, she of course told the whole street I was sick.

Beauty marks - are called tahi lalat (fly poos). Can you imagine the first time a masseuse told me I had a fly poop on the back of my leg?

And last, but not least - my all-time favourite: The Lasers stop the rain. People are referring to the large searchlights at beach clubs etc. It is a very common discussion on the Bukit, lack of rain and blaming the lasers. Those bloody beach bars on the cliffs have stopped the rain again!

13 January 2019 - Does Ibu Have Facebook?

So, I have been doing a bit of detective work, and Bapak seems to have two Facebook pages. I cannot find one for Ibu. It did seem strange that she would have one, as she does not have a smartphone and she cannot use a computer. Ibu often says to me, "How many bookings do we have on DOTCOM?" Or: "No staff here today, can you look up DOTCOM?" Which can mean anything from Sari hunting, to finding a picture or checking various booking sites to see if her hotel has bookings. I tried explaining the internet to her, but I think she is too young, she needs to be in the Bapak and Ibu Dua age category, to pick it all up quickly.

It reminds me of many years ago when Ibu Dua rang me at work and announced: "I'm on the net!"

After some clarification, I found that she meant she had learnt how to use the internet. Ibu Dua had gone and done a TAFE course to learn how to use the internet, good on her. This led to, of course, the need to buy a home computer and all that jazz. Which some nice young man set up at her home for her.

I asked her what internet provider she was with. Ibu Dua went into a story about how 'It was a sign.' That she had seen an advertisement on television for an internet provider, then heard the advertisement for the same provider on the way home in the car. When she got home, in her letterbox was a small card, an advertisement for the same internet provider. It was a sign! She just had to go with that company.

At that time, I had a three-month contract job, with a small Australian Internet start-up company. My job was in marketing. Our task was to get this small telco from 45,000 clients, up to 100,000 clients in three months. We used a basic marketing 101 method, and targeted demographics, with the TV/radio/letterbox drop. So, I asked her again about which company. When she told me, it was the company I worked for, so I said, "Do you not know where I work?"

Ibu Dua was a little distracted with her exciting new computer and did not get the connection at first. So, I asked what internet plan she purchased. She told me, the dial-up one, as that was all she needed, and it was cheap. I said, "Give me your details, and I will have you upgraded to broadband."

"Oh no," she said. "I don't think I want to be that fast, the plan I have is fine."

I told her it would be free, but she insisted she did not want to go too fast. Then Ibu Dua told me that she had a webpage. I was a little surprised, she then went on to say she built it during her internet course. So, I asked for the web address. Ibu Dua, got excited and said: "Do you have a pen?"

I said, "Yes, mum", even though I was going to type it straight into my browser.

So, Ibu Dua excitedly started to give me her web address, but ever so slowly. "Ok, got a pen? Now, write this down, it's W.W..."

I rudely interrupted, I was a bit busy at work, and I said, "Just give me the name."

Ibu Dua got a bit flustered and said, "Now I need to start again. It's W. W..."

Me being the typical going one hundred miles per hour person I was back then, interrupted and said, "Just the name is fine."

Ibu Dua started again, "it is important you put in, the three W's, now W.W..."

"Okay, mum, sorry."

Ibu Dua, now getting shitty she had to start again, "W. W. W. dot, now have you got three W's? Now, make sure you have a DOT after them. Then you put, [spelling out her full name], and then you have another dot. Then you put, [spelling out TAFE], then you put another dot, then C.O.M, no spaces and then a dot and then A.U., no space and no dot after that, and don't put any spaces, you can't have any spaces. Would you like me to repeat that? Make sure you have three Ws, and no spaces, and the dots are important."

"Yes, mum, I have that."

Nowadays, Ibu Dua is my go-to-person for Facebook and Bapak hasn't lost his password for about a year now, he must finally remember what year he is was born, and he's even got Instagram.

So, back to Ibu having a Facebook page... I think it may be Bapak spying and relaying everything to her. He's picked it all up, in only twelve months. Amazing that this generation grew up without computers, yet they pick it all up so fast. After four years of having a Twitter account, I still cannot understand Tweeting, and I am just getting my head around Instagram. Ibu is under seventy years old and over thirty so like me, she's not in that 'genius with Facebook' generation.

21 January 2019 - Ibu Is Being Nice, Why Am I Suspicious?

The other night Ibu rang me, quite late and said she had forgotten how much rent we paid on the house in the village, and how long the lease was. *Being that the house does not belong to her, it really is none of her business. However, it is no one else in the village's business either, but of course, everyone asks questions like that.*

The landlord had put the rent up, as we only rented it for one year this time, as opposed to the original ten years when it was for the childcare centre. So, it is now a whopping four million rupiah a year, yes around four hundred Australian dollars. I answered Ibu's questions, and she said, "Oh yeah, I forgot", and then hung up.

There is no point in not answering, and we do not have any secrets, with Ibu, or with anyone in the village. Who can, when they are up in your business, with every move you make? *What are you up to now Ibu?*

I told Hubby, and he said that Ibu had just purchased some land in the village, and when he asked her what she was going to do with it, she gave him a cheeky smile and said nothing else. I did not think much of it, until two days ago.

Some of our guests were doing an offering making class, and I noticed Komang had left them alone, so I went over to chat with them while we waited for Komang to return. At the same time, Ibu approached from the other direction, and we both met at the table at the same time. *Ibu greeted the guests with such a welcoming smile and greeting that she must have taken her happy pills.*

It turned out one of the guests spoke some Indonesian, so Ibu could chat away with her. Ibu put her arm around me, yes, a big squeeze, and told the guests I was her daughter number two, her first daughter was called Wayan, and I am Made. Well, I was a little taken back as she continued the arm around me, head on my shoulder, as though I was her favourite person in the world.

Komang returned, Komang's face also told the story of the confusion with Ibu's behaviour. The class could continue, so Ibu and I left them to their class. I went in the opposite direction to Ibu, not thinking too much of it at first.

On the way home, I asked Hubby, "Was Ibu overly friendly to you today?"

He said, "No, just the usual. We don't usually talk much, I usually talk to Bapak."

I asked if she insulted him today, he replied, "I can't remember, probably." Then he paused and said, "No, actually, I don't think she did! What the hell's up with Ibu?"

Now, the relationship between Ibu and Hubby is a love/tease each other thing. They greet each other, insult each other, then both laugh, and that is generally about as deep as they get. For example, the other day, we showed up, and Ibu was wearing a new sarong. I commented on it, asked where she bought it, etc. Hubby told her, "It's ugly."

Ibu replied, "If it is ugly, then Ibu will throw it in the bin."

Hubby said, "Great, then Rach can have it."

We all laughed, and then we went about our day.

Only the week before, Ibu had asked me about my new sarong, where I bought it, etc. I answered, "Hubby bought it."

She said, "It is cheap looking, from a supermarket and he is a cheapskate."

So, she can insult Hubby indirectly through me as well.

In Ibu's opinion, Hubby is too hairy, too stupid, wears shorts too often, and is just downright ugly, and I should have married a Balinese... that's generally what she tells him every week.

So, Ibu not insulting Hubby is a sign something is up. We are unsure of what is up with Ibu, but we are very suspicious. We think she has one of her ideas in her head. This could be a 'build us a house to rent' idea, which we have now been through many times with Ibu. However, there is never a correct day in the calendar, or our birthdays do not match, or something else comes up, and the house is never built. Or, it is a completely off the scale, 180 degrees opposite to what we would ever imagine it to be... I am presuming this niceness will not last, so we will enjoy it while we can. I mean, Ibu did not get hit by a car, or anything to cause a complete personality transplant, like one of the grandmas has had. We will just have to be patient and wait and see.

27 March 2019 - Chinese Travel Agent

I was contacted late last year by a Chinese Travel Agent (TA) who works in Singapore with Chinese Mainland Clients. My Chinese is not that good, it is limited to, 'Don't do that', 'That no good', 'Please line up', 'You stood on my foot' and 'Don't talk so loud.' Luckily, the TA spoke Singlish. My

Singlish is much better than my Chinese, you just need to add La to the end of everything, Okay La, Jam La (Traffic Jam), it is a bit like my French, I just add La or Le in front of everything.

So, we arranged a meeting for when she was coming to Bali with her husband. Travel Agents do well out of popping in a business visit on holidays. Just claim the whole trip on tax. I wish we could do that, alas, cannot with the Indonesian Tax system. We arranged for her, and her husband to accompany us up to the village. I also arranged a time for Ibu to meet with the TA, look at her hotel rooms, and discuss room contract prices, etc. I reminded Ibu, I rang the hotel three times this week to remind Ibu. The staff said, "Yes, Yes," including when I rang, the day before.

We personally went to the TA's hotel yesterday, to meet with her.

As, the night before she confirmed a few times on WhatsApp (WA), I thought, I would let her know via WA, that we were five minutes away. 'Good morning, we will be there in 5 mins... see you in your hotel lobby.'

TA replied: 'OK.'

Then I received a serious of messages:

TA: 'I am in the toilet.'

TA: 'Stomach pain.'

TA: 'see you later.'

I sent back: 'Oh, dear...we can make it another day if you need, we can discuss when we get there.'

We arrived, no sign of anyone... We waited five or more minutes then I sent, 'I am in your lobby, are you ok?'

TA: 'I am fine.'

TA: 'I am coming down.'

TA: 'Just yesterday, eat a lot of chilli.'

Okay, then.

So, they arrived ten minutes later, and off we headed.

When we got in the car I spoke to Hubby in Indonesian, mentioning something along the lines of 'too much information', will be a long day, etc. Oops, it turned out that Chinese TA's husband was from Malaysia. Although he does not speak a word of English, he spoke Malay, which is very similar to Indonesian.

So, I pretended that he did not hear a word I had said and proceeded to talk in Indonesian. He thought that was wonderful, as now he could understand, and asked me to then translate to his wife. *Oh, boy, I have only had two coffees, and this is a two-hour drive.*

So, I spoke in Indonesian, then translated to Singlish, then they talked to each other in Mandarin. I think that was the longest two hours ever.

Luckily, I knew they would sleep the whole way back, I could put money on it, the Chinese always do...*I hope so, as I will need to sleep as well.*

We made a few unplanned sightseeing stops along the way, with the TA making a few comments, not about the scenery, but comments such as, 'You are so pale still, after live so long here.' *I have not had enough coffee for these types of comments.*

I used my nod and smile approach. Bloody long photo stops for Chinese, what happened to the good old days of click and get back in the car to sleep?

These two had to get the right photo. Not a Peace sign in sight and they did not fall off anything taking selfies, so I was impressed with that, and believe me, they gave it a good try. No fear of heights, unstable ledges, rice field edges, 40-foot drops, fuel pumps bursting into flames by photographing that close, cars on highways, while standing in the middle to get a photo of a statue, or on wobbly walls with these two.

We finally arrived in the village and went straight to Ibu's hotel. I asked the staff, "Where is Ibu?"

The reply, "Bangli".

The staff aren't big conversationalists in the mornings, nor am I, until I have my third coffee. "Okay, when will she be back?"

Answer: "I don't know."

So, the TA and husband were going off to try canoeing, and I settled in for a coffee (a big coffee) and banana pancake. I was just about to eat and I got called down to the other office. I told the restaurant staff, "I will be five minutes, can you just cover my pancake, I will be back; I do not care if it is cold."

I returned in five minutes, grabbed another coffee, and my pancake had gone. One of the staff suddenly got talkative, "Oh, we make you a new one, that one was cold, it went in the bin, you can't have a cold pancake."

"Agus, you ate it, didn't you?"

Cheeky smile and he replied, "Another coffee, ooh, you must be strong."

Please God, give me the strength to get through today.

So, while I waited on a new pancake, and I finished coffee number four, I went to find Nengah, who was meeting me at 9.00 am with Ibu, no Nengah. So, I asked a few staff, "Where is Ibu?"

Same answer from all staff, "Bangli."

Me: "When will she be back?"

Same answer from all: "Don't know."

So, I asked, "Where is Nengah?"

"Don't know."

Okay, I will rephrase the question.

"What time is Nengah working today?"

After a few 'I don't know', Komang finally answered, "Oh, maybe after

1.00 pm."

There goes Nengah meeting with the TA at 10.00 am.

"Okay Komang, what time is Ibu back?"

"I don't know."

Why do I bother asking? We are here all day, so, not a problem.

I am used to Ibu not keeping appointments. We could just keep the TA busy doing activities in the area and feeding her, minus the chili.

Twelve noon came, and no sign of Ibu, or Nengah, so we sent the TA and her husband to the Hot Springs, they could have lunch there as well.

At 1.30 pm Bapak's car arrived, it had started raining now, and he was tooting madly in front of the restaurant for someone to come and bring an umbrella. Well, he presumed we all knew that was what that tooting meant. *I wonder if the guests in the restaurant understood what that meant? I wonder why he needs to continue to toot? We are not deaf. Is the horn stuck? I can also see you there on the CCTV Bapak, and the restaurant staff can see you, as you have practically pulled into the restaurant. Bapak STOP with the bloody tooting!*

Eventually, Kadek slowly walked to the car, with as much enthusiasm as he has doing any task. He's not as slow as Pak Jero, but he's a close second. He held the large umbrella over the back-passenger seat, and Ibu stepped out of the car, very slowly, looking very weary. I was very impressed with the back door, and got a little focused on the way it automatically closed, it was a sliding door. *I never knew Bapak had that on his car...oops, back to Ibu.*

I was on the laptop, so could not get up to greet Ibu straight away. Actually, I was on WhatsApp on the laptop to the TA, who liked to hit send, then send another message, then another, then another.

Hubby had come in before Ibu, to say Ibu had been in the hospital for five days with kidney stones, then he went straight back to watching sport on his phone. I stopped answering the TA for a second to fuss over Ibu. They brought Ibu into the office, she sat in the guest chairs. I went over and sat with her and held her hand while my phone was going off as bad as Bapak's tooting. Ibu asked me solemnly why I had not visited her in hospital...*Oh, dear, here we go!*

I told her, "Well, it would help if someone had told me, such as in one of your staff in the many phone calls I had made in that five days, or maybe even that morning."

Ibu understood, she did not get angry at all. *I hope the Doctors sent her home with a huge supply of whatever they have her on.*

Ibu excused herself to go get changed, and I looked at my WhatsApp, it was a running commentary on what the TA was doing. By her sending separate messages my phone had sent beeps for each one, such as:

TA: 'I have ordered my meal, my meal is not here yet.'

TA: 'I can see waterslides next door, how much are they?'

TA: 'Do you have other guests here?'

TA: 'I think I can see them'.

Then she started sending photos with captions, of random tourists at the Hot Springs

TA: 'Is this them?' (photo)

TA: 'Maybe this is them?' (photo)

TA: 'Are we under same transfer Back?'

TA: 'U may contact them if they want to go back earlier?'

TA: 'As they are already sitting.'

TA: 'I am waiting for the meals.'

Imagine what the tourists are thinking, bloody Chinese Tourist taking photos of us. Leave the poor tourists at the Hot Springs alone.

Now, I was not sure what the guests looked like, so I had to go and find the staff to make a positive identification before she filled my phone with random shots of tourists. The staff made a positive ID one photo. I sent a WA to the TA, 'Yes, same transfer, they will be ok.' *I hope she leaves them alone now. I had mentioned earlier we had American tourists visiting the Springs today (silly me).*

TA: 'Ok, later after I finish my meal, I will ask them.'

TA: 'How Long can the driver get here?'

TA: 'If they agree to go earlier?'

Me: 'he can be there in 20 mins'

TA: 'Ok.' TA: 'I will keep you posted.'

TA: 'Their meal just come.'

Me: 'Ok'

TA: 'The driver contact is your phone number?'

TA: 'I need to double confirm it is 3 of them, correct people.'

Me: 'LOL'

TA: 'My meal has now come.'

TA: 'I will eat my meal and let you know.'

TA: I will swap my fish meal for my husband's chicken.'

TA: 'as the chicken meal is more food.'

TA: 'Can we come back after we eat?'

ME: 'just let us know when not a problem.'

TA: 'Okay, I will let you know when I have eaten.'

TA: 'What driver will you send?'

Meanwhile, Ibu had changed her clothes, and she wanted the office rearranged, so she could lie down in the office, next to my desk! *She probably wants to spy on the CCTV. Boy, she must have missed five days without spying.*

I went to find what drivers were available. The problem was that all our drivers are Mangkus and there was a large ceremony, no one knew who was available, a lot of blank stares. Then Ibu started calling me, with her latest pronunciation of my name: "Ratchett, Rachtett, Ratchett, Ratchett, Ratchett."

How the hell can she keep that going for so long?

I was yelling out, "Please just wait, Ibu", my phone still beeping with every WA message, then Bapak started tooting again, as he wanted help to get stuff out of the car, so Toot, Toot, Toot, Toot. Beep, Beep, Beep, Ratchett, Rachett. Ibu was getting louder over Bapak's toots, then with the intensifying sound of the rain on the tin roof, it all seemed to get faster and louder. *Or that's just all that coffee?*

Back when I was younger, or pre-pain medication, I could cope well with multitasking. I would have turned off the sound on my phone, cut the wires to Bapak's horn, and put a sock in Ibu's mouth, without blinking an eye. *Today was just all a bit too much.*

I was still trying to ask the staff which driver could go, Ibu was keeping on par with my WhatsApp beeps, and Bapak's tooting. The rain was doing a good job of competing with her...*Is there a hole I can crawl into?*

I finally got back to Ibu. I sat down, and she asked me why she got Kidney Stones and an infection. I looked at her as in, 'you were in the hospital for five days, with professional Doctors?' *Did they put her in the wrong hospital?*

Bangli has the only Psychiatric Hospital on the Island. Maybe that's why the staff did not mention the hospital and just said Bangli?

So, I tried to explain to Ibu that all my nagging her about drinking water, I was not just nagging. Meanwhile, my phone was still beeping, Bapak had parked, so the tooting had stopped, and the rain was not as loud.

Suddenly, in started walking every single staff member, with shopping bags in their hands, one by one they came through the office door. Ibu started directing them where to put all the bags. *Ibu must have had a lot of clothes taken to the hospital, as she had no suitcase.*

She has never been anywhere to need a suitcase, so I presumed the plastic bags must be her clothes. The bags kept coming and coming.

I soon realised that Ibu had been shopping. As you do, when you are lying in a hospital bed.

I was now confident that she was not in the loony bin, and in the General hospital. *As, what Psychiatric Hospital would allow a shopaholic to do this much shopping?*

I should look further into that Psychiatric Hospital, though, for myself.

Now, I will not bore you with the other 39 WhatsApp messages from the TA, but let's put it this way, our other guests at the Hot Springs were very smart. They decided to stay three hours longer, a great way to avoid coming back to the hotel with the TA. I still got the commentary from the TA's every move from: 'I am getting in the shower' right up to 'I am walking to the car' and 'Ok, I got into the car.'

When they got back to the hotel, I opened the door, and they were asleep in the back. *Ahhh, I just knew that would happen, praise the Lord.*

So, I said goodbye to Ibu, she was in good hands. Nengah, the cook was busy massaging her in my office, while the whole family had arrived to support Ibu. Most were sitting around in the restaurant, glued to their smartphones, including Hubby. Ibu continued directing staff where to put the couch, pillows, new shopping, etc., at the same time watching the CCTV and directing Nengah to what spots to massage. *She has multitasking down pat.*

Hubby and I made our escape. Hubby and I chatted very quietly on the way home (it was the first time we had a chance to speak to each other all day), allowing the TA and her Hubby to snore and sleep, as long as possible.

It was a peaceful hour; they did not wake till Denpasar. My fault, I asked to stop to pee. *I should have bloody held it another hour.*

So, I will keep you updated on Ibu's recovery. She was excited that Ibu Dua is coming back to Bali in three weeks, probably just so she can nag me about Ibu Dua moving here to live with me.

2 April 2019 - Ibu update

I am sitting with Ibu... she will not stop farting. That is all.

7 April 2019 - Ibu Dua Is Coming

You may remember on Ibu Dua's last visit, she brought magic sponges to clean my already clean walls. Well, Ibu Dua arrives tomorrow, and we fly out after that, as we must renew our visa, that is done overseas every six years, so she can clean to her heart's content.

Last time we left for overseas, we rescued a puppy a few days before, and poor Ibu Dua was cleaning up puppy pee for one week of her holiday.

Last night we rescued a pup that had been dumped in a rice sack, and it has taken up half our day to get it to the vet, etc.

I have not told Ibu Dua about the new puppy yet.

16 Apr 2019 - The Good Daughter

So, I have cleaned the house from top to bottom. No, I do not have a maid. I decided to be a good daughter and leave Ibu Dua some dirty spots on the wall, so she can use her magic sponges.

25 April 2019 - Ibu Dua Is Here, Who Needs Ibu

I have not been writing much as Ibu Dua is here, and I promised I would not embarrass her, by writing about her.

The kitchen cupboards are very clean; the magic sponges did their magic.

Ibu Dua went off on an adventure to other parts of Bali for a week and got back to our house last night. We were having dinner, and I mentioned that as the raining season seemed to have officially stopped, we needed to be careful with water again. Although my hair was dirty, I was giving it one more day before I used the precious water to wash it.

Ibu Dua then got all sentimental and said, "I remember when you were a baby, you were so cute, you used to get very bad Cradle Cap, and you smelled just like a chicken."

A chicken?

Hubby asked Ibu Dua, how did she know what a chicken's head smelled like.

I asked, "Roast chicken or a live chicken?"

I presumed Ibu Dua was only tired and did not mean that I smelled like a chicken. Ibu Dua proceeded to say, "A live chicken, not chicken poo, but like a chicken."

I burst into laughter, and said, "You know this has to be an Ibu Chronicles."

Ibu Dua looked at me in horror at the thought of me writing about her, and tried to backtrack by saying, "It wasn't an unpleasant smell."

That was too much, "Sorry, this is an Ibu Chronicles."

Ibu Dua does not like to be in the Ibu Chronicles. So, she tried to backtrack some more, but dug herself in deeper, by saying, "Well, you know your Aunty, her baby was cross-eyed and ugly. I thought you were the most beautiful baby with your hair that stood straight up and your big blue eyes. Your Aunty used to say to me: "You think she is so beautiful, but she looks like a Monkey."

So, there you go, I was a beautiful baby, that looked like a Monkey, and smelled like a chicken. Who needs Ibu?

Chapter 13 - Back in the Kampung

1 May 2019 - I Have Officially Morphed Into A Dadong

A Dadong is a Balinese Grandmother, some of the younger grandmothers prefer to use the Indonesian word for grandma, 'Nenek'. Dadong is usually only used for the older grandmothers, you know, ninety-plus years old, no teeth, or maybe one or two, faces with wrinkles etched from history.

How I came to this conclusion, that I have morphed into a Dadong? Well, I was up in the village last week, for one night by myself. It was lovely to be greeted by the neighbours who asked, "When did you get home?"

Sometimes Balinese, when they have not seen an expat for a long time, will talk to them like they are a tourist, no matter how long they have lived in Bali, saying, "Oh, when did you arrive, or when did you get to Bali?"

Meaning, I haven't seen you, so I presumed you went 'home' to your country. Being that Bali is my home. The very rare occasion that I have had that statement said to me, usually in a tourist area, it grates at my heart a bit when I feel like this is my home. So, when I arrived back at the house in the village, after six months away in the south of Bali, it was so nice to be greeted by the neighbours with a 'welcome home'.

The house was a bit of a mess, no one has lived in it for months, and Wayan seemed to have forgotten to cut the grass. So, I pushed my way through the jungle and decided to start with sweeping the front porch. I threw on an old, oversized t-shirt, I already had on a sarong, I pulled my hair up into a bun and started to sweep.

Across the road is a small warung. It is really set up so the old ladies in the street, have somewhere to sit and gossip. *I am sure of that, as it is only open in the afternoon, with no set times, just when they need a gossip.*

I was sweeping away, when I heard one of them say, "There is an old person sweeping at that house."

The next person asked, "Where?"

The first lady said, "There on the porch, with the broom in hand."

155

Now, Balinese do not really have his and her, so it was just an old person. *Geez, I know they are losing their sight, but they have about 40 years on me.*

After sweeping, pulling weeds, and giving up, I decided to go and get some food. The temperature had dropped, and it gets dark quick with no street lighting, so I thought it best I jump on my bicycle and pop down to see Ibu and grab dinner. So, I went to my winter wardrobe, that I just leave in the house. I grabbed a hoody, and off I went.

I was riding along passing lots of Dadongs and then I realised, I was dressed exactly the same as them! *Oh dear, I am morphing into a Dadong!*

I said Hello to them all, and one yelled out, "Halo Dadong."

That's it, it's official!

I went back to the South the next day, and did not think much more of it.

A few days later, I went out to lunch with a girlfriend, after going to immigration, so was in my mandatory business attire, heels, and skirt/shirt etc. The Balinese owner of the warung, I had not seen in a while, said I was looking younger. *Now, that is the look I was going for!*

So, yesterday, I arrived back in the village. Hubby had a meeting, so I went along.

He had stayed one night and went back to the south, leaving me, as I must meet the job candidates Wayan has already shortlisted, with his interviews for new staff.

As soon as we arrived, we went straight to the meeting at the village heads' office. I was sitting there next to one of the office girls, and she was playing with my ponytail. *As you do here in government meetings, or have bra fittings.*

She looked at me and announced, "You know, you aren't a tourist, you are a Balinese person. Actually, you are a Kedisan village person. So, that means when you die, you can be cremated with the rest of the village."

Now, after only just coming to terms with the fact that I am now a Dadong, you would probably think when someone is planning your funeral this early, that you should worry. However, it is a great honour to be able to be cremated with the rest of the village. I will be buried first and dug up a few times, but they are welcome to it. They may 'Weekend at Bernie's' me a bit before they bury me, but that is fine. I will make sure I have on clean underwear.

So, that's me sorted, I looked across the meeting room at Hubby, and nothing was mentioned about him. *Where will they put him when he dies?*

I took the opportunity to mention to her, that Hubby had often said that, when I got old, he would just throw me in the volcano. She shook her head disapprovingly, a bit like Ibu does, probably a relative. *Well, now Hubby does not have to do that, throw me in the volcano, which is a good thing, as he fears heights, and he always worries he must pay someone to take me up in a wheelchair and push me in.*

So, I am officially a Balinese, a Balinese old Grandmother, but what is Hubby?

Well, the answer came from Ibu today. I took the potential staff members to meet Ibu, you must get a sign off from Ibu, even though it is our business, not hers, it is Ibu. So, potential candidates met Bapak first, and then out came Ibu. Well, Ibu began to tell them that before they accepted a job, they must meet Rach's husband, or maybe they would be too scared to come back to work. *Geez, thanks Ibu.*

Ibu went on to say that I was family, and I was a Balinese, but my Hubby was harsh, aggressive, scary, and Dutch. *She could have just said Dutch.*

I assured her that Hubby had popped in for five minutes at the beginning of the interview process and had met the potential candidates. She just shook her head and told them "This is Boss, Rasch is Boss."

I confirmed with the candidates that Hubby is the boss, I am second in charge, then Wayan... Ibu said, "No, this Boss", pointing her bony finger quite hard in my shoulder.

Poor guys were so confused, they may withdraw their application after this.

Interviews all over, and I came home to write my epiphany, that I have become a Dadong. While writing, Hubby rang me from the south and said I needed to go down to the hotel immediately, as Kadek was texting him and annoying him about something. He could not work out what he wanted, he was busy, and did not want to be disturbed... I think he was just at the hardware store. Although, I do not like to be disturbed at Ace Hardware, either. It was pouring with rain, so I told him I could not go right now. He is Dutch, they ride bicycles in the rain, sleet, and snow, so he was not taking no for an answer. *Bloody Bosses.*

Then the clouds separated, and the beautiful sun started to shine. So, off I went riding along, looking at the beautiful stillness of the lake. The clouds were coming down over the lake, the air so crisp from the rain. Then the Dadongs started to come out of their makeshift shelters from the rain. All Dadongs were using the towels that they usually have rolled up on their heads to carry baskets, as covers from the rain, so they had them draped over the heads. *Ahh, I have not yet succumbed to the towel on the head, there is hope for me yet.*

I got to the hotel and went straight to Ibu, to see what she wanted so urgently.

She told me Hubby had already answered her question, she had no idea why I was there. *Aduh.*

And, then the rain came again, and boy did it come down.

So, after hanging around for thirty minutes for no reason, I decided to order my dinner to take home, so that I did not have to go out in the rain again. I put a plastic bag on my handbag and pulled my hood on my hoody over my head, and off I went.

I could not ride the usual downhill, easy five-minute ride home, as a new lake had formed where the main road used to be. On a staff member's suggestion, I rode up the hill of the caldera and across the back of the farms and back down again. *At least this way, I would not bump into anyone, and no one could recognise me anyway, with my hood on.*

Halfway up the hill, a lady came out of the bushes, carrying a lot of cut grass on her head. Up here they take the grass to the cow, not the cow to the grass. I said, 'Excuse me Madam' (in Indonesian), as I passed her. *Not sure who was under that grass but pretty sure it was a woman.*

I rode on further to a steep hill, where I started to lose some momentum. *I am not as fit as I used to be. I really need to get fitter.*

I then heard the walking grass yell out in Balinese, behind me, "Careful, slowly in the rain, Dadong."

So, there you go, I have morphed into an old Balinese Grandmother... and Hubby is just Dutch.

2 May 2019 - Someone Went And Died

When your day does not go to plan. Wayan's mother-in-law died. Just burying her now.

Added: she was eighty-four, so I think it was the mother of the mother-in-law, everyone was explaining it, but then everyone was also related to her somehow. Amor ring Acintya (R.I.P).

I have walked back from the cemetery alone, as Ibu nearly pushed me in a drain three times on the way down to the cemetery.

Busy day today, four guests are out canoeing, and our staff are all busy at the cemetery. They have closed the office... hopefully someone will be back there when the guests come off the lake, and someone can take them back to their hotel.

So, glad a new staff member starts tomorrow. He is from Jakarta and does not have any family members in the village, so he can't close the office every single time someone dies.

12 May 2019 - In Tune

We were supposed to have a business meeting today with Ibu and Bapak. Hubby had some new ideas he wanted to run by Ibu and Bapak.

However, the meeting was abruptly stopped when Ibu said to Hubby that he was too greedy. Hence, she moved from a meeting to making offerings.

We had to follow Ibu to the kitchen and Hubby had to have a lesson, well a test in making offerings.

I knew all the parts of the offerings. Hubby just said 'uh ah' a lot while Ibu and Bapak spoke over each other trying to explain to Hubby what everything was called.

Then Ibu said she would talk to the Mangku first about our ideas, and then talk to me, not Hubby, as 'Ibu and Rach think the same'.

It's happening, I am becoming Ibu! Must be the Dadong coming out in me, I am now in tune with Ibu! Oh, dear!

15 May 2019 - That "Aha Moment."

That moment when you know your staff are really paying attention, and actually learning something new.

I was just doing a basic first aid lesson with my new staff member. We were discussing flushing out a wound and keeping it clean. He nodded and then pointed outside the office and said, "So you would use that, in this situation?"

I looked over to see our Mangku putting black volcanic sand from the new concreting in his son's knee. His son, nine-year-old, had just fallen off his motorbike trying to avoid our new wet cement. *Absolutely nothing to do with his feet not being able to touch the ground and he usually grabs the pole that is no longer there, to stop.*

The Mangku poured the black volcanic sand in the rather large wound, and he is currently blowing the sand dry.

Why do I have all this first aid stuff here, when, if our guests fall off their bicycle, we can just use black sand?

20 May 2019 - I Just Need Coffee, Kopi Dulu

My plan this morning was that I would get some work done at home, before going into the office. *Always nice, when you can stay in your PJs and Ugg boots, as it is effing freezing here at 5.00 am.*

However, I slept in. Not sure how, as the temple music and prayer start at 5.59 am, it is louder than the alarm on my phone.

One of our dogs woke me at 6.45 am, with no uncertainty, that there was a need for me to get up. Not a nice way to wake up, as she tends to only bang on the door at this house when there is an earthquake. So, when my brain worked out, it was her, I woke up in a bit of a panic.

You see the house did not fare well from the Lombok earthquakes, it is basically falling down, but not a problem, I have the escape route planned, and she is a doggie radar. No earthquake, she just must have realised I was still asleep and thought that was strange, so she banged on the door and then satisfied I was up, she went back to her bed and fell asleep. She sleeps twenty-two hours of the day, it was twenty-three hours in the South, but the cool air up here must agree with her.

All good, needed coffee first, make dog food, then I would get into it. Having special needs dogs, means cooking fresh meals twice a day, of a variety of choices, and hand-feeding some... thus, the reason we rarely go on holidays.

I had just sat down to work, and Hubby started sending me photos of a wound on the neck of his cat. (I say his cat, as I never wanted to keep him after I rescued him.) *How can one cat make so much noise?*

So, we spent thirty minutes going through the right antibiotics and dosage to give the cat.

Finally getting into the swing of work, and a friend in Australia, sent me a picture of cheese. Now, the picture was of lots of cheese and she asked if Hubby ate Dutch Smoked Cheese? *Huh, must be a joke, or a tease?*

Hard to concentrate on work now, but it did help me realise I had forgotten to eat breakfast. *Now while writing this, I have just realised, I have forgotten to eat dinner.*

Since it was obvious that my friend was out shopping, by the said photo, of a shit load of cheese, it popped into my mind that she mentioned t-shirts would soon be on sale in Australia. As I had seemed to have outgrown my only two decent t-shirts. Yes, you can say 'outgrown things' still, at this age. Now that I had succumbed to the fact that I had been dressing like a Dadong, I thought it was time to purchase something a little younger.

I do not like to shop, cannot stand it, love that my friends are willing to do it for me. I once, in my past life, when I worked in Corporate, had some very important clients pop in without an appointment, on casual clothes day. I asked my PA to run across the road on Collins Street, and just grab me a new suit. From that day on, I realised other people could shop for me, and I would never have to step foot in a store again. *The problem being now I do not have the corporate budget, and I do not have a PA, so I just do not shop.*

Then, I got a call from one of my staff asking where I was. I looked at the time, and I was late, the Mangku was waiting for me.

I had a five-minute shower, okay when you use a small bucket over a larger bucket, a one-minute water blessing.

I got dressed, ran out the door, grabbed my bicycle, and raced down the hill to work, racing past everyone. I was not racing anyone in particular, however, since my new staff member had his first training session yesterday with Wayan, on how to change brake pads, I could have actually won any race, as the brakes on my bike were not working.

So, in record time, and some amazing manoeuvres around the corners, while wearing a sarong mind you, I finally slowed down on the small rise to the office.

It was a very important meeting, as we had to move a tree. I had to say goodbye to the tree, give it a hug, give it a kiss, etc. None of this has anything to do with living in Bali and all that spiritual stuff. I just had not had my third coffee yet, and I still had not eaten. I was holding onto the tree, accidentally tripped a bit, kissed it and hugged it for balance. I then needed to say goodbye to it, and to the Mangku, as I had to go get something to eat.

Okay, food in tummy, still not a third coffee, as the water at the office was not hot yet. *FF sake, it is 9.40 am, and the water is not hot yet?*

I explained to the new staff member, that I was non-coherent until coffee number three. This was particularly important for him to take note of, especially as I usually could not speak English until said coffee was consumed. So, I explained to him if a guest ever came in, and the water was not hot yet, and I was speaking gibberish, he needed to step in. I also explained to him that he needed to make sure the water was hot before I arrived, or he may not enjoy working here. I also suggested he check brakes before handing over a bike, especially to the person that pays his wages.

Tree sorted, and the rest of the day was normal, as normal as my life is.

I left my bike to have the brakes reattached, and I started to walk back home. As there was a ceremony, I could not walk more than five metres down the street without getting invited in for a coffee. *So, finally, someone has the water boiled, I should have walked to work and had a coffee first.*

I declined many invitations until the temptation was too great, and I had managed to move at least one street closer to where I was going.

Lots of chats and catch-ups with other Dadongs and a few Bitch ladies.

Then one Dadong approached me in the street and asked me to drop in. She told me she was a relative of Ibus', and she wanted to ask me about her goitre. *Being that I am a Doctor, and all that jazz.*

We went down a gang to her, 'who would have known there is a house/little warung back here', and she told me, that finally, after five years, she had gone to the clinic, and the Doctor had told her it would probably need to be operated on. It was quite a big goitre.

So, I drank more coffee, sat with her, helped her make her offerings, and reassured her that she would not die in the operation. *Well, as long as she does not have the operation, I wouldn't be lying.*

As I was sitting there making offerings, my friend started sending me photos of her husband modelling t-shirts for me to buy for Hubby. *I forgot about the t-shirts.*

So, I video called her and showed her the goitre, as you do, and told her I would ring back later about the t-shirts. *I keep forgetting she is not working this week and shops are close to her. She had literally gone straight from cheese to finding t-shirts.*

After leaving the old dear, well, I had made 50 Canang (offering bases) for her, so that was enough. I had to call one of the staff to come and pick up all the fruit and snacks she had given me. I couldn't carry it. I told her it was too heavy, but she insisted. Since one of my staff was fasting, and I think he was just eating rice and eggs at night, I called him to come and get the fruit and told him he could have it for tomorrow morning.

Thinking back at this right now, I should have kept some. Oh well, Ibu gave me an apple when I left the office, and he did have a cycling tour today, so he needs to get back his strength. I seem to be fasting without meaning to. Seriously, I could do the food fast, not a problem, but the no coffee or water, no way.

I made it back home and grabbed my laptop and was finally able to head to the office, after what already felt like a long day. *I really need to get that work finished from this morning.*

I had just sat down in the warung next to our office, ready to turn on my laptop and two of Ibu's staff started arguing with me about the tree. *You do not want to argue with me now that I have had too much coffee.*

The long story short, the tree was being moved from our carpark, so the Mangku could drive his car on our land to get to his garage. So, I was not paying to fill the large hole that removing the tree made in our carpark. They said, 'Talk to the Boss'.

Being that Ibu is the Mangku's mother, I would go straight to the Boss. I packed up my laptop, took another bike, checked that the brakes worked and headed to the hotel. *I will just work there instead.*

I found Ibu and Bapak sitting in the restaurant, and I sat down to ask how they were. *I will discuss another topic first, butter them up a bit before I mention the hole.*

I asked about Ibu's relative with the goitre, and tried to get some history. Turned out the lady has had it for twenty years. Then Ibu said, "I think I am getting one."

I had a look at her throat, and sure enough, she was getting a goitre! So, I rang my Cheese/t-shirt Personal Shopper, who is also Ibu's beautiful Australian Doctor. We started discussing how many people in the village had goitres and the three types of goitres, etc.

Then Ibu asked if there was a pill to get rid of her kidney stone. The Beautiful Doctor, my Personal Shopper, yelled out in English, "WATER IBU!"

As we were on a video call, everyone in the restaurant heard. Ibu got up, as I was in the middle of translating for the Doctor. We were still on the video call, so I got up and followed her. I lost her in the hallway for a moment, but found her out the back, filling up her water bottle and looking sheepish that she had forgotten to drink water. So, I had to prove to the Doctor that Ibu was drinking water, by showing her drinking water on the video call. Ibu drank so much in one go that I think she may have forgotten for a few days.

It was a lengthy call, Bapak had gotten up early during the call and left. I returned to our office unaware that Bapak had still been listening to our conversation about goitres and treatment. *Well, it was a bit loud.*

When I went back to our office, to get back to work, Bapak was there and he started saying, "Goitre is Gondok in Bahasa Indonesian", and "Nengah's real name is Gonok." (Their Nengah has been having an unreasonable number of days off lately and was not at work again today.)

So Bapak kept saying "Yes, Nengah is a big lump on Ibu's throat Ha-ha" and "We just need to give Nengah Iodine to get rid of him Ha-ha", "Nengah is a pain to Ibu, Ha-ha." He just kept going and going.

When I presumed Bapak finally had that out of his system, since he was in such a good mood, I approached the conversation with Ibu about tree removal. I showed Ibu and Bapak the video of it being moved. All good, they agreed the Mangku would pay. *My plan worked.*

Then Ibu asked me when I was going to have my Melukat, (Purification ceremony) and asked, had I talked to the Mangku about it yet. I told her he was a bit busy moving the big tree. Then Bapak started laughing again, saying, "Melukat Pohon." (Although Melukat is, in this case, a Balinese word. In Indonesian, it translates as 'rolling' and Pohon is a tree). "Ha-ha, Melukat Pohon" (rolling tree), "Melukat pohon." *He's cracking himself up with his one-liners today.*

Bapak finally calmed down, and we all got back to work; he seemed busy doing his own work and had gone quiet. However, when I was chatting to one of my staff on the phone, and I said, "Tamu Mau Book?" which is a lazy way of saying 'The guests want to Book?' Bapak started again. "TAMU MABUK HA-HA", (Mabuk means drunk, so he was saying, 'The Guests are drunk HA HA'.)

I was trying to have a serious conversation, and Bapak was pissing himself laughing.

It finally stopped, but then later he heard me on the phone ask "Tamu Book?" (did the guest book?)

He cracked up, and was repeating, "TAMU MABUK, TAMU MABUK!" (Guest Drunk, Guest drunk.)

Either Bapak has had too much coffee, or he is 'mabuk.'

I am going home to work.

27 May 2019 - New Kid On The Block

Being the new kid on the block can always be a little daunting. I moved around a lot as a kid, so know what it is like to make new friends, a new town, etc. Being the new kid on the block in this village was a little daunting for me. Okay, a culture shock, probably, because I did not speak the language and I was a Princess.

We have a new staff member, Ari, he is from Jakarta, and he is Muslim. He was only in Bali four days when he started working with us, and moving to a Traditional Balinese Hindu village was a brave move. He is settling in very well. He does not have a relative die every minute, so it is working out just fine. He had to fit in quickly as we have had so many ceremonies in the past few weeks, and he must wear Adat Clothing (traditional Balinese clothing). He looks good in it, but I did have to get the other staff to dress him properly a few times. He seems to have the hang of it now, but he keeps forgetting the most important piece of the outfit, his udeng (Balinese Men's head-dress) and wears his work cap instead.

He is living alone in the staff accommodation at the back of our rental office, and although there are two other rooms for staff, he is the only one in there. The pool table in the staff common area goes to waste a bit when you only have yourself to play with. He has also been fasting, which means he must cook alone at night, so it must be a bit lonely. This could be why I get quite a few messages at night, not late, but he is letting me know he is there.

One night, the message was asking if he could get a dog to keep him company. I do not think it is the right living space for a dog, so, I have been taking one of ours down to visit him. Also, one of our other dogs just drops into the office, after he has rolled in roadkill, and covered in mud, just to give him something to do.

Unless there is a ceremony, it is eerily quiet at night where he is, as he is not in the kampung like I am. He is on the main road, where there are only commercial properties so, he just hears the lake, wind and maybe a random motorbike passing occasionally.

Last week, the power went out in the whole village. At first, I thought some idiot was setting off fireworks, as at the back of Hubby's family's greenhouse I could see sparks and heard noises for quite a while. Then with a big bang, the village was in darkness. Five minutes later, I got a message from Ari in English: 'The power is down there also?'

I explained 'Everywhere, and then it might be off a while, as something just blew up.'

I got back, 'Ok Ibu, I hope this not last until morning, I am afraid of ghost.'

Poor guy, it would be very dark over where he is, and all those bloody ghosts around would be scary. So, I sent him back a message saying, 'It's okay, all the ghosts are back in the cemetery, everyone was down there yesterday just making sure.' The whole village had been digging everyone up and reburying them. Okay, there may have been a few restless souls, but I did not want to scare him. I chatted with him for a while, just to keep him distracted.

The power was off the next day as well, but he seemed to have settled in with the Ghosts. At least he had someone to play pool with.

Then the riots started in Jakarta; contrary to the Australian news, there were no problems in Bali. However, on Friday night, I received a message 'Good evening, Ibu... do you hear the men yelling?'

I sent back, 'No, I can't hear them, but there is a ceremony.'

He sent back 'Oh, you are very lucky, I hear them very clear.'

I worked out what it was, and I assured him it was a ceremony, and it was just two men over a loudspeaker doing a 'Jero Jam', like a radio play for the Gods.

He sent back, 'Ooh good to know that. I just worry if that sound of riot next to me'—*poor kid.*

I sent Hubby a message telling him that our new staff member thought there was a riot in the village. Hubby thought it was hilarious and commented, in the South of Bali, it may be possible, but up there, no way.

So, I spent another night having a conversation on WhatsApp with Ari, assuring him it is just up at the Bali Banjar (like an open town hall). If he wants to go and watch, he can. He just must put on his Adat clothing, everyone will welcome him. We have already introduced him to the village heads, and he has had his big lecture from the village head on how he must assimilate into the village, blah, blah. Ibu now has two Muslim (Balinese) staff of similar age, so we have introduced them to Ari, and they have clicked already. We have had a big wedding and two other ceremonies, so the loudspeaker has been going for days and days. Did I mention, days? I am so accustomed to the sounds of ceremonies that I probably zone out.

Ari cannot understand a word they are saying over the loudspeakers, as he does not speak Balinese. I remember what that was like, so I spent the time trying to explain it all to him, as best I could. I encouraged him to go up and have a look. He wrote, 'It is kinda awkward for me to go alone, you said yesterday sometimes they ask you to dance.'

He was referring to a Joged dance, which I had told him, if he gets asked to go to, he may want to be prepared. Hubby has been pulled out of the crowd by one of the girls we fostered for a while. Being that she was only twelve years old and was doing a provocative dance around Hubby, I thought this single kid fresh off the plane from Jakarta, may have a bit of a culture shock if the same happened to him. I assured him there was no dance tonight. I told him when Hubby was back in the village, he could take him to the next event at the Bali Banjar, as Wayan was a bit busy contributing to all that noise Ari could hear.

So, the next day I made a little joke to Ibu, that our new staff member was having a rough time, what with all the ghosts and riots. She demanded he come down to our office immediately and talk to her and Bapak.

Ibu was lovely and motherly and told Ari that as he worked for members of her family, then if he was scared, he should feel welcome to come down to the hotel any time. Or go see the Mangku if Hubby and I were not in the village. She explained to him that there were weddings and other ceremonies in the village this week, so he would hear noises, but it was all safe. She double-checked with him that we had bought him rice and given him a bike, and made sure he was looked after. *She's checking up on me, I knew she did not believe me when I said we had him all set up with everything from plates to sheets etc.*

Ibu did get off the track a bit about her opinions of city folk. How it is much better to live here in the country in a community, as in the city there are bad people. *Ibu you have never even been to the city.*

She went on and on, as she does. How he will be looked after, everyone knows who he works for and what we have done for the village etc. blah, blah.

It did go on for about one hour, but at least I know now he is feeling loved by all.

Good on you Ibu 💜

30 May 2019 - Ibu Update

Ibu is sitting next to me at my desk, looking over my shoulder at my computer screen, burping. There is nothing on my screen that she needs to look at. Burp, after burp, after burp, right in my ear.

I am going home to work.

31 May 2019 - Ibu Update

I just told Ibu she could not dye her hair in the restaurant handwashing sink.

So, she has moved to the edge of the Temple, in the middle of the hotel gardens.

Chapter 14 - You Can Put on the Red Light

5 June 2019 - The Red-Light District

Ibu's hotel is empty at present. Well, one room has one guest, staying twelve days. That is thirty-three empty rooms. So, she asked me for some assistance to get more guests. Ibu was begging, "Help Ibu, help Ibu."

I have tried to help her with suggestions before. I was not looking forward to helping her again. She does not really listen to any of my advice anyway. I reluctantly agreed, since we are not that busy either.

Ibu got out a pen and a notebook and asked me to go into every room and look at them as though I was a tourist and write down what needs improving. A great idea, in theory. I know she really did not want to know what was wrong, and was probably hoping I would just come back saying housekeeping needed to clean something.

I started on her four front rooms she has just renovated. *Can't go wrong there, I guess?*

Wrong! Okay, housekeeping needed to get in there and clean up a bit after the renovations, but it was not the cleaning. *Seriously Ibu, when you renovate, you really need to pay attention to all the details.*

The first room I looked at I wrote down: 'the basin tap needs replacing, there are no shades on the ceiling lights, bathroom, or outside lights, just bare bulbs'. I found the same in the other three rooms. Two of the four rooms needed new toilets.

Ibu looked at me as though she was regretting her idea. Ibu focused on the cheapest points on my list, 'Where to get light-shades?'

The next day, Hubby and I were off to Tegallalang (about 30 minutes away, on the road that goes to Ubud), to buy her some light-shades. *How the hell she has convinced me to go shopping for her, I do not know!*

We stopped at a few stores; they were a little more expensive than I had first thought. I mean, I don't shop, so it had been years since I had been there. I had told Ibu that I thought they would cost around IDR 30,000 ($3) for a small bamboo shade. *Bloody inflation, they are now IDR 50,000.*

The problem with the shops in Tegallalang, you really need to order, made to order. You know; you order, they make. You can even have Antiques made to order in some of the shops. We stopped at a few shops, but no stock, 'You order, we make.' 'Ok, can you make like this?' 'No, we can only make like that.'

So, I was ringing Ibu, and Hubby was sending one of her staff photos of the shades on WhatsApp, of what was in stock. In one store, they had sixteen small shades in stock, at only IDR 15,000 each. So, I rang Ibu, and Hubby sent pictures. I was standing in the store, while I was on the phone to Ibu and Ibu started shouting at me. *She just wants to make sure I can hear her, as I am twenty kilometres away.*

The lovely Balinese shop keeper was posing for photos with her handmade shades. Proudly made by her husband, and Ibu was shouting in Indonesian "UGLY, UGLY!"

Oh, kill me now!

The poor shop keeper was trying to keep a smile. Ibu was shouting: "NEXT WEEK BAPAK WILL GO TO DENPASAR AND GET SOME, DON'T BUY THEM!"

I thanked the shop keeper, with my very Balinese uncomfortable smiling, and left. *There is no way I am letting Bapak buy any in Denpasar, last month he bought thirty plastic tissue boxes to use as napkin holders on each table in the restaurant.*

They are lovely shades of bright pink, green and light blue, with pretty pictures on them, and writing, such as 'Back to school', or 'Hello Kitty'.

The next shop I got to, I found four nice lampshades, and Hubby sent the picture. Ibu liked them, so she shouted, "GET TWENTY!"

"No Ibu, I can get four, and you can order more when the owners get back from holidays, and you didn't give me enough money for twenty."

So, shopping done for Ibu, we continued to Ubud to go to the supermarket. I have not been into the Delta supermarket for ten years, I don't do any food shopping. When I say I don't shop, I literally mean I don't shop. Hubby hunts and gathers, I cook. I walked into the supermarket and thought I was in a Western country, I could not believe how fancy it was. *I really must get out more.*

Back to the hotel to give Ibu the light shades, to find she had sent Bapak to Denpasar to buy toilets. *Poor old man. Ibu also sends her husband to hunt and gather.*

Ibu did not even know about Tegallalang village (a thirty-minute drive from her village that she has lived in, all her sixty-four years). *She gets out less than I do.*

Ibu asked her staff to put the shades in the four rooms that needed them the most. This took some instruction, such as, "How about you clean the dust off the cable first, untie the cable tie, and the big knot in the cable?"

This proved to be too difficult, as housekeeping had tied up the long cables, so that when they make the beds, they don't hit the lights with the sheets...*Aduh.*

Ibu decided to indulge housekeeping, and the solution was, that they would look nice on the porch of the four rooms facing the restaurant. *Well, at least that will be an improvement.*

Hubby insisted they at least cut off the cable ties to the ones in the rooms. Reluctantly one staff member obliged. Hubby commented he would have fired all Ibu's staff by now, and decided it was at this point he would go and have a coffee, or take her staff out one by one in a canoe and throw them in the lake.

While one of the staff was hanging the light-shades on the porch of a room, Hubby was sitting in the restaurant having his coffee and asked, "Are those globes red?"

I went and took a closer inspection, and low and behold, three of the rooms had red globes, and one had green. Now, I have not been at the hotel at night for over six months, but I knew that Ibu had gone overboard with her Christmas lights in July last year and I also knew that guests had complained that they had lights shining in their windows all night, changing colours. *Some travelling salesperson was at fault there, obviously.*

So, I said to Ibu, "You know that a red light outside a room is a sign to say the room is for sex, you know a brothel has all these coloured lights at the front." *Could this be the reason the hotel is so quiet, people are too scared to go into the Brothel?*

Hubby tried to explain to Ibu how, in Denpasar, and the outskirts of Sanur, the same travelling salesperson years ago, must have set them up with a similar light display. He then explained Amsterdam, so Ibu laughed her head off, she then started to ask Hubby if he ever frequented one of those places before he got married. Then she cheekily asked if that was where we met. *Oh, Ibu, funny, not.*

The conversation somehow just ended up in the gutter, as it often does with Balinese. Although I was trying to get the staff to replace the red bulbs with clear ones, Ibu was too focused on teasing Hubby. She was relentless, she just loves to tease him.

Eventually, after a few hours, the light-shades were up, and the cables all cleaned, and of the same length, however, the globes were still red, they replaced the green one.

I guess Ibu thinks, at least she can rent out the rooms in some capacity.

5 June 2019 - The Brothel

We have arrived at Ibu's hotel tonight, to have dinner with the Beautiful Doctor and her hubby Santa, as they are in town. The red lights are on in front of the rooms, in all their glory. And the front sign to the hotel has coloured lights twinkling and going around the sign, aka Brothel.

I guess we just wait to see what clientele show up tonight.

7 June 2019 - Deep Fryer vs Pie Warmer

We were at the hotel to catch up with our friends for dinner, and some drinkies and Ibu received a delivery from Jakarta; however, the instructions were in English.

So, although I was enjoying my wine with good friends on their room porch, *actually wine without friends is good too,* one of the staff came over to say Ibu needed me, now.

Ibu needed me to explain to her what the hell she had sitting in a box.

Now, I'd had quite a few wines, so, I saw the huge box, and my first thought was, another bloody pie warmer, so I teased her a bit. Ibu ignored me, told me I was drunk, to just shut up, and just read the instructions. I could not read the instructions, not from the wine, I did not have my glasses. *Okay, from the wine.*

However, one of the twins had opened the crate and popped it on the counter, and it was quite obvious, it was a deep fryer.

Now, having a large commercial kitchen, I stupidly presumed Ibu would know what a deep fryer was, or one of the staff would. Wrong!

I explained what it was for, and how it worked, but somehow Ibu thought, since I was drunk, I was just pulling her leg. Ibu asked if she could make soup in it. I laughed at her and explained she could make French fries, and spring rolls, fried chicken, etc. When I explained that you put in a lot of oil, and then you need to change the oil regularly, she said, "Oh, yes, daily."

I said, "No, not daily, just when it starts to get a bit old or changes colour."

Well, Ibu started screaming that I was drunk. And, who on earth would use oil the next day? And I was disgusting. (Balinese don't do leftovers.)

So, I went and got reinforcements. Ibu generally believes everything the beautiful Doctor and her husband, Santa, say.

So, I asked them to come into the kitchen. Hubby came as well, but she never believes a word he says, so it was up to the Doctor.

We all entered the kitchen to find Ibu clapping her fingers on her right hand together, making the motion of a duck quacking. Saying, "Rachet Mabuk, Rachet Mabuk." (Rach drunk, Rach drunk).

Ibu asked the Beautiful Doctor what this strange contraption was for. There was a lot of translating, a lot of laughing, me at Ibu, Ibu at me.

Finally, Ibu believed me, well, not me but the Beautiful Doctor.

I looked up the price of the machine for Ibu on Google, as I am very nice. Not really, Ibu just kept screaming at me to look it up on the Sari shop, what the price was of the Deep Fryer. So, I had to oblige to shut her up, so I could get back to my wine. Ibu cannot differentiate between different shops advertising on one online shopping website. So, to Ibu, if it came from Jakarta, then the Sari shop will have one.

Ibu just loves the fact that if she points at the computer screen and says, "Ibu want, Ibu want that Sari," we print off the bank slip, she sends Bapak to the Bank, and five days later her shopping comes. She generally does not like it and sends it back, but it is so much fun to her, not to Bapak, nor to anyone else.

The Deep Fryer turned out to be about five million rupiah (about $500), a very generous gift from one of Bapak's friends living in Jakarta. As Ibu did not purchase it from any travelling salesperson, or from the Sari shop, she was not overly impressed with the present.

Finally, she allowed me to return to my wine. *Oh, and friends, of course.*

That was one week ago. I just found it out the back, and I mean out the back, in the graveyard for stuff from the hotel, back in its crate/box. The pie warmer, however, is still proudly positioned in the restaurant, although I will not let her use it.

28 June 2019 - Ibu, Ibu, Ibu (Me Shaking Head)

Just some inappropriate, but very Ibu comments she has made this week:

Our new staff member is thirty years old, and not married. Comment from Ibu, "Ibu knows why, as he looks like a Bengchong." (Ladyboy.)

And then an array of comments to me:

"Why have you lost weight everywhere in your body, apart from your stomach?" (Ibu grabs my pot belly.)

"Have you lost weight also in your...?" (Ibu points to my privates)

"Does your husband like you having it skinnier down there?"

"You need to get rid of your fat stomach though, so he can see it better."

All comments made while she was peeling vegetables, in a kitchen full of staff.

That is all.

1 July 2019 - It Is Currently 12 Degrees Celsius

When you have no heating, and no insulation in your home, and some of your windows are made of cardboard, it can get effing freezing up here in the village. One of the lovely Gossip Warung ladies' husbands, just offered me a place to sit by their fire. Which has now filled our house with smoke. They have built a nice warming fire across the road from their warung, against the bedroom wall of our house. *So, kind.*

2 July 2019 - The Secret Of Youth

Hubby just told me, how last night, when he went up to the warung on the main road, to buy us three beers, the owner asked if two were for his wife, and one was for him.

Hubby laughed and said, "Yes, she always drinks more."

The old man asked, "Why not four?"

Hubby said, "Well, three is enough, four is a hangover."

The old man laughed and nodded understandingly.

Hubby got chatting with him and asked the old man how old he was. He proudly told him he was seventy-nine years old. Hubby asked him his secret of looking so young.

The old man's words of wisdom were: "Don't let yourself worry about the problems around you, and when your wife wants to fight with you, just seduce her."

24 July 2019 - Ibu Has Discovered Yoga

So, contrary to what many believe, Yoga is not a big thing to Traditional Balinese. In fact, it was not really a big thing on this Island until after the bombs, when the American expats in Ubud decided they needed it to relax.

Then, of course, that bloody book came. You already know how I feel about the influx of thirty-something females to Ubud. Riding their bicycles, carrying their yoga mats, looking for their Brazilian lovers.

Ibu did not really know about, 'Yoga for exercise' before now, she knew about Yoga being performed on certain days in the Balinese Calendar.

The calendar will say, 'today is a good day for those that require Yoga, or those close to death to perform Yoga'. This kind of yoga is nothing like the modern Lycra pants, chai drinking yoga of today. Balinese Yoga is for purification, to get the fire out of you, and to visualise the water coming over you to obtain smoke – it symbolizes body purification. The 'yoga of dying' is built on the belief that the soul will leave the body when the body cannot sustain itself any longer. This yoga comes into the picture to prepare one's self before finally leaving the mortal realm. The other style of Balinese yoga is more tantric. It is lovemaking mixed with meditation— *no yoga studio needed for that one, or any of the Balinese types of Yoga.*

The Traditional Yoga of Bali is worlds away from the Indian Yoga. All forms of Yoga to the Balinese are a connection to God, the connection to God is the utmost of importance. Yoga is to be done in a Temple, or in a Mountain Cave. Anywhere that there are no people, and no water, nor close to a fire, and you should worship the Supreme God. *There goes the idea of sitting in a class full of sweaty people in Ubud, following a teacher.*

You will find more and more Balinese Yoga instructors today. They have adopted the new modern Indian method; just to get in on the action of this money-making venture, that brings thousands to Bali in the hope of spirituality. And why not? They should get in on the action, rather than the money going to some illegal Hippy chanting 'Namaste'.

Namaste is an Indian word, not Balinese, and it is one thing that I must admit, annoys me. *I am working on it, being that my Mangku says, 'I should just let it go.'*

So, Ibu and her girlfriends have discovered Yoga, as a form of exercise, in no way related to Balinese yoga, she just thinks it has the same name. It will not last long, the aerobics classes only lasted a few weeks. I have not gone to see what they are wearing, or what they are up too, but she's excited and tells me every day, "Ibu do Yoga."

27 August 2019 - What Is In A Name?

Just chatting on WhatsApp with our Mangku's wife and she called me 'Ibu Risel'. That's a new one to add to my list. I am now known in the village as either Chul, Bram, Grees, Richrd, Rachett, Rash, Rasch, Ricel, Sibram, Bu, Ibu, and of course Dadong. It is fine, I have never been attached to my name. My mother tried to name me Rebecca, but my Romanian grandmother interfered. My father said, "Rebecca, Rachel, as long as she marries a Goldstein."

6 September 2019 - Now!

Ibu rang me in a frantic voice: "Rachett where are you?"

Me: "At the Village Head's Office."

Ibu: "Bapak needs you now!"

"Ok, it is a bit busy here, so I will come down, then come back here."

Me: Rode a bicycle in heat, there in a record 5 minutes.

Me: "Where is Bapak?"

Ibu: "You took too long, Bapak has gone."

Me: Blank stare.

"It is very rude to show up here puffed, you should sit down, get a drink of water, slow your breath down, not so frantic, and then speak."

"It's hot outside, and you said now!"

Ibu pushed my shoulder down, "Sit first."

Me: Got up: "Call me when Bapak is back."

Me: Left.

I am back at the Village Head's office, and now there are even more people in the line. *Aduh.*

10 September 2019 - Fifty Shades Of Grey

I thought since my hair was so grey, I should do an Ibu and dye it.

Maybe everyone will stop calling me Dadong?

I will not use the restaurant hand washing basin, though.

I am at the store where Ibu told me to go, they have a lot of stock. The choice of hair colours to choose from are the standard black of course, and then we have blue, green, purple, or pink, only IDR 15,000 ($1.50).

So, I can't go wrong really.

12 September 2019 - I Can't Win

I just finished our committee meeting at the school, so I thought I would pop in to say Hi to Ibu.

I rode to the hotel and calmly walked up and said, "Good afternoon Ibu, how are you?"

Ibu looked at me strangely and said, "Why are you not all flustered, and puffed as usual?" Then proceeded to imitate me puffing, and then walkd off.

Aduh.

12 September 2019 - Death And taxes, Again

Death in our village is a certainty, taxes not so much. Death happens quite regularly, with such an aging population. I am quite certain people in the village look at it as a great excuse to stop work, have a gossip, well, Wayan does.

We had a death the other day, that was not as well planned, and Wayan disappeared. It was quite dramatic. I was standing at the warung next door to our rental office, talking to the Mangku and his wife (Ibu Mangku), and suddenly everyone came running out of the harbour. I mean literally running, hailing down motorbikes to get a lift, speeding off in the direction of the only road out of the caldera. We just stared across at the harbour, I was looking for smoke. *Maybe a bomb had been reported?*

Wayan jumped on his motorbike and took off without a word.

One Dadong was hobbling past us, as fast as her little legs could take her. All the motorbikes had already left, but she was determined to get to wherever everyone else was going. Ibu Mangku yelled out to her to ask what was going on. The Dadong yelled back, "Jero has fallen out of a tree, and everyone is scared he is dead."

Jero is what we call all Mangkus, so which Jero, was not yet known, I mean we only have about 200 Jeros in the village. It is the same as when they say Wayan died, we only have 450, ok 449, Wayans in the village. Ibu Mangku shook her head and went back inside. The Mangku did not seem too fussed, so we continued our chat. The harbour lot, being the harbour police, warung owners and the annoying bracelet sellers, all thought it was very important to head over to the base of the tree. *Maybe to help kick him to see if he was dead?*

The majority of those that went to the tree do not have smartphones, so, no selfies. In Indonesia, stopping to see a dead person, and checking they are dead is compulsory, especially to get a selfie, or film it and put it on Instagram. Causing major traffic jams is just par for the course. *We don't have traffic in this village, but someone has to check if he's dead, don't they?*

Then Hubby called and said he was back in the village, and there was a lot of commotion in our street. I told him how a Mangku had fallen out of a tree.

Wayan's wife then stopped in to tell me it was a person who lived in our street that had fallen out of the tree, and Wayan may not be coming back to work today. I asked her if the Jero had died, and she answered, "Not yet."

I could hear the sirens of an ambulance coming, so presumed with the sirens on, he was still alive—*no need to be in a hurry and use the sirens if he is already dead.*

Then Hubby sent a WhatsApp (WA) saying the Village Head was in the house across the road from ours, and the Ibu there was screaming, so it had to be serious.

Then Ibu Mangku came out, and I said to him; "I don't think Wayan's coming back to work."

Ibu Mangku replied casually, "He will, he's not yet dead."

Another WA from Hubby "The neighbour is throwing things around the house."

I answered, "Well, she is a crazy, so it's probably triggered something."

He answered back, "Yeah true."

Now, she is officially crazy, I was not being rude. Her Hubby told my Hubby, how he took her to Bangli Mental Hospital, and she was pronounced crazy. He brought her back. *I guess he just needed confirmation.*

I once heard her talking to the Gossip Warung ladies, and she said, "I can't go back to the Mental Hospital, or I will die."

Our front doors face each other, and sometimes when I come out, she is just standing there, she just stares at me with crazy eyes. *I know how you feel darling.*

Another WA from Hubby, "She just yelled out, My Jero is dead."

Well, there you have it, now Wayan will not come back to work!

A few more messages back and forth and I was getting so confused, I said to Hubby, "Where is her husband?"

He sent back, "Umm, I guess he's dead."

Hubby had said it was the neighbour across the road.

Never get directions from Hubby. He will send you to the wrong place.

Across the road and 100 metres up, is to him across the road. So, here I was thinking that the father of the crazy lady had died, as he is also a Jero. But no, it was the husband of the lady three houses up the road. The man had been climbing up a tree to pick fruit. *Not in his own property though, so not sure what was going on there.*

He fell out of the tree and was knocked unconscious. *I do hope all that kicking did not add to his demise.*

Now, back to taxes, some interesting developments in Indonesia with taxes in the last few years, especially in the village in the last few months. Ibu hates taxes, tells us we are stupid for paying them... everyone loves taxes, not.

When I lived in Australia, I used to look forward to tax return time. Waiting for that huge cheque, meant I could plan my holiday, and no, not to Bali. I really did not mind taxes back then. I mean you could claim for everything, and boy, did I claim. Having a lot of property meant you paid at a lower tax rate, so of course my friends and I tried to buy up a small city block. I remember one friend. When we all went out to a restaurant for dinner, he would jump across the table to grab the bill so he could claim back the cost of 10-20 friends having a meal, as a 'business dinner'. We certainly spent a lot as well. *Gee, back then I would not blink at a $300 bottle of champagne, now I wait all week for my $3 Bintang allowance.*

It does not work that way in Indonesia, you do not get a tax refund.

In our village, not many people have had to pay taxes, they have paid donations to the Temple, village, etc., but that dirty word 'tax' is not used.

Even at the very beginning of starting our business, we would try to explain the expenses of running a business. As soon as they heard the dirty word, they would say, "Oh, you don't pay that."

Ibu has literally called us stupid for paying taxes. She gets so annoyed when we pay her rent on the office, and then send 10% to the tax office on behalf of Bapak, as Bapak will not do it, and we are not getting in trouble, again... Yes, in the first three years of renting an office from Ibu and Bapak, the tax man made a visit and said they had not paid tax on the rent, so we had to pay a fine. Ibu told us we should have just bullshitted the man and we should not have shown him anything. *Aduh.*

Now, do not get me wrong, Bapak pays the taxes monthly, as we do. I know, as he has his spreadsheet set up, and I have to work elsewhere, as he sings his figures. He then announces he is off to the tax office; it is a whole day trip for him. I presume they help him lodge his taxes online. He has probably been visiting that tax office for fifty years, and he does not understand that he can just do it from his office, with a few clicks of a button. I presume he just does not mention the dirty word to Ibu. He is clever as he always returns at the end of the day with an oleh oleh for Ibu.

It was lemons the other day, big, yellow, expensive ones.

Two months after our staff member Ari started, Ibu asked him to go down to see her after work, it was the third time... I was very suspicious, thinking she was trying to poach him, and gave him a bit of a hard time about it. I grilled him on WhatsApp, and he told me, "Ibu wants me to delete all the taxes."

I was like, 'What the?'

He tried explaining it to me in person, but in the end, I said, quite aggressively, "You do not go down there until I have talked to Ibu!"

So, when I was back in the village for a night, I called him to come down to my office, so Ibu could explain herself, as to why she kept calling my staff member, as she was literally calling him daily.

It turned out Ibu had a box, that the tax man put in a few years back. It recorded the restaurant food sales and calculated the tax. It took us a bit of time to work out that Ibu did not want to cheat the taxman. Ok, a very long time, as she kept saying, "Delete the taxes." Then she said, "Just delete five percent."

What seemed to have happened, is that as none of her staff knew how to use a computer very well, they all did manual receipts, then someone entered them into the computer. Someone, no one admits who, was entering them in at 15% tax instead of 10%. We really could not solve this problem for her, and told her to just call her Account Rep at the tax office. She asked if she could just buy a new system and start again. We advised that we could not advise her, only the tax office. She was not impressed, she had that look of, 'I will just throw the damn box in the lake'. The *same look Hubby gets with Ibu's staff.*

A few months back, land surveyors were in the village, oh the talk of the town, everyone was going to get titles to their land. Actual, registered titles, not just a hand-drawn map at the village head's office, and a handshake on who owned what. Hubby laughed, the first thing that came out of his mouth was, "Now, they will have to pay land tax."

The Gossip Warung buzzed for nights and nights. Talk of how they could go to the bank and borrow money, and fix up their homes, etc.

Then they found out they had to pay tax. Hubby just laughed. For at least another week, the Gossip was all dirty talk, 'TAX, TAX, and TAX.'

So, the other day, Wayan had to take the day off to collect his land title, as you do. A large meeting was held at the Bale Banjar, information was given over the loudspeaker about how to pay your land tax. And that day men were walking around the village, all carrying pink folders, containing their land certificates, all with solemn looks on their faces. *They look less solemn when someone dies. Clearly, no one has heard of Benjamin Franklin.*

A few days ago, I was in the office trying to concentrate on a quote for a travel agent, and Ibu came in with a piece of paper and sat down. Paper held up in front of her, reading out loud her list of titles. She had given one parcel of land on the main road, and one parcel of farming land to each child. She listed off fourteen titles. Ibu was reading out all their names, and then the tax figure next to them. She was not impressed that her taxes were adding up. I said nothing. *Geez Ibu, you have gone all these years without paying land tax, and now you are complaining about it.*

Later, as she was distracting my work, I jokingly said to her, "Being a landowner, must be so stressful."

She peered over the top of her paper and gave me the evil eye.

17 September 2019 - Oops

Just left a ceremony. An old lady insisted I go in, she was pushing me in. She said to take my guests in, to see the Gamelan... *Well, I thought that was what she said.*

Once we went in, I was told sternly by an old man, to go out the back and get coffee and snacks for my guests... *Well, I thought that was what he said.*

My guests sat and watched the Gamelan and enjoyed coffee and local snacks, it was lovely for them.

As I was taking the empty coffee cups back to the kitchen, the original lady said: "So, did you get your dogs out?"

Two of our dogs were under the food table.

How embarrassing.

Note to self: Learn the old Balinese language.

20 September 2019 - Ibu Wants A Bicycle

I just popped into the office for fifteen minutes. Bapak was sitting on our guest chairs. I said hello, sat down at the computer, and was writing down some dates of tours for the staff. I was finished and about to leave when Ibu said, "Rachett" quite loudly.

I nearly jumped out of my skin, as I had not seen her on our day bed, she must have been asleep. Ibu asked me if I had met with the Mangku today, and I told her that he had to go to Bangli. She nodded and went back to sleep. I said goodbye to Bapak and quietly walked out, so as not to wake Ibu.

I got on my bicycle, I was nearly out of the driveway, and Ibu yelled across the restaurant, across her restaurant guests. "Rachett, where can I buy a bicycle? I want to get fit."

I stopped and turned around, wheeled my bike back to the edge of the restaurant and said she could borrow one of ours.

She screamed out, "No, it would be broken quickly, I want to buy my own. How much are they?"

I told her the price of a standard bike, and she replied, "Ooh, so expensive."

I said again, she could just borrow one of ours. Then I asked her if she could even ride a bicycle. She told me she could.

I said, "Ok, show me, try mine."

Ibu stated, "No, not now, as I might fall, and it's hot, and I don't want to be all puffed and red in the face like you."

We talked a bit more about Hubby getting her a cheaper bike, and then I excused myself to leave.

As I was riding off, she yelled out, "Then Ibu can go all around the village with you!"

Gee, I am looking forward to that.

21 September 2019 - Ibu Does Not Like Me

Ibu does not like me at the moment. I popped into the hotel this afternoon for five minutes. Ibu was going on and on about her new staff member that went to a tourism university. I told her, after I had spent thirty minutes with him the other day, "I can tell you Ibu, there is no way he went to a tourism university."

She said, "He has a certificate."

I said, "He must have downloaded from the internet."

Then I said, "He has no idea, Ibu. He has never heard of the first things you learn in hospitality, such as 'The customer is always right', and 'First impressions are lasting impressions.' My staff, who have been to tourism universities, could quote that in their sleep."

Ibu replied with, "He went for three years and then got married, and it's been four years, so he must have forgotten."

I told her she's dreaming.

She is not happy with me; she would not even reply when I said goodbye.

She will get over it when she needs me for something.

29 September 2019 - Ibu Loves My Arse Again.

I woke up very tired, dreading going to the office, secretly hoping Ibu would not be there.

The reason for being so tired, was that Hubby woke me at 2.00am saying, "Get up, get up, something's going on, everyone is leaving. Didn't you hear the loudspeaker telling everyone to GO?"

I was in a deep beer-induced coma, so No.

Okay, Agung must have erupted, and we are evacuating again. It can't be an earthquake big enough for everyone to be told to GO, and the house was still standing.

I presumed it was Agung. I was not in the biggest hurry; all the windows still had the tape on them from last time. Probably safer to go back to sleep, no use being out there if the volcano's blown.

Hubby was yelling at me to get up, get dressed, he was freaking out. I could hear lots of motorbikes starting up, and taking off, and every dog in the neighbourhood was barking. *What's the rush? Just go and get the masks.*

Then he'd gone. Hubby went out to the street to ask what was going on. *I hope he grabbed a mask, might just lie down again until he comes back.*

He returned saying a house was on fire. I was finally dressed and looked outside to see smoke billowing up from the next street. Now, when I say street, I mean gang (lane), the homes are all compacted together, and access is by small gangs (lanes), not large enough for a car. So, even if we did have a fire station closer than 100 kilometres away, there would not be much use, as the house on fire was 300 metres up a small lane.

So, waiting up for hours to make sure everyone was okay, and then going to sleep at 4.00 am, to get up at 6.00 am, meant the thought of seeing Ibu, was a bit much.

No one was hurt, and they all got the fire out with buckets of water, all the men in the village, now that's community spirit for you.

So, this morning, I did not go into the office. I washed my hair instead. That took a good two hours, heating saucepans of water on the stove to carry to the mandi (square tiled box in the bathroom) and then scoop on to my head with a small plastic bucket with a handle. Any excuse and Ibu would notice, believe me.

I finally succumbed to the fact that I had to go in, to print some stuff, and to check with my staff, to see if our guests had come and gone, happy.

When I got to the hotel, Ibu was in bed, sick. She did not look too great, so I doted on her, and then said I would help her if she liked. I needed to print up some English translations for my staff. I told Ibu I could sit with her new staff member for ten minutes and see if he had any questions about correct English.

Well, after the lesson was over, which she could hear, as the bed is in the room behind our office, she then managed to make her way to the day bed and appeared next to me. She patiently waited for me to finish typing an email, and so sweetly asked me, if before I left, could I help Bapak pay his staff health insurance. I suggested I get my Rep at the Health Insurance office to ring Bapak. The Rep could explain how to set up an online account, being that the Rep is a native Indonesian speaker, and is actually from the Health Insurance Department. Ibu started smiling at me, the colour was returning to her face.

By the time I left, she was up, and in the kitchen trying to send me home with all sorts of goodies. She even took me to her special room where she keeps all her Adat clothing, to lend me clothes for an up and coming ceremony.

I came back home and told hubby, "Ibu likes my arse again."

He shook his head (like Ibu does) and said, "That woman is like the weather, you can never tell which way she will be from one day to the next."

She was probably making herself sick so that I would feel sorry for her, about giving her a hard time yesterday.

1 October 2019 - The Queen Is In Town

We had a large village ceremony today, everyone came, everyone was expected to attend. The Kuta to Seminyak beaches must have been a little quieter today, with all the Bitch ladies not at the bitch.

I received a call from a driver at 7.00 am, asking if he could bring five guests for an offering making class.

So, I rang Ni Nengah, as she is not from our village so did not have a ceremony. Yep, booked in for 11.00 am.

I headed over to one of our kid's grandma's house, took over some supplies, finished some offerings there, told them I would be at Temple late, and headed to the hotel at 10.00 am.

When I got to the hotel, Ibu was in a bad mood, nine out of her thirteen staff are from our village, so not coming to work, and now I had Nengah booked for two hours. Ibu proceeded to scream and make a big deal of it until 11.30 am (the first thirty minutes of the guests' class). I apologised to the guests; they have not read the Ibu Chronicles but were still very forgiving of this crazy lady screaming from the kitchen across the hotel gardens.

Ibu came out at 12 noon, dressed for Temple, and waved from the restaurant at our guests having their class in the garden Bale, like she was the Queen of England. Sweetly saying in English, "Hello, hello", waving her hand.

Then she came over and proceeded to demand I take photos of her with all the guests in the class. This went on and on, posing with each guest, then saying to me, "Another one", then "another one."

She then tried some English, finally stating "My English not too good" and then excused herself to go join the procession going past.

The guests had no idea who she was, or why they would want photos with her, but obliged.

I am starting to think Ibu knows she is slightly famous.

2 October 2019 - Ibu Update

Just a quickie, as will write up the rest later. We have to do brochures for the Batur Geopark. Bapak has just asked me to check if his brochure is correct English. I will need to fix it. As apparently, the hotel has 33 operating rooms, and the cool fresh air refreshes the body and soul physically and spiritually so that it stimulates a passionate appetite in the rooms.

I told Ibu, it does go well with those red lights out the front of the rooms.

3 October 2019 - Credit vs Debit

Yesterday hubby was in the village, so I asked him if he could drive me around to do a few things I needed a car for. He asked where, suspiciously, as he does not like going to the hotel.

I had 28 pencil cases with pencils, etc., to drop at the kindergarten, kindly donated by a friend, and I also needed to go to the village heads office.

He took me to Kinda and parked across the road. I went in and handed donations over, then I popped into the village heads office. Hubby waited in the car the whole time. When I got back in the car, he seemed relaxed, so I then asked him to take me to the hotel; we needed to pick up a desk I wanted to take home.

Hubby tries to avoid going there, as Ibu is always on his back about something, but he obliged.

When we got there, there was a large group of locals staying, with lots of minibuses in the car park, so we had to wait for the staff, so they could put the desk in the car. Bapak had kindly bought us a new tour desk, as Ibu said the one we had in the lobby was ugly. *Thanks for that.*

However, the staff had put our existing desk outside. Luckily, it is not the raining season, as all our receipt books and brochures were inside the drawers of that desk.

I told Hubby to come in and sit down and wait. Instead, he wandered around the hotel grounds a bit. I lost sight of him, even on the CCTV. *He is in the black hole somewhere the staff disappear to.*

So, I sent him a WhatsApp to say the coast was clear, Ibu was not around, the staff said she had gone to a ceremony, and to come in.

Hubby came into our office. As soon as he sat down, Ibu walked in from the bedroom behind our office, putting on a kebaya. Literally, putting it on, she walked in with only her bra on. I said, "Good morning, Ibu, do we have another ceremony?"

I looked at Hubby apologetically, he had his head down, looking at his phone, trying to avoid eye contact with Ibu's breasts.

Ibu ignored my greeting, and my question about a ceremony, and screamed, "DOTCOM say we owe them money, but Bapak has paid them, so Bapak has to go to the bank now, can you check!?"

There was no use me correcting her, she meant Booking.com or any of the other booking sites. *I will start with Booking.com.*

So, I obliged and opened their Booking.com account, to find they did not owe Booking.com, in fact, they had twenty credit notes from them. I told Ibu, and she screamed back, "No, no, we got a phone call!"

One of the young staff had taken a phone call from a lady claiming to be from Booking.com, who said they owe money and had to pay it to this other bank account, today, or their account would be closed. Some scammer had rung, and they literally had the cash ready to go to the bank. The same staff member that took the call, proudly showed me on Bapak's phone, how eleven invoices showed a CREDIT, and she had not been scammed. "Well, yes", I said, "they owe Bapak."

Well, Ibu was yelling out for one staff member after another to all join in this conversation, and six staff all agreed, that Bapak owed money to Booking.com. *Aduh!*

Bapak walked in, and sat at his desk in his undershirt, and a sarong, not yet dressed either. When I say undershirt, I mean the same garment Australian male tourists seem to love to wear in public, in Bali, often with a Bintang logo on it. Bapak would never wear his undershirt in public, only in front of family.

Well, it took more staff than it does to change a light globe, to have a debate that credit means they owe you, not you owe them. This went on for about thirty minutes.

Ibu and Bapak finally dressed, staff kicked out by me, Hubby could comfortably talk to them about Credit vs Debit. Hard to do when not wanting to look at Ibu's breasts.

He finally assured them that credit means they were owed, and so Ibu was left with 2.3 million cash in her hand... I am not sure what ceremony they were supposed to be going to, as the next thing, she had Bapak on the phone asking the price of a paint sprayer. They did not look in a hurry to go anywhere. Ibu now had cash in her hand, Ibu could shop instead.

I left to go see if the staff had put the desk in the car.

Upon my return, Ibu no longer had any cash in her hand, so the shopping must have been done. Bapak asked if we had done our brochures for the Geopark yet, and could I look at his brochure. Well, you know how great their brochure was... I had started laughing hysterically about the wording of their brochure. How it would go well with Ibu's red light theme.

It reminded Ibu that she wanted to tell us a story. About how last night she had gone to the Water Temple up the road after the ceremony. At first, I did not get the connection to the suggestive brochure and a Holy spring, so, I started checking my emails, and let her talk to Hubby. Until she started miming her experience.

We have a purification Water Temple just up the road, it is not for tourists, just for Balinese to do a Melukat (water purification). Ibu was feeling tired and sore from the walk to the cemetery the day before. Mind you, she had only walked from the hotel, everyone else walked from the village, so she had a good two kilometres less than everyone else. Bapak rode his motorbike.

So, Ibu decided to go to the Temple Springs to ease her pain, and to cleanse herself from being at the cemetery, just in case a spirit had possessed her. *Probably her mother, she would do something like that, she was bitch when she was alive as well.*

So, Ibu stood up behind me. Obviously, this story needed her to stand up, and start grabbing her breasts and almost twisting them off. I was in the middle of reading an email, so I missed the first bit of the story. *That's some serious boob twisting there, Ibu.*

She hit my shoulder to have me watch her performance, I was not paying enough attention. Mind you, I could see her on the CCTV.

Ibu was explaining to Hubby, how there was a Balinese couple together in the same section. (It's split into male and female pools.) Hubby had that look of, 'Why the hell did I come today? Why does Ibu have to always feel her breasts in front of me?' So, apparently, this couple was having a great old time, him grabbing her boobs. Ibu explained that this inappropriate behaviour went on for a bit longer. Ibu ignored it as much as she could, but then the girl climbed on to the guy's lap and straddled him at the edge of the pool, and then Ibu said, "Ibu was out of there!"

I double-checked with Ibu, that it was not tourists, and that Ibu was not actually at the Hot Springs. No, it was definitely a Balinese couple, at the Holy Water Temple Springs.

Ibu was so disgusted that she has banned any of us from going there. She declared. "Rachel will have her next Melukat in the hotel grounds and the Mangku can go and get a big bucket of Holy Water to throw over her head in the hotel garden!"

Gee, great, it's a not an Ice Bucket challenge Ibu.

4 October 2019 - Ibu Update

Glad Hubby was not with me when I just dropped into the hotel. Ibu was sitting in the Bale in the garden, I went over to be polite and say Hello. Ibu told me that above her breast was hurting. I told her it could be her bra. She said, "Nope, I'm not wearing one" and then lifted her blouse and showed me her boob.

I told her that could also be the problem, then I left.

Chapter 15 - Where The Wind Blows

20 October 2019 - Gone With The Wind

So, it is a tad windy in the village. Okay, maybe more than a tad, since the warung at our rental office has collapsed. Half our rental office roof has gone, trees are down, at least half the houses are missing roof tiles and the hotel grounds are covered in roof tiles. Oh, and a restaurant on the lake's edge has floated away.

It was a dark night, no power, no water, and very noisy winds.

So, we were all sitting at the hotel just now, discussing the damage, and when the winds will stop. Then we were discussing tax, *as you do when you are in the middle of a Natural Disaster.*

Hubby was telling Ibu off for muttering. (He says that to me too, as he has selective hearing). He told Ibu he could not understand what she was saying and that she should sit up to talk. Ibu said she was in pain and tired and started waving her arm around, ignoring him and complaining to me. Well, not entirely ignoring Hubby. Ibu yelled at him, saying he was stupid, and that Rachett understood every word she said, then she ignored him.

So, I asked her if she was wearing the bra top I gave her, and when was she going to the Doctor. Ibu replied, "Oh, I went to the Doctor yesterday, and he said because I planted a tree in a pot some while ago, and the root has grown through and breaking the pot, so I have the pain."

No use arguing with that one.

I am going home to let the dogs out of the house, as our back fence has blown away. (We have gained half of someone else's roof though.) The dogs are locked inside the house and will need to pee. Funny thing is, even when our dogs are outside, they have not tried to escape, but every dog in the village has come in.

21 October 2019 - Now, We Wait

I just rode my bicycle, at full speed, due to a large tree threatening to squash me, down to the rental office. The Mangku was standing on the street looking at the damage of our office and his warung. I pulled up, looked at him, and he very calmly said, "We wait till the wind stops."

So, we will wait. I better get back home before I blow away.

22 Oct 2019 - No More Wind

The wind has stopped. *Maybe not Ibu's.*

27 Oct 2019 - Ibu Really Needs To Get Out More

I just came back from a meeting in Bangli city, and was having a late lunch in the hotel restaurant. Ibu sat down next to me and said, "You can use our empty restaurant next to the warung for your guests' meals until we fix the warung."

I replied, "It will need to be cleaned up, and fixed first."

Ibu stated, "No, it is fine."

Yesterday bright and early, we started with the clean-up at the rental office, and at around 9.30 am, the staff had all the roof tiles removed from the ground. They removed the dangerous hanging awning roof and all the iron off the roof of the warung.

We were all standing, facing the office, surveying their work, and calculating the materials we needed. Then, we suddenly heard the wind coming. We all turned and looked at the lake, it looked like a tsunami approaching. Everyone ran home for cover; we did not go back.

I went to pick up the car this morning, and Ibu's restaurant two doors up from our rental office got hit this time. So, after I told Ibu the news, she started screaming for staff. We were in the restaurant hotel, but she was screaming out staff names.

When two staff finally came, and Ibu asked if the restaurant was damaged, "Yep", was the answer.

So, now her staff are there cleaning up. Now, the wind has finally stopped. (I was a bit too quick to announce that yesterday.)

Not Ibu, she is still full of hot air.

28 Oct 2019 - Ibu Has Lost Her Noodles

Poor Ibu, one of my staff called, and I had to go urgently down to the hotel.

There was a bad review on Expedia about the hotel, and the staff did not know what to do. Sometimes it is very hard for non-native English speakers or non-native complainers, to answer complaints.

An Australian hotel guest had given the lowest review possible for his one-night stay at Ibu's hotel. The review explained that his wife had ordered mie goreng (fried noodles), and God forbid the kitchen had used instant noodles, and there were only some veggies in it. His review ended in, 'my wife was furious about the appalling meal.'

Now, I completely understand, it really is upsetting to have a bad meal that costs IDR 20,000 (AU$2.00). I know, sometimes I pay as much as IDR 20,000 for a meal at a warung, and if I don't get the usual staple, or rock, or hair, in my food, I feel cheated.

Since Ibu's Chef of 30 years, passed away, Ibu has had to do a lot of the cooking herself, and I know I would be upset too if someone complained about my cooking. I am very fortunate that I can cook anything for Hubby. It can be burnt, undercooked or not aesthetically pleasing, and Hubby will always do a 'Darryl Kerrigan'.

He had never seen the Australian movie, called 'The Castle', when I first started cooking for him. Still, he has always complimented me on every single terrible meal I put in front of him.

I asked Ibu if I could see her menu, only to discover that there is a photo of the mie-goreng. Sure enough, it shows the dish is with instant noodles, and a small number of vegetables.

Ibu then went and got out the packets of noodles she used and started throwing them on the table. Then explained, well, screamed, that there is no other noodle type that you can buy here. I know she is correct, as we must go to Ubud (one hour away) to get most of our food supplies. The village is extremely limited, we don't have a supermarket. The small warungs only have that one Indomei packet, the same one Ibu was still throwing, one by one, across the table.

I tried to explain to her that the instant noodle is not used as much now in tourist areas. That a lot of tourist areas have gone a bit more upmarket in the past few years, and many restaurants use the fatter Chinese noodle.

Ibu gave me that look of, 'Where the hell will we find a Chinese?'

I tried to explain many places even cater for coeliacs (I am gluten intolerant), vegans, and other modern-day eating diets. I lost her on that one. She could not understand this whole 'people may die if they eat something'. She started going on about, 'When did this start? What the hell is wrong with this world? Why can't people just be grateful they have food?' *I will not tell her about Smoothie Bowls.*

The poor thing, I really felt sorry for her, her restaurant had always been famous for its food with locals. For three years in a row, they won an award for their grilled fresh fish in Balinese Sauce. Megawati (former President of Indonesia) still, to this day has that fish dish picked up, and taken to the airport before she flies out, when she has visited Bali. Bapak has a very large, framed photo of Megawati's first visit to the hotel restaurant proudly displayed in his office.

Nengah would have been the person who made the complainer's mie-goreng. Nengah has been in the kitchen since she was twelve years old, now. Nengah makes what she has been making for twenty-seven years. She still, after ten years is struggling to make toast though. So, trying to change a menu, or explain a vegan is exceedingly difficult, she will smile and nod, but the vegan meal will have egg in it.

After I tried explaining to Ibu about: 'The new tourist to Bali, the ones that want to change everything to suit them, or change food to be like it is back home', Ibu lost her noodle and declared, "I know, I will sell the restaurant!"

I asked how on earth she was going to sell a restaurant inside a hotel. I went through all the complications with that, such as hotel breakfasts, mixing two businesses on one premises, three businesses with ours as well. She said that she would build a small kitchen out the back for guest breakfasts. None of her ideas and ranting made any logistical sense. Eventually I, and the Mangku, (who was also there, as it was that bad, we had both been summoned) managed to calm her down.

Then Ibu just looked deflated, like she just wanted to give up. I suggested she go have a lie-down.

I answered the review as nicely, and with only a small amount of sarcasm as I could muster, and I left.

8 Oct 2019 - It's All Good

Ibu is okay now. I got to work about 10.00 am, and before I could sit down, Ibu started going on about how a guest ordered mie-goreng for breakfast this morning and commented how delicious it was.

At 10.00 am, Ibu decided to give me lunch since I had told her I had breakfast at 5.00 am. Ibu gave me a plate with red rice, mie-goreng, and fried chicken. I am allergic to wheat and a vegetarian...

Aduh

9 November 2019 - The Race That Stops a Nation

Well, a ceremony that stops a village. So, you know we had extensive damage due to some extreme winds, 114 kilometre per hour winds, apparently.

The staff started rebuilding, and then it all came to a grounding halt. Mind you, the staff assured me the roof was on. I saw the last panel go on, then everyone started ceremony stuff.

Then the rains came, and they came into the office like a five-metre-long waterfall down one wall.

Luckily, they have stopped, and it is hot again, so everything has been drying out.

I saw the Mangku's wife last night, at Temple, and asked her if she had checked her side of the wall, as I presumed, she also had a waterfall. She said she had not been into the warung since the ceremony started. *Who checks their business when there is a ceremony? Silly me.*

Today is the last day of a fifteen-day ceremony, which is why Wayan has not been to work, or answered his phone, or replied to any text messages. When I mentioned that to Ibu, she said he has just been drunk, but I had seen him playing Gamelan, and heard it till 2.00 am some nights.

A ceremony reminds me of the Melbourne Cup Carnival week of races. I used to attend every year; it was also like a religion. I was a VRC (Victorian Racing Club) Member. I went to every day of the big week, had far too many hats, and always bought a new outfit for each day. There was a lot of preparation for all my guests in my member's car park spot, and I took time off work for the week. So, a ceremony is very similar; women buy a new outfit for each of the more important days, get their hair done. *Okay, I do my hair myself, but at least I wash it.*

Just like the Melbourne Members Race events, at a ceremony, the men gamble, the women prepare lots of yummy snacks, dress up with amazing headwear. *Okay, in this case, amazing towers of fruit.*

Everyone hangs out in marquees, drink lots, have late nights, only to get up the next day to do it all over again, and never see a horse.

Ibu has been busy with the ceremony and on a roller coaster of emotions this past week. I have allowed her to scream, suck up, cry, and just huff, we are all tired.

Today after lunch, well after a drop into school, a run with the dogs, a procession, a bit of work, then lunch, I planned to go home and have a little nap. I asked Ibu if she was going to the temple tonight, as she was not in the procession this morning. She said if her afternoon staff show up. Ibu has also had a skeleton staff. Yesterday she had two out of thirteen staff show up. Bapak had a toothache and went home early from the ceremony. So, Ibu was working alone. She was so tired, that she fell asleep while talking to me. I tried to get a photo, but the flash went off and woke her. She went straight back to sleep.

I got some work done while she slept in the chair next to me. When she woke, I told her I was heading home for that nap now, and I asked if she did go tonight, could she ring me, so I could go to the ceremony with her, as I will be alone. Hubby is smart and escaped to the south. She huffed and puffed. It is the first time I have seen her not excited to go to a ceremony. *She probably hasn't had time to dye her hair, as the restaurant washbasin has been used by guests too often.*

I really want to go tonight, as they draw the raffle and I have ten tickets. I would be content with any of the prizes; I'd love to win the TV, as the lighting is too bad in the house to read a book at night, or the fridge, so I can stock it with beer, or the main prize, a motorbike. *We don't really need another bicycle. Pity there is not a toilet as a prize.*

I am also hoping everyone will be back to work tomorrow, so we can get the roof fixed, and Ibu can stop screaming.

Yesterday, I did go home to attempt a nap as well. I lay down and the next thing I knew Bapak was ringing me, and ringing me, and blabbering something about me having five guests. I said I didn't and Komang was there, so she could talk to them. I attempted to sleep again.

After four calls from Bapak just hanging up, then one of their staff calling from the kitchen phone, I finally turned my phone off to lie down and blocked them all out just for a twenty-minute power nap. The next thing I knew, one of the twins was in my house, saying Ibu wanted me back, and he was here on the motorbike to collect me.

So, I reluctantly got up, dressed in the temple attire I had been wearing earlier, as much quicker, and off we sped, and I mean sped. I asked him to slow down, but it was the Evil Twin. *Hubby would be so angry, as I do not have a helmet on, and I am sitting side-saddle due to wearing Traditional Temple attire. I look like a true Dadong on the back here.*

Arriving safely, after the whole scary 800 metre ride, I found Ibu had five Dutch guests booked into her hotel via Airbnb. I explained we don't use Airbnb, so they are not our guests. She said one of her staff, who was not there, had signed the hotel up for Airbnb. *Well, that's not my problem.*

But apparently, it was. I could tell that it was, from the amount of screaming Ibu was doing, and the fact that she was nearly hyperventilating.

So, I nicely spoke to her guests and asked them to please wait, and I would go and check their booking. *I am not sure what they would have thought about all the screaming.*

It took me ages to find their booking, as I did not know their password or which room, etc. It turned out Ibu's ex-staff member had advertised one room for six guests for IDR 350,000 with breakfast. *No wonder the Dutch snapped that up.*

Once I solved the problem, I told Komang that I wanted to go home. I told her that Kembar had brought me. (Kembar means twin, but that's his real name, we also call them Cheery and Skinny, which is nicer than Twin and Evil Twin.) So could she please find him to tell him to take me home. I walked out the front and hopped on his motorbike and off we went. *Gee, he is going slow now, he must have listened to me after all, or he is not in a hurry now, or Ibu has calmed down.*

I got off and said goodbye, he turned the bike around and smiled back at me... It was the other twin... *They always get me.*

৯৯৯৯

I am back at work again, major nap fail. There is a new drama. Ibu is reasonably calm, but Bapak is lying down exhausted. I am only here to make sure Ibu does not have a heart attack.

9 November 2019 - Thai Food

Komang called me yesterday, to say we had a hotel booking for twenty guests, one group from Thailand, and they had various requests for rooms that she could not work out.

So, in between temple stuff, I had popped down to help her. The requests were not unreasonable, just logistics of rooms being close to each other. Being a larger group, I upgraded some of the rooms, so that their rooms were all next to each other and I left.

Today I went to the hotel for lunch, Komang told me that Ibu had agreed, for the Thai guests to use the kitchen when they came, that they had rung and asked. I told her, "I hope you said No, as they are checking in at dinner service time."

Komang looked at me sheepishly and said, "Ibu already agreed."

Aduh.

I went and found Ibu, and told her that was not a good idea. Ibu told me, "Not a problem, they will just want hot water for their pop-mei-noodles."

Me: "Ibu, they are not Chinese, they are Thai."

Ibu assured me it would be fine, "They make Bakso."

No amount of convincing Ibu that Thais would not be cooking Bakso worked. Komang just shook her head when I looked at her. I told Ibu that I would have said no, and don't blame me, even if they booked through us, as I had already turned down that request in writing with their booking. I left to go to Temple, and hopefully to have a nap after that.

Komang rang me numerous times, while I was trying to nap, to ask me to please come down to the hotel, for when the Thai Group check-in.

Just twenty minutes, please people! Just a twenty minute nap. I should have turned the phone off.

I ended up going back to the hotel. The Thai guests arrived with drivers and large shopping bags of food. Komang went into melt-down checking them in, as they were all asking her questions at the same time, such as, 'Do you have a phone charger?' 'Can I move my room to be next to her?' 'Can I pay by card, but the other half of this room by cash?'

Komang walked out of reception, looking overwhelmed. So, I went in to help her. I greeted them in Thai, and of course they then all swarmed to me like flies, firing off the questions to me.

I helped them with all their requests, and then I got on my bicycle and went home.

I am going to try again to nap.

I managed a ten-minute nap, the Dadongs were gossiping too loudly outside my bedroom window, so I rode back to the hotel for dinner.

I walked into my office and through to the kitchen.

Ten Thai girls were using the whole kitchen, cooking up a three-course Thai banquet. Ibu was standing in the kitchen, watching over them with an evil eye. Nengah, whose kitchen it is, was handing the Thai girls anything they pointed at, such as cooking oil, woks, etc.

The Thai girls had started with a soup, they are now starting on a chicken dish, and Ibu is starting on a heart attack. They don't seem to notice Ibu's evil glare at all. *I have been on the receiving end of that glare, it generally does not end well.*

I guess I'm not getting dinner tonight. Although, I do love Thai food.

10 November 2019 - Winner, Winner

So, I did not end up going to the ceremony last night, as the staff had to wait for an hour before they could get into the kitchen to make my dinner, and then I was just too tired from lack of power naps. Also, Ibu did not want to go with me, as she was on Thai Patrol.

This morning I jumped out of bed, put on my Adat clothes, and went to check on the raffle draw.

The sun was just rising, I had not had a shower or breakfast, or even a coffee. *I will just sneak in, no one will be there at this hour, and I will have a look at the list, as I cannot wait to know the results.*

As I was walking down the lane towards the main Temple, I just had a feeling we may have won something... I sent Hubby a WhatsApp message telling him where I was going, and that I had this strong feeling, like we have won something, so I was going to check before I went to the office.

I walked up the steep ramp to the main Temple area, like a town square. I walked through the Candi (entrance), and the square looked empty, remnants of the previous night's activities still visible. At the entrance, just past the Candi was our 'Pecalang Lapor Pos' (visitors report post). Four tired-looking Pecalang were sitting at the post, they looked like they may have been there all night. I was not expecting anyone to be there, as the ceremony went on until at least 2.00 am. I greeted them and told them that I wished to check the raffle draw numbers. One pointed casually at the list posted at the 'Prize marquee', twenty metres further from where they were sitting.

I walked over, passing the empty VIP marquee and approached the Prize Marquee. All the prizes were still there on display. A list of the drawn ticket numbers was stuck to the door of the fridge prize. I got out my ten tickets and slowly read the list of numbers. I checked, and then I double-checked.

OMFG! We have won the motorbike! I air punched the air "YEAH!"... *That is my first air punch, ever, I have always wanted to do that since I watched The Breakfast Club.*

The Pecalang sprang up from their post and rushed over.

I declared, "I won the motorbike!"

One guy grabbed my tickets from my hand and checked the number, then checked again, then told me I had to go into the Temple to speak to the Head Mangku. *Of, course I do, I mean, who doesn't go to the Head Priest when you win a raffle?*

I realised I had forgotten to put on a selendang (sash around my waist), so pointed that out, as you cannot enter a Temple without one. They assured me it would be fine and to go in.

One Pecalang would not give me back my tickets, and escorted me in. *Don't get any ideas, mate, I know where you live.*

I entered the Temple, and all the Head Mangkus were inside. *Oh, oh, I hope I don't get in trouble for not wearing selendang, and don't you guys ever sleep?*

I greeted the Mangkus, apologised for my attire, and explained that I had won the motorbike. They looked at the Pecalang holding my tickets, and he nodded to confirm. They took me over to the VIP Bale and requested that I sit with the Head of the Villages while they double-checked my tickets to make sure I had not won anything else. I commented, "If I have, I will donate it to the village, a motorbike is more than enough."

I sat in the Bale with the VIPs, and while everyone was fussing around with my tickets, the Village Deputy Mayor asked me if I had dreamt that I would win the motorbike. I told him that I would have been happy to have just won the TV or the fridge, as we had neither, and that we did not need a bicycle, as we had twenty, but this morning I did feel like I had won something. He told me that he had also bought ten tickets and had dreamt every night for the past week that he had won the motorbike. I apologised to him that his dream was not correct and asked him if he did win anything. He sulked and said, "No. but, I can buy the motorbike off you cheap if you want to sell it."

I laughed and replied, "I would have to ask my Husband first." *Oh, shit. I forgot to ring Hubby!* I excused myself to get out of the Bale to ring Hubby, as they were still fluffing over my tickets. *They are not fakes, guys.*

Hubby answered the phone, and I said: "Baby, we won the motorbike!"

Hubby screamed, "FUCK YEAH, BABY!"

Oops, he doesn't know I am in the Temple. Everyone heard, luckily, they are Hubby's friends, so they laughed. After confirming that I had indeed won, we had to have the obligatory photos with me shaking the hand of all the Village Heads, thanking God, etc. *I hope that does not go on Facebook, I have not even looked in the mirror today.*

The Deputy Mayor then asked when Hubby would be back in the village. I told him he was due in three days' time. The Village Head said, "Okay, you have Sibran come to me when he is back, and I will give him the paperwork, and the keys."

Oh, yeah, of course, can't give it to a woman, but who cares, I won! Thank you, God.

11 November 2019 - Go Faster

I arrived at the office this morning, and the first thing Bapak said to me was, "Now when we call you, you can be here faster, too slow on the bicycle."

Twenty minutes later Ibu got back from Temple, hugged me, congratulations and said, "Now when we call you, you can be here faster, no more bicycle."

Aduh

19 November 2019 - Just Drink Beer

I had a government meeting this morning in the hotel restaurant, and Ibu wanted to know what it was all about. So, we sat in a garden Bale for a chat. Ibu and I were chatting, and then Ibu started going on, and on about, how tired and stressed she was about her staff. I listened to her whine, and then Hubby messaged to say he was in the village. So, I told her I was going home now to drink beer with him and discuss our own business. I explained to her, Hubby and I have the most enlightening business meetings over a beer. I can then go to sleep, not thinking about anything. Ibu said, "Can Ibu drink a beer, and she will be enlightened, and sleep soundly?"

I replied, "Why not."

She asked, if Bapak could as well. I said, "Well, it might help with his toothache, but Bapak told me he is healthy, as he has never smoked or drank, and besides, he is already asleep."

Ibu then asked if she could drink lemon beer. I told her, why not, but as half a per cent alcohol, she may need to drink double.

Ibu declared, "Ok, I will go wake up Bapak to drink beer."

I just went back, as I forgot some documents that I had left at work. Ibu and Bapak are both sound asleep in the office. *Not sure if they drank beer, but they look content.*

19 November 2019 - Yeah, Don't Tell Me

Did I fail to mention we have another ceremony in the village?
Nah, just everyone else did.
Three more days.

1 December 2019 - What's Your Name?

OMG, Komang has called me Rach for years, and now she just sent me a WhatsApp and called me, Risel.
Note to self: next staff meeting topic: Your Boss's name is?

8 December 2019 - Where's The Honda?

We cannot go anywhere in the village now without every single person asking, "Where's the Honda?"

Even within hours of winning the motorbike, we walked the dogs up into the forest, and an old couple came out of their grass hut, and asked, "Where's the Honda?"... *They must have Facebook.*

It is quite strange to everyone that we have not used it yet, but we have not renewed our motorbike licences.

One of Ibu's staff just asked me, "Why are you still riding your bicycle to work, when you have a Honda?"

I answered, "I haven't got a licence."

He said, "Nor do I."

So, I asked all Ibu's staff, and not one had a licence.

I commented, "It's okay for Balinese."

Ibu remarked, "Dye your hair black, so you won't need a licence."

24 December 2019 - Begpackers

I was just reminded of this little episode, by another tourist... well another tourist's strange comment. He just flagged me down in the main street, to ask where the Hot Springs were. He was a very happy tourist, carrying his child on his shoulders. I told him it was about four kilometres away, and if he went to our office, we sold discounted tickets. He then asked how did you get to the Hot Springs, and I told him he would need a driver. He answered by saying, "Ok, I will hitchhike."

Huh?

Which reminded me of two of Ibu's guests... well sort of guests. I had ridden my bike up to the hotel the other day, to grab some take away. I was not dressed to greet clients, so I just rode around to the back.

As I parked my bicycle, Ibu started screaming for me to come help, you know the drill. *That bloody CCTV, I should have snuck in via the blind spot.*

An elderly Dutch couple, whom I had seen eating in the restaurant, as I rode past, were standing at the cashier. Ibu's staff member had a blank look on her face. They were trying to explain what they wanted, but she could not work it out.

So, I walked up and asked if I could help them. It turned out they were asking if they could just leave their car in the hotel carpark overnight, and just use a shower and toilet. I said they could rent a room; *it is a hotel after all.*

They said no, they did not want a room, just a shower, and a toilet, they would sleep in their car... for free. *Bloody Dutch.*

I continued to offer them a room, *at this HOTEL.*

I advised them that they could rent a cheap room. They insisted they wanted to sleep in their car in the carpark. *Well, fine with me but nothing's free.*

Bapak was sitting at one of the tables in the restaurant and looked at me to explain what they wanted. I explained to Bapak in Indonesian/Balinese, that they were crazy, and asked him how much a room would be for just the use of a toilet and shower.

After we discussed for some time, the crazy people wanting to sleep in their car, and Bapak finally understanding what they wanted, he suggested a driver room.

I told the Dutch couple Bapak's offer, they thought that was reasonable, and I escorted them out the back to show them the room. They agreed on the price, with breakfast.

We walked back to the restaurant and then Ibu asked what they wanted, well screamed out the serving window from the kitchen. When I told, her she started screaming, "NO, NO!"

Too late, Bapak had already agreed.

I presumed the Dutch did not understand the language, but the screaming across the restaurant was pretty obvious. The Dutch were probably pleased they had secured their deal with Bapak, so the crazy lady screaming could not back out now. I then went to leave.

As I was riding out, I saw that it was not a car, but a campervan that the Dutch were sleeping in. They had parked it in the middle of the hotel carpark, on the driveway, parking across the first six parking spots. Blocking the access to the other car parking spots, and to Bapak's car garage. They were setting up their table and chairs, having a great old time. Looking quite pleased with themselves, thinking they had rented a whole hotel carpark for IDR 100,000, with shower, toilet, breakfast, and Wi-Fi.

So, I walked up to them and told them that they would have to move, so other guests could park. They were quite put out, that they would have to pack up their home and move, and started complaining that the ground was not level if they moved, so their bed would not be straight.

I told them, "Well, you are welcome to rent the whole carpark if you like, but it's going to cost you."

They moved.

Chapter 16 - Back on the Bukit

3 January 2020 - Cockfighting

One of the lengthy discussions Hubby and I had, before making our decision to move permanently to Bali, was, 'How would we deal with the animal cruelty?' Cockfighting being just one of the more well-known acts of animal cruelty on this Island. Although considered an important part of the culture, it was very hard for us to come to terms with.

The roosters for cockfighting are the ones you see in the baskets, not the ones roaming around through the garbage. For many Balinese, eating the rooster after its timely death, is the preferred meat over a free-range roaming chicken. Everyone knows the bird's meat is clean, as they are fed the finest grains, the free-range chickens eat garbage all day. It took me a few years to convince Ibu that when a tourist ordered chicken in her restaurant, they wanted chicken, not rooster. And how tourists would not identify the way her kitchen cut a chicken. When a tourist approached me in the garden of the hotel and asked me if the kitchen was serving dog, I thought it time to explain to Ibu that Westerners do not cut a chicken through the bones. Also, being a large rooster, it would look foreign, taste different, and somewhat scary to some less travelled tourists... I printed off pictures of chicken portions and how to cut a chicken, western style, and put them up in her restaurant kitchen to remind the kitchen staff. It eventually sunk in.

A cockfighting rooster's life is one of luxury, compared to his cousins that roam free. The cockfighting rooster is fed only the best quality grain, they are bathed, they are exercised, even massaged and groomed. When a Balinese boy is given a young rooster of good breeding, probably from a long line of fighting roosters, he is given the responsibility of caring for the animal right up until its fateful death. The death may be premature compared to his cousins, or maybe not. That will depend on how long his free-roaming cousin could outrun the local dogs, or cross the road to get to the other side, in Bali traffic.

We rescue a lot of dogs and then adopt them out. We usually only keep the ones with faults, 'The unadoptables' we call them. Such as our chicken chasing dog. She lived for one year on the Bali streets before moving in with us, she has the chicken dinner instinct ingrained in her.

When we first moved into the village we live in, in the south of Bali, Chicken Chasing Dog got off her lead on day two, and chased a free-roaming chicken around the village for about two hours. Three old Dadongs sitting on the side of the road laughed so hard watching the stupid Bule girl running past, chasing a black dog following a clucking white chicken, up and down the streets. The Dadongs seemed thrilled we had moved in, something new to break the monotony of their days. When the excitement finally stopped, as said chicken ran into someone's house for safety, I caught the dog. As I did the walk of shame past the Dadongs, I apologised, and politely asked them, "What would happen if the dog had got the chicken?"

One answered very matter-of-factly, "You will have chicken for dinner", and that was that.

In our village in the south, we do not have cages lining the streets containing cockfighting roosters, as we do in the village in the North.

Not that there is not cockfighting, I just think they ran out of roosters. In the first two years, there was a cockfight every single day behind our house (as in literally behind our back wall).

In the village in the north, a cockfight is only held when there is a large ceremony, to entertain the Gods. It is illegal to do it every single day just to gamble.

It stopped suddenly behind our house down here, after Hubby bravely went out there one day and confronted one hundred testosterone-driven men; to nicely explain the dangers of burning large piles of feathers after each fight. *To be honest, I think it stopped, as they ran out of cocks.*

In the village in the north, there is no shortage of cocks, baskets of cocks line some of the streets. Every afternoon the men get out their cocks, and wash their cocks. They lovingly massage their cocks, they slap their cocks up against their neighbour's cocks, to practice for the next big fight. The very old men walk up and down the street with their cock on their hip, lovingly stroking it, and showing it off to everyone they pass, with very strange grins on their faces.

I have been back in the south just over one week now, and it took me one week to work out what was missing down here. Apart from the absence of rain, I finally worked it out, it is the absence of cocks.

4 January 2020 - Finding Zen In 2019

This past year, I spent more time with our Mangku than in previous years. However, he did a lot less talking than in previous years. A lot of the time he was in his 'Zen moment'. Not that he uses that word, it is not a

Balinese word. However, Hubby and I described these moments as, his 'Zen moments'.   Like the times, I just had to sit in the Bale outside our rental office and watch the Mangku cut his bonsai trees for hours. *Not that there was actually that much cutting in my opinion, just a lot of him squatting and staring at the little trees.*

If you think of the Karate Kid and Mr Miyagi, there is no wax on, wax off, but I know I am supposed to learn something from all of this. There is me sitting there, moving around uncomfortably, as I cannot sit still for longer than five minutes without being in pain, patiently waiting. Okay, impatiently squirming around, waiting for my enlightenment or my lesson to start. *Or, for him to at least bloody talk.*

Sometimes I would just go off home, have a coffee, and then come back, and he was still in the garden, in his zen moment. *I am not sure if he even noticed that I was gone.*

For four days, I had to watch him make a little white statue out of rice and plaster. That was at least more interesting, as I could see the statue forming, but still, he did not speak... even Hubby, watched that one for a while.

Occasionally, the Mangku would just get up from his bonsai watching squat. Walk past me, cross the road to the lake, get in his wooden canoe, and paddle off, and not come back for thirty minutes or so, without uttering a word.   He would then come back with a fish, take it in for his wife to cook and then go back to his little statue, still not uttering a word.   His wife did not utter a word either, she just went about cooking his lunch.

None of his five children talk much either. It is like pulling teeth to get his wife to talk sometimes, unlike Ibu. It is hard to believe he is Ibu's son, although he is adopted, he grew up in her house. *Well, Bapak does not speak much, so he gets it from him, I guess.*

The Mangku walks in such a calm and graceful manner. Unlike myself, who is always being told off by everyone in the village to slow down. No matter how long I have been here, I still move at a faster pace than the whole village. The Mangku, with the flowing whites he wears seems to just glide everywhere.   He is young for a Head Mangku, much younger than my previous teachers, but he has this old soul thing about him, probably all those past lives. When he does talk, it is usually just to tell us how to do something in our business. Or, to have a bitch session about how much Ibu thinks too much about money. Or how his wife thinks she always needs to buy a new outfit for each ceremony.   I do love the fact that when he takes off his white turban-like cloth from his head, unravels his long hair and tucks it up into an oversized cap (trucker cap), he switches out of Mangku-mode into Human-mode and talks like everyone else.

I explained to the Mangku, how 'I find my Zen moments in a bottle of beer.' He listened with great intent, just as Ibu had, when I explained to her my enlightenment found in beer, and he seemed to understand. Although, just like Bapak, he does not drink.

A lot of the Mangkus do drink, some drink a lot. It just seems that the ones that are at a higher plane than the rest, do not drink, they find their enlightenment without needing a drink to get up there. Bapak was a Head Mangku in the village. He was also a teacher at the religious university, where Head Mangkus study. Bapak has taught some well-known people in Bali and very respected in the Bali government. Being very small and cute, and old, Bapak reminds me of a Mr Miyagi, or dare I say, a Ketut Liyer, with better teeth. Our Mangku is taller and skinny, so he has more of a young Gandalf thing going on, minus the beard, but he does have the hair down to the ground, having never been cut.

So, the lesson I learned in 2019 is: Until I can sit still, I will still need beer to find my Zen!

5 January 2020 - New Year - New Name

Just adding another version of my name to the list. Bapak just sent me a WhatsApp. Bapak has signed many documents with my name on them... but no, today, let me be called RICHELT.

30 January 2020 - Life's A Beach

I have not written much lately, don't worry, Ibu is still there, I am here.

I am in the south enjoying beaches and sunsets, and Ibu is still up in the village, doing her usual thing. It is the quiet season, so I do not need to be up there, Komang has everything covered. *Well, Komang may need to go on stress leave.*

Our daily WhatsApp messages (starting at 7.00 am from her home, through to 9.00 pm), mainly involve Ibu and the crying emoji.

One day of being with Ibu, she even sent, 'I just want to go home.' -poor kid, I sent her home. I even got one message from Komang yesterday, saying she doesn't understand Ibu. Now, this is from a Balinese, so I am glad I am not the only one.

I ring Ibu almost daily. Usually, one topic involves five calls, as she has a habit of hanging up on me mid-conversation, or just putting the phone down and walking off.

I went up there last Sunday; it was the first time since we left on Christmas Day, and I caught Ibu sitting behind Komang at my desk, using my computer, with a guilty look on her face. Ibu had her traditional medicine gunk on her forehead. Instead of saying 'Happy New Year. How are you?' etc., she immediately said, "Oh, I have something in my eyes, and it hurts."

I looked at her, with that 'well, yes, you probably do with all that gunk falling in your eyes' look. But then I looked in one of her eyes, to make her feel loved, and noticed she did look like she may be getting a cataract. So, I felt sorry for her and let her off.

I made Komang get off my computer and close the online shopping site, so we could get some work done. Ibu must have told Komang to tell me she was starting at 10.00 am, as when I told Komang I would finally come up, after three weeks of her begging me to come and rescue her from Ibu, she told me she was not starting until 10.00 am. So, when I walked in at 9.30 am, that was a bit of a surprise, to all of us. Ibu has a habit of manipulating my staff. Poor Ari has been dragged down there at night to help Ibu and ended up sleeping in reception, as the rain got too heavy, and he could not get home.

After I did a bit of work, Bapak came in, and he looked a bit deflated. He's a bit overwhelmed by the whole 'Indonesia is going online' thing. Many Expats here that run businesses are thrilled that everything is finally going online. For a seventy-six-year-old Balinese man trying to run a business, that he has been running the old way for 36 years, it is all a bit too much. Bapak is used to, for example, going to the tax office once a month and sitting there half a day. Then going to the bank with cash to pay his tax and then going back to the tax office to prove payment... this month they told him to do it all online. *Poor Bapak.*

Also, he must pay his staff's health insurance and work insurance, etc., all online as well. Ibu started going on about **BPJS** (workers' insurance/pension) and how she will be 'rugi rugi', meaning she will make a loss.

At first, I thought she did not want to pay it, like she does not want to pay taxes. It turned out, Bapak has been paying for the insurance for years, but when he went to BPJS on Friday, they said he had not. They gave him a username and password to check his account, and he left.

So, I asked him for the username and password. He could not remember what he had done with it. So, I told Komang to ring get him to BPJS on Monday, and get a login for the online system, and we can sort it out for him.

Well, yesterday, we finally got into his account, only to find the system says Bapak has not paid in two years... However, he has been paying, he has the receipts, from an extremely helpful person at the local bank that helps him every month.

So, I now must work out where all this money has gone, and I mean a lot of money. Komang is being very helpful and trying to explain to Ibu and Bapak what's going on, and that we will find the money.

Komang has strict instructions not to do online shopping, and so does Ibu!

18 February 2020 - Elvis

Tomorrow is Galungan, it is a particularly important day in the calendar, a bit like Christmas to Christians. Everyone will be in the village, our whole family, all the kids, everyone coming home from all over Bali.

At 8.30 am, I rang Ibu to discuss this important day. She answered the phone, did not say hello, put the phone down and screamed for Komang, then screamed some more. Komang finally came to the phone, I asked her to get Ibu to call me when she was not so busy.

At 9.30 am, I rang the hotel phone. Komang answered the hotel phone. *I know Ibu is flat out, she has been for three days, preparing for tomorrow, but when Ibu or Bapak want something, they will ring me at any time of the day or night.*

As Komang has tomorrow off, we discussed for Wayan to get my offering supplies in the morning before we get up there, and for Ibu to call me back.

I rang Ibu's mobile at 10.30 am, the phone rang and rang, and then all I got was Elvis music.

I rang at 11.30 am, Elvis serenaded me again.

I rang at 12.15 pm, Elvis has not left the building.

I rang at 12.30 pm, I am getting sick of Elvis.

I just rang the hotel directly, and Komang answered again (after two tries). She does not know who Elvis is, or how Ibu managed to do that to her phone, as she said she has seen Ibu answer it this morning. I know Ibu does not even know who Elvis is, or Angeline his Sweet, Sweet Angeline.

I guess I will just see Ibu and Elvis tomorrow.

20 February 2020 - Galungan, A Day To Worship The Dead.

Well, it is a little bit more than that. Basically, the dead ancestor's spirits are called down, from where they are waiting above Mt Agung until they are reincarnated. To be ceremonially bathed, fed and entertained for ten days. The Penjors (bamboo poles you see lining the streets) representing the shape of Mt Agung, are the invitations to the spirits to come down. *A bit like putting balloons on your front gate when you have a party.*

The poles have a little house-shaped basket, a bit like a bamboo letterbox, where you put food for the Ancestors. This food needs to be replaced regularly every day, for ten days, until the last day, which is Kuningan, where you send them all back. *As enough is enough guys, we must get back to work.*

Ibu, of course, like all Balinese had been busy preparing for these ten days of the Ghosts on Bali. Ibu was a little too busy for me, but Elvis was still available when I tried phoning her, as we arrived in the village. We headed up early to the village yesterday, we had no staff working, and it really was not a day to work. However, we had invited three guests, one a regular visitor, to join in the family fun. Hubby was happy, as he had three extra cougars for the day.

While our Cougars were having breakfast, Hubby and I rushed to our house, as the landowner needed to get into our House Temple. She had rung, saying no one seemed to have a key to the front gates. *Oops, I did, the kids did, but they were not there yet either.*

We needed to get dressed properly, greet all the neighbours, check on the neighbour's puppies that had been sleeping at our house, etc.

The village was buzzing, not a spare car park anywhere, so Hubby slowed the car down, and I did a tuck and roll near the school, to get out and walk up to the house. Greeted by all the Dadongs along the way, with "When did you get home?"

The usual, everyone else arriving from the south getting the same question. Everyone parking cars wherever they could, and unloading baskets of offerings.

Once I finally got to the house, I discovered we now have two cats. *Hmmm, great.*

Our landlord, Komang, was supposed to meet me there to do the temple. *She was obviously having trouble finding a park as well.*

I opened the gates, and then the Dadongs just followed me into the house. I ended up doing the typical Bali thing of getting dressed in front of everyone, while they all just chatted away. *Don't you have some praying to do ladies?*

Luckily Wayan had climbed the fence and cut the grass the day before, so we could get to the front door (as the rains cause the grass to grow if the gates are locked, and no one can get a cow in to keep it down). But he had not done the backyard, so no one was getting through that jungle. *We will need some cows back there.*

Hubby arrived, like everyone else, he just parked wherever he could. He chose right in the middle of the cockfighting baskets, so the old men, just moved to let him in, and continued to bang their cocks in front of his car.

Hubby got dressed, and then he left to go to the car, as we had our guests at the hotel. Then Hubby yelled over the fence to inform me the Barong was heading to the hotel. *We just left everything open, no use worrying, no one's going to steal anything, the Dadongs will slowly make their way out. Then Komang and a cow can get in.*

The Barong is similar to a Chinese dragon, that walks the streets, clearing it of bad spirits. I mean when you invite down a whole bunch of ghosts, you have to expect some others uninvited to tag along.

Ibu had only one staff member at work, Kadek, so I had him set up our offering for the Barong. As Ibu was not there, we did one for the hotel, and one for our business, and Hubby provided the cash for both. (We give money in our offering to a Barong.)

I helped our guests get dressed in Adat clothes, and then I asked Kadek, "Where is Ni Wayan? She is supposed to be giving my guests an offering making class, while I go pray with the kids."

Kadek said, "Well, um, she's not coming, Ibu will do the class."

Ok, now that was a surprise, not sure how she would fit that in, lovely of her though.

Thirty minutes passed, I was collecting flowers in the garden, and I heard Kadek on the phone to Ibu. Well, I heard Ibu screaming, and then I could see that Kadek had the phone held away from his ear, so he wouldn't burst an eardrum. Ibu was not coming. Kadek said he would do the class, and that Nengah (the cook) was now in the kitchen. I asked him if all the components for the class were ready, and he looked at me blankly.

So, I ran around with Nengah, getting more flowers, all the components for the offerings and then realised I had not had any breakfast or even a coffee. *What was I thinking? Kopi Dulu, Rach.*

I yelled for Kadek to make me one very large coffee and something for me to eat. So, the guests made offerings, learned to offer them. I managed a coffee, a very large coffee, and a very small Balinese pancake. Then Hubby called us, as the Barong was coming.

We headed to the hotel driveway entrance, for a village Mangku and the Barong to do their thing. All cleansed, money taken, good to go.

Just as I was walking back in, I saw one of Ibu's grandchildren sneak into the hotel, stealth style. *Ibu must be close.*

Ibu had made Bapak pull up the car outside the hotel, and hide in a blind spot, as she had forgotten something and did not want me to see her. I ran out to the street, stuck my head in the car window, and surprised her. Wished them both Happy Galungan, good health, etc. Ibu stated, "Must pray first."

Yep, I know that Ibu.

They were headed down to the cemetery. A couple of family members have not been cremated yet, so they were probably hanging out at the cemetery, wondering if they were invited to the festivities. Ibu and Bapak had to go down there to make sure they were not feeling left out.

I had not seen the kids yet and promised to meet them at 9.00 am, it was nearly 11.00 am. *Oops. Oh, well, we wanted our guests to see as much of the village as possible, they can meet the kids anyway...I just missed a bit of prayer, my knees are grateful......*

20 February 2020 - Meet The Fockers

Galungan Day continued... Now, many people have dysfunctional families. I grew up with one, and I have one now in Bali. For example, my mother Ibu Dua went to visit my stepmother Ibu Tiga (number 3), and my half-sister in Adelaide the other day.

It gets a bit confusing when we mention family here, as we have Ibu and Bapak, being our adopted parents (under village customary law only). Then we have all our adopted kids (under village customary law) and their families, some of whom are related to Bapak, some are not. So, we have a lot of grandparents, and that makes it fun, as you really need to visit them as often as possible, or you get told off.

After the Barong, I asked Hubby to drive the ladies and me up to the village, to as close as he could get us, and he could go off to do whatever he had to do. *Knowing him, he probably has hiding to do.*

The ladies and I, got out on the main road and walked up a small lane to get into the village. The first person we came across, well actually I did not see him at first, we had walked past a house, and just heard a voice yell out behind us, "Rach, when did you come?" in Balinese, "Where are you going?"

I looked back to see a very short man I did not recognise. He had a distinctive look, not one you would forget. All in white (so, a Mangku) and dreaded hair, well just a big clump of matted, knee-length hair. *Not sure how he knows me? Then again, the ghosts are in town, so, it could be one of them.*

So, I answered him, and we continued. I had warned the ladies that all the Bitch Ladies were in town, so they may get, "Where you from?" in English, and "Come to the Bitch, I work on the Bitch"...we did not get that once the whole day. We only had a lady stopping to take her large basket of food off her head and give my guests some snacks. *These are the snacks the ghosts were offered but did not want, so the ladies were having the Ghost's leftovers.*

Also, the ladies met one of our neighbours in the street. She has one of the pups that we had had sterilized a few days before we left, and had been caring for. I asked her where was Melly, as my Hubby was looking for her earlier. She said, "She died."

I was like, "What?"

"Yeah, she got sick and died", and she kept walking, she had human dead to visit, and all that.

If only I had known yesterday, *I could have called Melly down today.*

So, I rang hubby and said, "Melly's dead."

He did not take it well, screaming a bit like Ibu.

So, I hung up and let him deal with his grief on his own. I had guests, and the streets were full of people wanting to say Hello.

Then the rains came, oh boy, did that clear the street. It went from having to move every minute, to get out of someone's way, to deserted streets.

The ladies and I sheltered for a while, until we thought, 'This is silly!' so, we rang Hubby, who took some convincing to come and rescue us with umbrellas. He may not have been over his grieving stage yet, he seemed to be at the angry stage, and there was some confusion as to which small lane we were in.

He finally found us, he had to ride a bicycle with a poncho and a sarong. The minute he handed us the umbrellas, the rains stopped, of course. *He showed up with a smile, so he must have finished all stages of grief and moved on.*

Thanking Hubby, with a smile, I announced, "Right, now we will go over to three of the kids' grandparents' houses," as the whole family, will be there (three of our kids are from three houses all in the same block of compounds, so we get to see all three families in one go, and we just mix it up a bit), and we can sit and have a coffee.

The houses were at the other end of the village, so the ladies followed me through the rabbit warren of streets, passing everyone praying, as the 12-noon prayer had started. Music filled the streets from the main temple and a priest over a loud speaker, chanted the daily prayer (well, three times a day prayer).

Whenever I arrive at the little block of three compounds in one, I just arrive and let the Grandmothers fight it out with each other over who I came to see. Luckily the first two houses were busy praying, and we got house Number three, my favourite. *It's a good day.*

We made our way around to the back of the house, through the little maze of walls, and broken paths, to get to where the family hangs out. Passing one of the Aunts in the very skinny laneway, who was excusing herself to pray. I hugged her and said I'd catch her soon. As we turned the last corner to the back of the house, I immediately saw two brothers sitting there. Wayan, being the father of one of our kids, and his youngest brother Ketut, they were drinking Arak with Drunk Uncle. I had always called him Drunk Uncle, as I did not know his name, and was always drunk. *I was surprised to see Drunk Uncle, as I was sure he was dead, but then again, this was his day to visit.*

Wayan's pregnant third wife was there as well, and their adorable little daughter. One of Wayan's older kids from the first wife was there, but someone was missing, Miss Fourteen from wife Number Two. *You know Wayan, the one you gave us as a baby, and we gave back to your ex-wife when she was six, and you were supposed to collect and bring up today?*

So, I mentioned that Miss Fourteen was missing. And Wayan started going on, how he had asked me to borrow our car, and then Ketut got in, saying I should have lent Wayan the car, now that I have a motorbike. Then Drunk Uncle got in on it and how they all came up with three to a motorbike. We are only two, and that she had not been collected from Denpasar... so, a little miscommunication as to who was bringing Miss Fourteen today, poor kid.

However, we gained one. One of our other girls from House Number One, Miss Nineteen, has been working overseas for one year and had failed to inform me she was back. So, that was a very pleasant surprise, she wanted it to be a BIG surprise, so everyone was sworn to secrecy. I would have preferred to have known earlier, as I was having nightmares that she had been sold on the European sex market, as I had not heard from her for days.

So, we all had coffee, snacks, and laughs. One guest tried some arak, just a little sip from the lid. *It is 5.00 pm somewhere in the world.*

Then the teasing started, as you do at family get-togethers, today it was my turn to be teased. Grandpa did not need to go on as he usually does, how God hates me as I had not been pregnant, as Wayan decided that it was his turn for that topic of conversation. Drunk Uncle likes to bring that one up as well. (Later in the day after talking to the ladies, I had realised that he had not been speaking in English, so most of the time the ladies had no idea what he was on about).

The conversation that continued, about me turning Fifty next year, and how young my husband was, and how Wayan just gets newer younger wives, etc., was not actually filtering down to the ladies, so I had no one to come to my defence.

The ladies were busy being entertained by Wayan's gorgeous four-year-old daughter; she was stealing the show. Miss Four said to me, "Aunty Rach, what is that lady's name?" Pointing at one of our rather tanned guests. I told her the guest's name, and Little Miss Four said to her in English, "You really must buy some sunscream," (She said sunscream, not sunscreen.) Everyone laughed, Miss Four entertained the ladies while the men continued to tease me.

Another brother soon arrived, Made. Grandpa and Grandma were fluffing around having so many guests. Made has five young sons, they were hiding in the background, his wife got back from praying, the porch was running out of carpet space. There were three chairs in the whole house, plastic ones that wife Number Three had bought. I'd given one to one of our guests with a bad knee, as getting down on the carpet, she may never have gotten back up. Pregnant wife Number Three had one, and Grandpa was carefully balancing on the other, as it was broken down the middle.

We all chatted for ages, the men drinking and teasing, Miss Four entertaining, and then all the village men were called to a town meeting.

Wayan did not look like he was moving for anyone, but we thought this was our call to leave and let Grandpa have a chair with four legs. Wayan said he could not get up, so he could not go to the meeting. I told him with that fat gut, I could see why.

As we were leaving, one of the ladies, the one that must buy sunscream, realised that one of the men had left for the meeting, wearing one of her black Havana flip flops. She was left with one Havana and one large men's Adidas flip flop. So, we decided to walk past the meeting on the way to lunch, and swap it back. As we were leaving Little Miss Four yelled out: "Bye, don't forget to buy sunscream!"

It was drizzling, so we were glad Hubby had found us with the umbrellas. We walked through the town square to the Bali Banjar (like an open-air town hall), and there was every man in the village, that was not too fat, too old or too drunk to attend, sitting in the Banjar. We tried ever so Ibu-stealth-like, to sneak a look at the flip flops on the stairs. Someone was talking on the loudspeaker, I did not recognise the voice, and could not see through the crowd. I thought all eyes were focused forward. Ever so quietly, I snuck closer to the stairs, this secret men's business meeting was strictly no women allowed. And then suddenly, "Rach, what are you looking for?"

Me frozen like a little mouse caught trying to get the cheese, looking up at, at least thirty pairs of eyes, staring back down at me. *Why does everyone know how to say my name apart from Ibu and Bapak?*

I quietly and apologetically explained the situation, and the men closest to the edge of the Banjar welcomed me to look through the piles of flip flops on the steps. *Nope, not there.*

So, we tried the back steps. Again, trying to attract as little attention as possible, "Rach, what are you doing?"

Seriously, that's about the twentieth time today, someone - I have no idea who they are, has got my name right...Nope, not there either.

So, our guest now has a souvenir from her visit, and a bit of a funny walk. As we scurried off from the 'no women's zone', one of the ladies commented how that meeting must have been bloody boring, as a lot of men were more interested in me finding the flip flop.

We popped into the school on our way back to the hotel, so I could show the ladies the renovations to the school, and the lovely choice of lime green paint. As one of the ladies said, 'Must have been a sale on green paint.' Hubby was at the school, with the car parked in front of the school gate, so we could get a ride as it was raining again. We headed back to the hotel for lunch.

We arrived at the hotel, and although I had rung the kitchen from the school to order lunch, so we did not have to wait.... it was not ready yet. I had rung Ibu's phone first, and let Elvis serenade the ladies, but as Elvis would not take a lunch order, I then rang the hotel, then the kitchen.

Hubby went to the kitchen to see what was happening, came back and told me Ibu was in there.

I walked into my office, greeted Bapak, who was very friendly, then I walked through to the kitchen and greeted a few relatives along the way. There was Ibu in the kitchen, already out of temple attire, on her phone... and not talking to Elvis. So, I walked back out and went to wait for lunch with the guests.

My lunch came out, but it was lacking in something, besides not a great deal of food on my plate, there was no chilli. I commented that Ibu must have put me on a diet again, as my lunch was a third of the size of everyone else's.

So, I walked to the kitchen serving window, and Ibu was no longer on the phone. I yelled out, "Hello Ibu!" Ibu ignored me and started picking up plates and moving them around. I ordered some chilli sauce from Nengah, and while she was cooking it, I yelled, "Hello Ibu!" again.

Ibu ignored me, so I blew her a raspberry. Ni Wayan was standing next to me and laughed, but then saw Ibu's face and stopped. I started yelling, just like Ibu does to me, "Ibu, Ibu, Ibu, Ibu!"

She finally acknowledged me, by snapping, "Ibu Capek." (Ibu tired.)

I grabbed my chilli and went back to the table to sit down to eat. I told the guests Ibu was tired, and not in a speaking mood. Hubby commented, he thinks she's going through Menopause but has been for fifteen years.

After lunch, I was in my office, and Ibu came in, yelling at Bapak and ignored me again. Then she went straight out and said, "Hello", all nice and sweet, to one of my guests, who she recognised had been up many times.

I walked out past Ibu, back to the table, and finally, Ibu came over to me. Only, to tell me off for wearing a kebaya without a corset, and that she could see my fat roll through the lace. I explained that I had been ringing her all day yesterday to ask for a corset. Her answer was that she was busy and tired.

Then Ibu started to ask what bra I was wearing and started poking my breast to see if it was padded. When she discovered it was not padded, she wanted to tell all my guests that my boobs were big. Ibu continued poking my boob and asked me to open up my kebaya, right there in the restaurant, to show her what bra I was wearing. Ibu repeated to our guests that my boobs were big and continued poking mine. She decided to do a visual demonstration for our guests, by grabbing her own breasts (braless) and flopping them up and down.

So, after the boob check, I asked Ibu if our regular guest could have a photo taken with her. (Someone on Facebook had challenged her to get one with Ibu.) Ibu put on her best smile, after complaining she was not dressed appropriately for a photo. Ibu had her photo taken, and then I thought I would see if I could get one, and to my surprise, she obliged.

Before we headed off, Ibu chatted with Hubby for some time, Ibu complaining about my lack of staff, and saying she knew more about what's going on with them, than we did, blah, blah. *Well, she does gossip more.*

Ibu said that we should be in the village more regularly, blah, blah. Ibu does not understand the whole 'foreigner bosses in Indonesia rules', the government appoints, so thinks we should be in the office twelve plus hours a day like her and Bapak. *She is just pissed off I am having a three-month holiday, well that's what she thinks I am doing. A bit hard to have a holiday when she is on the phone with me every day.*

As I was saying goodbye, I asked Ibu where she got the Elvis music from. She said she had no idea what I was on about, or who on earth Elvis was, and that her phone worked fine, and that she was tired and that was that, and for me to go home now.

10 March 2020 – Kuningan

So Kuningan has come and gone – just like the Dead. Up early last Saturday, like many good Balinese, off to their parents' house for the last day of this ten days of Christmas. *No, not Christmas, but the same pressure to see family, prepare food, travel home, get dressed up, drink too much, etc.*

We headed to the village. Along, with what felt like half of Bali, dressed in Adat, joining the lines of cars and motorbikes on the highway heading to their villages. We did not have any guests. I knew Ibu's hotel was empty, so we took our Chihuahua Fred with us. We are not small dog people, but this rescue dog stole our hearts, and the fact that he does not yap or even bark, and just sits on my lap (as I don't own a handbag), he's easy to take to work... to piss off Ibu. Ibu does not like dogs, especially dogs inside, especially in the office, and especially inside a bedroom, which was why we got 'kicked out of home' years back.

So, running late due to a few pee-pee stops, one for the dog. Our landlord rang, frantically asking where we were, as she wanted to get into our house temple again...*mind you, she did not get there till 1.30 pm in the end, so not sure why the rush...although half her friends and family did.*

We went and opened the house, turned on the water, etc., and then I was walking out our gate, and people were just piling in. *No idea who they are but dressed to bless. Good thing I just swept the floors.*

On Kuningan Day, most people finish the last lot of praying quite early in the morning. Also, this morning there was a State-wide Basa Bali

(Balinese language) competition. It started at 9.30 am, the kids all over Bali were competing to show their Balinese writing and speaking skills. Our school should be up there at the top of the state, as we never took Basa Bali out of school. The previous Governor removed it from many schools, being that Balinese children were the minority in Bali, but we kept it in school. The latest Governor has brought it back in. All government offices must use Basa Bali on Thursdays, also in all businesses, schools, etc., and everyone must dress in Balinese Adat on Thursdays and full moon. I love that concept.

We went to see Ibu and Bapak at the hotel. I wanted to tell Ibu our news that the landlord had just said that she did not want to renew our contract, and we would have to find a new house. It will be weird and sad, as it was our childcare centre for ten years, then our kampung house for three years. It is going to be hard to find another vacant house, as everyone in the village uses any empty houses when they come up for ceremonies. Rent is cheap, it went up slightly after ten years, to four million ($400) per year. Many people have offered us houses in the past. Still, they want to stay a few nights when they come up for ceremonies. That is fine, and the family do offer us the homes for free, it is just that we need to find a place with a wall around it to keep in all the dogs, so we will start looking next week.

We found Ibu, she glared at Fred, then glared at me for bringing a dog. I mentioned to Ibu that the landlord did not want to continue the contract, and I had to start looking for a house. Ibu laughed, then looked at me very suss and asked, "Where would you look?"

I said, "Here, in this village of course."

Ibu looked at me with her nose in the air and walked off to get a coffee, so we went and grabbed a coffee ourselves.

Then Hubby asked Ibu if she had any guests, knowing she did not, and commented that it was probably due to the Coronavirus. Ibu answered, "No, we only get Chinese from June to September."

Ibu seemed to not really understand the Coronavirus. Or, that Bali had been greatly affected, not just by no Chinese coming, but other tourists cancelling their travel. We tried to explain to her that any elderly or low immune system person of any country could get it, not just Chinese. That it was contagious like the flu, and that there were no cases in Bali yet. I told her the reading I had done about the virus, so far indicated that it would not probably survive well in Bali, due to outdoor living... unless people were in a crowded area, such as a shopping mall with AC or someone with the virus coughed on them, etc. Ibu sort of understood, but then thought it was silly someone with the flu would be shopping, and that I was spending my spare time reading about a virus.

Ibu pondered her newfound knowledge. Then declared it was absolute nonsense, it was quiet as it is February, and that she had always been quiet in February, and so have we. We basically shut down our rental office every low season. We only do tours if booked, there is no point having it open during low season, it always has been too quiet. That did not stop Ibu telling Hubby off, that one of her guests was angry as we were not open. Ibu was angry that our rental office manager could have time off to go Java. She was angry that the one guest she had that whole month, could not rent a canoe on that one day. Ibu had also sent one of her staff to Java at the same time, as he is friends with my staff member who is getting married. I told Ibu it is the same as the warung next to the rental office was closed, and she said, "Yes, it is closed as there are no tourists, its low season."

Aduh

After the ceremony stuff was completed, and everything quietened down, we all headed back to the hotel. It was getting colder, so Fred put on his little red puffer jacket that has 'Born to Be Wild' written on the back in bling. *Well, he does not need to be wearing Adat, the Ancestors have been sent home.*

Hubby soon followed Fred's lead and changed his clothes, then everyone seemed to follow Fred's lead, apart from Ibu and myself.

Ibu has started renovating the hotel, and I had no idea it had started until Hubby told me the other day. *Best I have a look at the renovations and tell Ibu how wonderful they are. Get in some brownie points with Ibu, she will soften, I know her.*

Fred and I went off through the gardens to check out the new rooms. Two old rooms and an old shed have been demolished, where four new rooms are being built, it looks like they will be a great size. Fred wandered in and out of each room just to check them all for me - yep, all good here Mum.

So, Fred and I went back to tell Ibu and Bapak how wonderful the renovation was looking. Fred had to inspect and water all Ibu's new plants on the way back as well.

Fred and I went into the office, and we sat down. Bapak proudly told Fred and me, how the other two rooms would also be demolished, and a new private garden would go in. This is great news, as those rooms have not been done for thirty-six years, and they were so bad...*Mind you, Hubby, and I lived in one of them for six months.*

Then Bapak said that they had also renovated two other rooms on the other side of the hotel. So, Fred and I headed off, to go and see those as well.

While I was in one room, getting Fred's opinion, it seemed Ibu had followed us. Her stealth movements were detected by Fred, who alerted me to her presence. I called out to her quite loudly, as she was hiding behind a wall, "All great, everything looked wonderful."

Apart from the tacky blue plastic toilet roll holder, she had done everything I suggested.

Ibu came closer and showed herself. Ibu had started to warm up to me again...*I will mention the toilet roll holder, cannot let her get too cocky.*

Before we were to have lunch, I went into where the family were all seated, and I sat next to Ibu. I put my hand on her leg, one of their sons was opposite us on the other couch, with his hand on Bapak's leg. This is a real bonding thing, and Ibu knows it. A few other family members were also just hanging out. Ibu said nothing at first and then said to me, "You really should not have worn that Kebaya, you need a longer one, the one you are wearing shows your fat stomach. And, you should have worn a wider selendang like I am wearing!" (A Selendang is the sash that goes around the waist over your kebaya, or with men it often ties over the top of their kemban, which is like a sarong)

So, I told Ibu that her selendang looked like a beach towel. She then asked, "What is a beach towel?"

So, we all had a conversation about that there are different types of towels, this went on for thirty minutes.

Hubby came in, so did Fred, who sat on the floor in the middle of the room, surrounded by family, as though he owned the place. Fred, not Hubby. Ibu ignored Fred. She even ignored his very cool jacket. The rest of the family giggled and commented on it, not having seen a dog wear clothes before. I said he was cold, that he had Corona. Ibu, back to ignoring me, and Fred, even though I was sitting right next to her, said to Hubby, "So, you have other work when you are not here?"

And then a light bulb went off, in my head, not the room.

I had forgotten that a few years back, someone from Denpasar had told Bapak a story, while they were carrying a dead body to the cemetery, that we had rented a house out near the Bamboo Forest, and that we had started another business without Ibu and Bapak. A totally fabricated story, but Ibu and Bapak believed them, and it took a lot of convincing to calm them down. So, Ibu had her nose out of joint, as she did not believe we were having a break due to low season, she thought we were starting a new business behind her back. It probably did not help that I had stopped ringing her daily, but that is not my fault, I gave up talking to Elvis...

Chapter 17 - The Rona

16 March 2020 - Toilet Paper

I rang Ibu this morning, to see if she needed disinfectant, etc., as we were heading to the big warehouse supermarket, Lottemart, where you buy everything in bulk. Ibu answered. *Elvis has left the building.*

Ibu was all good, one of her family had already bought her lots, she is prepped and squeaky clean.

Bapak, on the other hand, was sending me recipes. I would send him a government notice update on WhatsApp, about Corona, he would send me back a food recipe. *We are not on the same wavelength.*

It is only my second time in a supermarket in twelve months. I went prepared with a mask and Dettol to wipe down the trolley, Hubby, etc. *My usual routine, not a Corona thing.*

I was dreading it, as I do not like crowds or spending money. I had seen videos of Australians fighting over toilet paper, so I was prepared to see the craziness. We drove into the supermarket carpark, Hubby said it looked busier than usual, as in maybe five more cars.

Hubby grabbed a trolley, I smacked him, and disinfected him, and then the trolley, and then we made our way in - all calm, lots of toilet paper, a whole aisle to the ceiling of toilet paper... but someone has bought out my favourite coffee... see we have priorities here in Bali.

20 March 2020 - How's Ibu doing?

What does Ibu think of Corona? More importantly, what does the BIG Ibu (Mother Nature) think?

A few days ago, we made the decision to officially announce the closure of our business for a while. First, I had to break the news to Ibu before we made a public announcement.

We had, last month been discussing with our landlord, how we wanted to rent the house up there for one more month, while we searched for a new one. Then everything changed, for the whole world. Lucky for us, although we had already made this arrangement with our landlord. She was wonderful, when we said we had changed our mind, and said no problem, just give the key to the Headmistress of the school when we move out. That sorted, it was time to let Ibu know.

I rang Ibu Wednesday night, before the gossip reached her, as I had just told our drivers, staff, and the landlord, Ibu would know in a minute. Ibu answered the phone, after a short Elvis serenade, and said, "Where are you? Are you sick?"

After assuring Ibu I was not sick, Hubby was not sick, we discussed what was happening, and all the latest updates. Which, of course, changed every few hours, but at least I could get her up to speed on events until that moment. Ibu had no idea that tourists could not really come in after 20 March, without strict rules, such as health certificates, pre-purchased visas. Ibu had no idea that countries apart from China could not enter. All my WhatsApps to Bapak had being negated with food recipes. *I guess we all deal with things differently.*

I asked Ibu about the very large loan she had just taken out from the bank to renovate the hotel, and if she was going to stop renovating, and pay back what was not spent. Ibu said, "No, no worries, the renovation will be finished in two months, just in time for July peak season."

That's when it got real. That Ibu has no idea how bad this is! So, I do not like to be a pessimist, but it was time to tell Ibu the hard facts that hotels were closing, and peak season may not happen. I said, "Peak season may be delayed, it could possibly happen later, say in October, but who knows."

Ibu laughed. Ibu asked if we were starting a new business in the meantime... Ibu still did not get it. Ibu asked if we had any friends that wanted to buy the warung next to our rental office, or maybe we wanted to take it over... Ibu still did not get it. I told Ibu, we would come up for one day, just to pack up the house, and close the offices, but we wouldn't stay. I mentioned that it could get down to regions closing borders, Bangli may not let us in. Ibu laughed and said, "No, Bangli will let you in."

I put Hubby on the phone. He explained to Ibu that governments could no longer hold meetings, as they could not have large groups. Ibu said, "No, we have meetings booked here for next month."

Hubby answered, "Well, maybe it's different in Bangli", knowing all too well, that it is not.

Ibu is in a blissful bubble, I have decided to let her stay in the bubble, and the reason why may be explained further down.

Ibu and I chatted a bit more, about how the neighbours down here were now out of work. At least the people up there had vegetable farms, and that there would still be a demand for vegetables, so that was great.

It got me thinking how the Traditional Balinese that have not been caught up in the Western way will not really be affected by this, if they are not infected. The traditional Balinese do not go to supermarkets, they do not care about toilet paper, or hand sanitizer shortages. They have never been to an airport, they do not have fridges, do not use fuel, they still use wood for cooking, etc. They would be just doing their usual routine of heading to the farms every morning, making fresh food daily, fishing, etc.

Our main reason for closing, besides everyone cancelling, is we do not want tourists visiting there. So, the villagers can be left alone, and hopefully away from the virus. However, a lot of their families work in tourism. They may return to the village, so there is a risk of the virus heading there, which would be devastating. There is also not enough farm land for everyone to work.

There are still many extremely old people in the village, and they have survived many hardships in their nearly 100-years during this visit to earth. Their beliefs are something we may all wish to consider. Traditional Balinese believe that everyone must feel suffering in their lifetime, or you will not appreciate the good times, you become complacent. They believe that Mother Nature, (well, God to them) applies the Rule of Balance when you are not looking after the Earth. They believe in plagues (viruses) that will affect people, or nature, or animals which come when there is an imbalance in nature due to human activities.

Their simple lives with no mortgages, or cars, TVs or smartphones, mean that, if there is no virus in their village, they will not really suffer, apart from those who depend on their families that work in tourism and send money home. They have seen suffering, but they have always seen the positives that come after, so they believe, there is always a reason for everything.

There was a rice shortage in the year 2000, due to a thirteen-month drought in Asia. Many people in the village did suffer then, as crops needed water, and they could not afford to buy rice, but they learnt to grow cassava (a starchy root vegetable that did not need much watering), and they lived off that. Some did not live, a great sum, but that was due to their sugar levels being put to the test, causing diabetes. It is often talked about, the drought that made people starve to death, but it would have been kidney and liver failure, not actual starvation. They believe in reincarnation, so they will see their family members that passed, again. That drought caused the lake level to drop considerably, revealing fertile soil right on the lake's edge. When the drought ended, the water level did not rise again that year, or the next, and they were able to farm the land. Farming soon became easier, no more carrying water up the hills, and now there was more land, so more vegetables, so more income than before.

Every few years, God does take back the land with heavy rains, and they patiently wait for God to let them use it again.

Their village was covered in ash and huge rocks in 1963, when Mount Agung blew, and they had to leave for eighteen months, many walking to

Singaraja and Denpasar, a four-day walk. The village was covered in seventy centimetres of ash. Today, the remnants of that event are seen in the vegetation. When they returned there were only a few trees that survived, poking up through the ash. So, they built Temples under the trees, with only a single stone chair for God to sit in and admire the tree, as God obviously wanted those trees to survive. The government planted Dutch Pine trees and Australian Ghost gums to rejuvenate the vegetation. So, the whole caldera and the other side to the slopes of Agung has a completely different look to the rest of Bali, and no Koalas.

That ash made the farming soil rich in nutrients. When they returned they had their best crop that year, better than any they could remember before that event.

Of course, in 2017, Agung went again, and a blanket of ash came down, not 70 centimetres, but it did its best to cover everything, and that stuff can stick around. To this day, the ash still falls out of the grass matting ceilings every single day. *I hate that stuff, sweeping it out every day.*

Still, everyone appreciated the great crops produced again. So, what's a bit of ash in the lungs, hasn't killed anyone yet?

We had to close our business for two months then, I will never forget Bapak putting locks on the doors of our office, as he had never closed it in thirty-six years.

Agung erupted a few more times. (We closed again for one month in July 2018.) When I tried to evacuate a ninety-three-year-old lady in 2017, she told me she had outrun it last time, she will outrun it this time. Then she told me it was not her time to lose her house, it was my generation's time. I nearly thought that was going to happen when the Lombok quakes happened.

The Lombok quakes in 2018 were devastating to the people of Lombok and Gili's. I must admit for the first time it made me fearful of quakes. The constant quakes, and thinking the house would collapse on you, so strategically placing your mattress in a spot that the wall couldn't hit you. We spent so many nights outside with the neighbours in the ten-degrees cold waiting to go back inside, and every time thinking; will this house stay up? I went in much earlier than the old Dadongs, as I am a wimp when it comes to cold, and even with a beanie and gloves, and jacket and Ugg boots, I kept choosing the house falling on me, over the cold.

We just lived, probably like many people, with an emergency plan of where to run in a quake. We slept fully clothed, including shoes, and we had a great dog radar, who woke us at least two minutes before every quake. *I think she's broken; she was downstairs and outside before the 6.6 mag quake at 1.45 am the other night, and didn't let us know on her way out...little Bitch.*

The landlord has a lot of repairing to do on that house now, they will need to demolish half the place. Still, they will have to remove all the duct tape from every window, and door, as that's how the house had to be, due to sneaky Agung. So, the positive is, they had always planned to renovate, and now they may save on demolition costs. Especially as, I think that duct tape is holding the whole house together.

The old Grandpas also turned behind our bedroom wall into a makeshift kitchen at that time, where the whole street cooked every night, another reason for the duct tape, all the smoke. This way, as little time as possible, was spent in any part of your home that could fall. Now, the Dadongs sit at their warung every night, while their husbands grill fish. It has turned into a real social place for the oldies to hang out, the Balinese version of going to Bingo or playing Bridge. They have talked to the same people for decades; however, they are highly social, never feel alone, and have no need to talk to people on a little screen.

They have had other significant events in their lifetime, in the area around them, living inside a volcano will do that.

In October 1963 Batur also erupted, and today the black scar is always a reminder of that event, as you drive down to the lake. Millions of tourists would have photos with that permanent mark, that also changed the shape of the lake, giving it two extra little peninsulas. No one was there at the time, as they had left in March. Now, they use that lava rock to build more solid homes, as there was no wood left for rebuilding when they returned. God obviously said, 'I do not want you to cut down my trees to make wooden houses as you did before, I want you to make your houses from this now. Save the trees for your cooking only, build houses that are stronger and warmer in the cold nights, and cool in the hot days.'

In 1926 Mount Batur erupted, and the lava began its fast descent towards the village of Kalang Anyar, that was located at the southwest base of the volcano. Villagers refusing to leave, staying to pray; as in 1917, Batur erupted, and the lava stopped at the Ulun Danu Batur Temple doorstep. Our village and others helped the villagers relocate. Still, they prefer to say the Dutch forcibly removed them, (they did send the Army) and relocated them to the caldera ridge, where the village remains today.

The village is now called Batur. Well, it is Bali, you do not use many different names.

The village they left behind was covered in lava, but they were not impressed with the Dutch, as they believed they should have all stayed, and praying would have stopped the lava flow. (There were still a lot of casualties.) The eleven-tiered shrine that survived, (and was transported to the new village) has been built into a magnificent temple. The government also paid for new housing and better infrastructure than their previous village. The villagers have witnessed many landslides below them in the last 100 years, that would have taken out their previous village multiple times.

They are also now closer to God, being higher up, and have the best view in Bali, of the caldera and the lake, also called Batur, of course. So, every day they can be reminded, and appreciate what God gave them.

In 1917 the eruption was in the main large crater of Mount Batur, that tourists climb today. However, three more eruptions formed craters, uniquely named, Batur One, Batur Two & Batur Three.

We were here to witness Batur Four open a vent in 2009, and she still steams to this day.

They believe these events all have a purpose, that when landscapes change, that is God rearranging things. *A bit like Ibu moving furniture. We may not know why she does it, but she does.*

They believe that if God, or what some of the world refers to as 'Mother Nature', takes lives to do this, then it is not their place to question that, we are guests on this Earth. If God wishes to kick a few of us out, then God can do that. *Governments are doing that right now, kicking a few out, not letting some in.*

Some Balinese beliefs are a tough way to look at this virus, that many Westerners would not understand at all. Such as, there is a village across the lake, that has had the same population for nearly twenty years. *They obviously have an in and out system going on.*

So, talking to them about all the elderly around the world dying, or just people dying, they think that there must be too many people living, when they should have already passed. God already made them sick, (such as with Cancer, etc.) Doctors kept them alive, so then God had to give them a big boot to say, 'no, sorry, really it is your time, see you in your next life.'

What the world's already seeing after this virus, is rivers clearing, and skies turning blue. All this talk in the media of Coronavirus, has replaced the talk of Climate Change.

Did Mother Nature just get sick of everyone talking about Climate Change, but no real action?

Is Mother Nature saying, wouldn't it be nice if you stopped spending all day at work, and spent some time with your families?

Is Mother Nature saying? 'You know what guys, it's simple, stop all this flying your little metal things through my clean sky. Stop cutting down my trees and putting concrete everywhere, to drive around in your little metal boxes. Stop wanting things you do not need, that make you build factories, that send all this shit into my clean sky. I am getting a respiratory problem from it, I am coughing, I have a headache, I can't breathe. Do you want to know what that feels like?'

Is Mother Nature saying? 'You know, I gave you some beautiful landscape, in walking distance to where you are, why did you f#%k that up, and then have to go searching for what you destroyed, in other countries?'

Is Mother Nature saying? 'What the f#%k gave you all this strong need to stay indoors, and stare at little screens to talk to strangers so far away, while you are living next to a person, that you could be talking to? Shall I force you all into physical, social distancing, just to make you crave physical contact again?'

Is Mother Nature saying to us? 'Guys just go back to basics, you really do not need all this materialistic shit you buy, build, accumulate. You are here for a very short time on my planet, yet you make a dent like you bought my planet, and you think you can do some remodelling.'

Will the Traditional Balinese even notice any difference in the world? Will they just continue to live their lives in the same way as always, with the smallest footprint on the world? Continuing to make their offerings 'Canang Sari' every morning, before they go to work in the farms, to say thank you to God (Mother Nature) and the universe, and everything on this Earth that you have supplied.... and that ain't toilet paper.

22 March 2020 - Dog Fight

You may be wondering how our village is going up there. I cannot give an update at this stage, so I thought I would give an update of our other village, the one we live in, in the South of Bali.

Some people probably believe all expats live in fancy villas, with restaurants, spas, and other expats nearby.

We did not choose to live in Bali to live a Western life, or with Westerners. So, we live in a rural village in the South, surrounded by cows and some lovely locals. Not a big village, it is basically housing built on a subdivision of an original Balinese farm. The original farmer still walks around in his sarong, grass hat and no shirt, taking his cows from paddock to paddock, or your driveway. The cows follow me when I am out, we still do not know why, but it is a problem, as I keep getting the herds mixed with the next farmer's cows. There is only the one original family, then there are very small houses, built by a developer, or people who came from the north of Bali to work in tourism. There are also some people here from other Islands.

We chose the area, as everyone had dogs, important to us, so we can walk all our rescue dogs every day, with no problems.

On the 16th March, something dawned on me; more dogs were following us on our walks than cows. More dogs were fighting. More dogs were just roaming around the streets, even in the heat of the day. Then I realised; they were hungry. They had started fighting at night for any scrap of food. Rubbish bins were turned upside down. Rubbish had also not been collected daily, as it usually was from some homes. The night before the whole street was out at 3.00 am breaking up a dog fight over one piece of garbage. I had to bring in a dog to our carport with a huge wound, and just let it get over the trauma. *He's doing well, I have him on antibiotics.*

People obviously cannot afford to pay for rubbish removal anymore and they were not feeding their dogs as much either.

So, I put out a call to friends, and they sent me money to buy dog food, and I have been visiting the homes to feed their dogs daily. We are also now paying for the neighbours' garbage to be collected, so it does not collect in large piles out the front of their homes. It allows me to chat to the grateful owners about Corona, and here are my observations so far:

No one, not one person has complained or cried 'poor me' since they lost their jobs. The people here have all discussed it, and they are mutually in agreement, that they will not go back to their villages, here in Bali or in Java. So that they do not take any risk of taking Corona with them to the elders. How long that will last, I don't know and also will depend on a few factors, like, we have no running water in this village, and the rains seem to have stopped. It costs 300,000 IDR to buy one tank of 5000 litres of water: no money, no water.

The other consensus in this village seems to be, 'close all country's borders at once, so this virus stops spreading, and stop letting in tourists.' These are people that make money in tourism, but they all agree that lives are worth more than the money.

While I was feeding an old man's dog yesterday, another woman came to give him a small bag of rice. She is not a relative of his, she just said he's all alone, as his son lost his job early in all of this, and went looking for work, and they have not heard from him since. This old man sits every day on his porch, weaving baskets, awaiting his son's return. The first day I went to feed his dog, was early in the morning, and he got the dog out of his bedroom. He's been sleeping with his dog, unusual for Balinese to do this, so that surprised me.

One other observation is that when Hubby has said to a Balinese here, 'It's sad times for Bali', they correct him, and say, 'It is sad times for the world'. The houses in our village are not close together, so we can keep our distance, daily chatting in the street is still happening. This morning on my early morning walk, I just chatted to a neighbour from behind his garden wall, he used to come out to chat. Neighbours' kids are yelling out 'Hello' through their gates, instead of coming out to pat the dogs. Last night a four-year-old went to give me a hug, out of habit, and the look on her face when I backed away, (as her mum is pregnant, so I need to think about protecting them), was heart-breaking. I bet many people are feeling that one around the world. How do you explain to a four-year-old to not hug? Everyone is really helping everyone here in this community, there is so much they are all doing for each other, there is too much to list. The main thing is not one complaint. Not one 'poor me', not one 'this is sad for Bali', not once since this all started. Remember we got quieter in Bali when China closed, impacting here early.

22 March 2020 - New Normal

Ibu just rang me. Everything is normal up there... apart from no guests, of course. I told her how today our large local fresh produce market down here, was told to close, so that's a worry for the locals here. She did not quite understand why, as everyone grows their own vegetables up there. So, she said to go to Indomaret (mini-market). She rang to see if we had masks for everyone in the family, as people from Denpasar are returning and she does not want to catch anything. So, she does get it. I told her to stay at least one metre away from people, and she said she was already standing two. *She's never been an affectionate one, so that's a normal distance for her.*

She thinks it will all be over in a month and has prepared a room for me to sleep in when I come home.

Oh Ibu ♥

24 March 2020 - Nyepi Eve

Just got back from walking the dogs and had two cute things said to us.

Old Balinese Farmer, "You can't go out tomorrow!"

We assured him we would not.

From the neighbour in the next house, twenty-five metres away, "Did you get rain last night?"

Tomorrow is Nyepi (Balinese Day of Silence). Nyepi is held once a year, in the Balinese Calendar, Nyepi Day is the new year, it will be the year 1942 in the calendar. *It feels like 1942 in the village.*

On the Island of Bali, no cars are allowed on the roads, the airport is closed, there is no internet or electricity, there are no fires allowed, not even a candle, for 24 hours. It is a day of silence, a fresh start to the new year. If we are quiet enough hopefully the bad spirits will believe the island has been deserted and move on.

It is also a day you are to reflect on your past year and plan for the next. We will certainly be doing that tomorrow. Who knows what the next year will bring, but I wish you all good health, and don't sweat the small stuff.

For those in Bali, enjoy the stars tomorrow night, soon the whole world will see them as we do, on this special night. Remember, if you are separated from your loved ones, like we are, just look at the sky, and know, no matter how far away you are, we all share the same sky.

26 March 2020 - My Corona - Necessary Travel

We have been staying home as instructed. Hubby going out once a day, wearing a mask, to the market. Me, only leaving on foot, wearing a mask to feed dogs.

I woke up early on the 24th, the daily 5.00 am earthquakes seem to wake me, even though I do not really feel them. There was a WhatsApp from the Village head in the north, saying we all needed to open our gates, so our houses could be disinfected on 24 March. That we would need to stay inside. We had gone to bed early, so I had not seen the message. It was already 6.30 am, I'd walked and fed the dogs. Hubby had woken and walked into the kitchen, and before he even had his coffee, I said, "We have to go up to the village today."

You should always let someone have coffee before you talk to them, not sure why I broke that rule.

So, after Hubby had his coffee, and calmed down, he could digest that information. We realised this may be our last chance to get up there, and we could not leave the house up there full of our shit, for the landlord to worry about where to store it for us. So, we had to do 'necessary travel'.

Our plan was to just pack up the house. Even though the lease had still one month to go, there was an indication from the village head, that this would be the last opportunity for us to pack up, see the kids and go. *Sneak in and sneak out Ibu stealth style.*

Many of the high school kids, including ours, had been in the village since 13 March visiting Grandparents. However, this time they did not return, as we got the notice that all schools were to close from the 16th. So, our kids were still up there.

Hubby jumped on the motorbike and rushed off to the market to get us some food, as we had to be in our house for two days, Nyepi and the next day. (The Governor had announced a two-day stay inside notice.)

I pulled the car cover off and put what we would need for the move in the car, removed the Chihuahua a few times, as this was not a day for him to travel.

Hubby came back, and we jumped in the car.

It was weird being in a car, after so long. The roads were quiet, as we made it to Jalan Uluwatu, a police car went past slowly with a loudspeaker, giving information on staying home, etc. *What if we can't get back?*

A stop for fuel, we do not pump our own fuel here, all attendants wearing masks.

Every person we passed was wearing a mask, apart from some tourists on their bikes, but they were not even wearing helmets, so why would they wear a mask. Even women praying alone at shrines along the highway were wearing masks.

The roads were quiet, not one truck or bus or minivan, mostly motorbikes.

We made it up there in record time. It felt like over ten years ago when we used to live up there and come down on weekends on the motorbike, to stay in Kuta. It felt safe on a bike back then, until large vehicles were allowed on the Island, then we gave up the motorbike, until now. We feel truly blessed that we won a motorbike, as Hubby has been using it to go to the market since this thing started.

We passed two tourists on their way out of the village. I guess they didn't get the memo about no unnecessary travel.

They were not wearing masks, but they did have helmets on, at least.

Driving into the village, the only people on the roads, were those allocated to disinfect.

Pulling up to the house, one of the old Dadong neighbours said, "When did you get home?"

We were wearing masks, she was not, but she was the only person out on the street. The little gossip warung closed, all doors to houses closed. *Now, that is social distancing.*

We quickly put the little fridge and my desk in the car, and we took them to our rental office.

As we were unpacking them at the office, one of our girls went past with her family, on their way to temple for a private ceremony. I noted it was only immediately family (but not all of them) hanging off the back of the little pick-up. They slowed down, and all waved goodbye, knowing they could not stop for the normal hugs. I waved with a tear in my eye, wondering when we will see them again.

We brought everything in from outside the office, that normally sits at the front, and took the signs off the door. N*o theft up here, but best not to leave it outside.*

I said goodbye to all the equipment. I know - weird, saying goodbye to bicycles and canoes. Hubby put a big padlock on the door, and closed the door, for who knows how long.

I stood at the car and gazed out at the lake, which was so calm, the water like a sheet of glass, no fisherman out, there was just silence—a surreal moment.

We went back to the house and grabbed the full gas bottle to take to the hotel, to leave there with the other bottles, as it is not safe to leave it inside a building.

We thought we could sneak into the hotel Ibu style and sneak out again.

We pulled into the hotel, everything was closed, a box on the cash register, the server window to the kitchen closed, my office already locked up.

Ibu's renovation half completed, it was like everything just stood still, the hotel was deserted, we did not expect anyone to be there.

As we walked silently around to the back, to the gas bottle area, Ibu called out from the kitchen, she was in there alone, wearing a mask. Ibu was trying to talk to us, yelling from the kitchen, while frying some vegetables.

Bapak then popped around the corner, and yelled out, "Rachel, your

Balinese is getting so good."

He meant my writing WhatsApp messages to him daily, in Balinese. (I had never needed to write it before.) They were both yelling at us at the same time, excited to have some company.

I had found some masks at the house, from Agung days, a pack of twenty, so I had brought them, thinking I could leave them there and then tell Bapak by WhatsApp where they were. So, I put them down on a bench outside and told Ibu I would just leave them there, and that there were some alcohol swabs in the bag too. Ibu wanted a demonstration on what to do with an alcohol swab, so I showed her from a distance, handy just to carry if you need to scratch your eye, to clean your finger first.

Ibu started repeating what she had been saying when Bapak was also talking, "So glad you are home, now you can stay here, in the hotel, with Ibu and Bapak, for free of course."

Ibu and Bapak are living alone in the hotel, which is the best place they can be, away from the rest of the world. Their children that live in Denpasar, are staying in Denpasar, so they do not risk infecting anyone. We feared many would return to the village, but it seems like many are aware they could risk the elders' health.

Hubby asked Ibu if she could make him a pancake for breakfast. Ibu said, "Make it yourself!" and got out the eggs and flour.

Hubby explained he did not want to go into the kitchen, just in case. Ibu said, "Oh well, go out to the restaurant, and make yourself a coffee, and wait till my vegetables are cooked. If I had known you were coming, I would have cooked earlier, you will just have to wait!"

Hubby replied, "It's okay, Ibu, coffee is fine."

We went back out to the restaurant and wiped down the table and chairs with my Dettol mix. I made two coffees at the coffee station, wearing my mask and surgical gloves.

Then we waited for Bapak to have his shower, so we could say goodbye at a distance, and we could go get the rest of the stuff out of the house and go.

We finished our coffee and went around to the side of the kitchen, Bapak was in his towel, brushing his teeth down the back. We stood two metres from Ibu, I sprayed my hands, as I do what feels like, every five minutes. Ibu stuck her hand out for some. I sprayed her hands, she smelled it, and said, "Arrgh, it smells like a hospital!"

Hubby discussed with her for a while about disinfectant, handwashing, etc. She explained her daughter Kadek, had beat him to it, with this lecture. We talked with Ibu while waiting for Bapak to clean himself and put some clothes on. Ibu said if Hubby should go to find some work, then Rachel can live here with us for as long as it takes, free, we are family, and we need to look after each other. Ibu was happy that three of her children have government jobs. Another one is a Doctor, and one is married to someone in Government, so she only has us to worry about.

We talked some more about how we have not been able to get in contact with our staff member, who went to Java with her staff member. I knew they were going to Mecca before he got married. I know they went as he posted pictures on Facebook on 24 January 2020. Then there were no more postings. I presume his wedding was cancelled, as weddings are now banned. I worry for him, as his mother has a bad heart condition, we talked about when we would hear from the Java boys again. I had sent my staff member money for his wedding, I hoped he received it.

Bapak finally came, walking up the path from the shower getting dressed. We greeted him with the Balinese greeting of hands in prayer position, and then he did the normal 'brought his hands down and tried to grab Hubby's hands in between his.' Hubby pulled back and said, "No, Bapak, I cannot!"

Bapak was probably thinking he'd just spent thirty minutes scrubbing himself from head to toe and putting on clean clothes so would not be able to infect us, but we had to point out, we may infect him.

So, we stood there, the four of us, two metres apart in a square. Bapak began his speech/prayer of goodbye, etc., and then he burst into tears. OMG, I lost it. Ibu started crying, Hubby started crying, we all stood there, not being able to stop crying. Bapak was determined to finish his speech/prayer, but he could not, he had to grab his towel and wipe the tears from his face. It was too much for me, I have never seen Bapak cry, always the rock in our family.

Bapak excused himself and said he must go do private prayer now. Ibu crying, "The vegetables should be done soon."

We told her we thought it best we leave as soon as possible, she replied, "You should just stay here, live here, no need to go back."

I explained we have all the dogs. She replied, "No dogs, yes, you go back."

We left. I could not look back. We headed to the house.

We stopped at the warung at the beginning of our road, that I shopped at daily, when up there. I went in, as Hubby can't fit into the surgical gloves; I was using a new mask and new gloves for each stop we made. *Luckily, I know how to make masks now.*

I walked in, and the old Dadong said, "When did you come home?"

Holding back tears I bought Hubby his favourite biscuits. This was necessary shopping, as Ibu did not make him breakfast, and he gets Hangry. Still, I was not sure how to hand over the money. She did not want to give me change, so as not to contaminate me! So, she told me to take two of those peanut snacks, and that's 10,000. I had IDR 15,000, so she took IDR 10,000 out of my gloved hand. I put the extra IDR 5,000 on the table, and I said goodbye. I quickly left as I was about to cry again.

Her husband was across the road, so I did the Balinese goodbye to him from four metres away. This was getting real now.

Back to the house, everything in the car, I swept out the house. We had to leave our mattress, as it would not fit in the car, and it would just get mouldy in the rental office, as it is just a warehouse really. I then sprayed disinfectant over light fittings, door handles, the kitchen, the bathroom. I nearly couldn't breathe, so I started to pull a bit of the duct tape off, but was only from the low windows, where hands could touch, the house did not fall down.

The village men were coming to spray the outside, so we had to hurry. We closed the doors for the last time. Another final moment, the memories of thirteen years of kids in that house, the cloud and rainbow murals and some kids' names, still on the walls, we left the gates open. We still had to give the keys back, and say goodbye to our kids, I was avoiding this.

We could not go in the small gangs to visit one, as she was with her grandma, and it was too compacted in there. (I will talk with her on video calls.) Another had gone past to a ceremony, three more to go.

Keys first, we pulled up at the house where the landlord had said leave the keys, well actually Hubby missed the house, it is only three metres wide, so easy to miss. It is one of his best friends, but his mind was not really focused, lucky no one on the roads, so he could just stop in the middle of the road.

I walked back up the deserted road, entering the open gate. The door and windows were shut, and all their shoes were outside, meaning all shoes. I could smell the strong smell of disinfectant, so I knew the sprayers had already been. I yelled out, "Excuse me."

I heard back "What?"

Then at the window was one of our foster kids blowing kisses to me, yelling out to me, "Hello, I love you!"

I swallowed the lump in my throat, the door opened, my husband's friend opened the door. We fostered his daughter for one year, about ten years ago, until he and his wife could find work, and get back on their feet, and take her back, we are very close to this family. The look on his face, as I stood there in my mask and gloves. We did not know what to say to each other. He did not step out of his doorway. I told him that we needed to pack up the house earlier than we expected, and here were the keys to give to the landlord. I said we had already closed the business and could not bring tourists here. He quickly snapped, "No, don't bring tourists."

I could see a tear in his eye. I put the keys, and the electricity card on the porch, and said I have disinfected them, but please could they spray them again before picking them up. This big tough Balinese Trekking

Guide was choking on his tears. I looked again at the window, and his daughter was now bawling, trying to blow me kisses still. I lost it again. I realised I can't go visit our girls, I cannot say goodbye, we can WhatsApp, as we have been, but I can't physically hug the kids, for who knows how long.

We drove off, not knowing how long it will be until we return, the streets now deserted, everyone locked inside. Thank God, I had toilet paper, as the tears did not stop.

The roads on the way home were deserted. A few ladies carrying offerings, two metres apart from each other, was all we came across for at least one hour of driving.

It was the quickest drive from North to South, we have done in ten years. We made it back by 3.00 pm, with a car filled to the top with stuff, which we are slowly unpacking today, as yesterday was Nyepi.

When we pulled into the entrance of our village down here in the South, a Mangku was sitting in the middle of the road on bamboo matting, surrounded by offerings, and praying. There were at least twenty Balinese nearby, watching the Mangku, some with masks, some without. The only socially distancing seemed to be from the Mangku. The Pecalang waved us through when they recognized us. *Glad we could get back in.*

Yesterday was Nyepi, and today we cannot leave the house again, but we do have the internet.

This morning when I got up before sunrise, I heard the roar of the ocean, the birds were chirping, roosters were clucking, dogs were barking. I realised yesterday they did not do that, even the ocean took the Day of Silence seriously.

10 April 2020 - New Name

I could not get hold of Ibu last night, only Elvis. I had already had my daily check-in with Ibu Dua in Australia. So, I sent Bapak a WhatsApp to check in on them, as Elvis gave me nothing.

Bapak has managed to come up with a new name for me. I am now, 'Reshelt'. He even gave hubby a new name, we shall call him 'Cibranh'.

Stay safe everyone, may you soon be reunited with any family you are separated from.

21 April 2020 - Needs vs Wants

About ten years ago, Ibu Dua was coming to Bali, and found out we still did not have a TV. Ibu Dua, is very much into her tennis (playing and watching) and loves watching the Olympics. The Olympics coincided with Ibu Dua's visit, so Ibu Dua decided for Christmas, we needed a TV. *This obviously has nothing to do with her upcoming visit in the following year.*

I personally cannot stand watching sport. I am not good at sitting still long enough to watch TV. It also makes too much unnecessary noise. I prefer to hear nature and am so blessed down here, to hear the ocean, the birds, monkeys, and cows. Oh, and my dogs when a stranger is in the street. I don't have the Gossip Dadongs down here, so it is very quiet, which I love.

Sometimes, when our Western family come to stay, they do go a little crazy with the quiet and play music on their phones etc., but we never do. We do not even have a stereo or any music device.

So, back then, for Christmas, we got a delivery truck to visit on Christmas Day. In those days, Christmas Day was not as celebrated in Bali as it is now, it was hard to find a tree, decorations, etc., and department stores were open, just like any other day. The TV arrived in a large box, and the delivery guy placed it inside, near the front door, and there it stayed.

It became quite handy to put your keys on, your mobile phone, etc.

Ibu Dua rang a few days later, to ask how we were enjoying the TV... Well, I had to break it to her, that it was still in the box. I explained to Ibu Dua that to enjoy TV here, you needed a satellite dish, or you could get an aerial and watch some entertaining Indian Soap Operas, Ibu enjoys them. So, Ibu Dua wanted to know how much it cost to get a satellite dish, we explained there were different packages. Ibu Dua wanted to know which one would have the news, oh, and the Olympics. As we intended on moving to a new house, I explained that it would not be a good time to get a satellite dish, and we could discuss it when we moved to the new house. We also did not have very high power to the house. As the rice cooker, toaster and kettle had just caught on fire when I plugged in the laptop, and melted all over the little fridge, one more electrical appliance may just burn the whole place down.

So, when we moved, Ibu Dua rang to see how our move went and had the TV come out of its box yet. We had become quite accustomed to the box being an entrance table, and we had it placed near the front door at the new house and put a sarong over it. *So, thank you Ibu Dua, it was most useful.*

Ibu Dua's trip to Bali was approaching, and the TV being still in the box, seemed to be of some concern. So, Ibu Dua offered to pay for a satellite connection, so we could enjoy TV. Ibu Dua insisted this would be good for our business, as we would be up to date on current world issues, and not just what was happening in Bali. This probably stemmed from my lack of knowledge as to who the current Prime Minister of Australia was at that time. *Can you blame me, who could keep up? I could get that information from the Balinese. Who needs a TV?*

Once I went to visit a friend at his tattoo parlour, and the first thing he said to me was, "Johnny Howard out."

We decided Ibu Dua should not have to pay, we would get it connected. So, we chose the cheapest package. *Hubby is Dutch.* Assuring Ibu Dua, that there would be Olympics.

The day came, the satellite dish installed. Hubby had taken the TV out of the box. I was not enjoying the box so much after that, it was not as sturdy without the TV inside. *Now, where will we put our keys, etc.?*

Hubby was not as impressed with the TV as he thought he would be. He decided he would really need a chair to sit on, to watch it, as sitting on the tiles was uncomfortable. Hubby had finally taken a chair from our dining table, we had always had a table to eat at, we were very civilized. No, not really, I just can't do the squat and eat thing. As the new house did not have a kitchen, well, I did nearly burn the last one down, I had turned the dining table into a makeshift kitchen bench, so a spare chair was available. Hubby then decided he needed to put the TV on a stand, as it was too low on the floor. Another dining chair was used. Then he needed a coffee table to put his beer on while watching the TV, and the box had since been destroyed by puppies. Another dining chair was used, and as the last chair was already being used for the rice cooker, we were suddenly 'needing' furniture. This TV was causing a chain reaction. Suddenly we 'needed' all this stuff we have never needed before, just to watch TV.

Ibu Dua gave it one week after the satellite dish installation, then she rang, bursting with excitement, to see how we were enjoying the TV. I said it was fine. Ibu Dua, seemed a little disappointed. Ibu Dua asked if we were up to date with all the latest news. I told her, "Yes, I was, but I was a little confused with the latest current world events", having had such a large gap of so many years, since watching the news.

Ibu Dua enthusiastically asked what I needed help with, in my current world events catch up. So, I asked her all the essential questions, such as: "Who the hell is this kid with the funny hair called Justin?" "When did Brad leave Jennifer, and have all these kids with Angelina Jolie?" "Was Madonna trying to copy the United colours of Benetton?" "Who is this giant woman called Kimora?" And, last, but not least, "Who the hell are these Kardashians, I can't keep up?"

Ibu Dua said, "What on earth, are you watching?"

I answered, "E-News, that was the only news that came with this satellite package."

Now, we are in a different house, and we still have that TV, it is behind the door in the spare bedroom, we stopped watching it about eight years ago. Hubby was finding he was getting addicted to watching TV and not doing much else, but he had learnt how to do a 'Smokey Eye' and how to 'Smize'. I was not aware how much newfound knowledge watching TV had brought Hubby, until some tourists once asked if he could take their photo, and instead of 'Cheese', he said "SMIZE." He also once said to a tourist "Easy Breezy Cover Girl"... that was when we had the satellite turned off.

Lately, Smize has been an essential skill that we learnt, so the TV did give us some knowledge. When you wear a mask, you need to know how to 'smile with your eyes'. I am so used to smiling at everyone I pass, I now go out without sunglasses on, so I can still smile with my mask on.

I always believe everything happens for a reason, and what I had hoped for during this Rona time, is that more people would start getting back to Needs vs Wants. However, it seems not everyone sees it that way. I read a comment, in an article yesterday, how in a Western country, a landlord had threatened to turn off the cable TV, if a tenant did not pay their rent. Now, kicking them out would be totally unreasonable during this time, as a roof over your head is a need. But a comment from one woman was, "That was totally unreasonable, as Cable TV was essential during this Pandemic, as it was needed to get through this staying at home during COVID-19."

I am starting to see clearly now, why Climate Change was such a problem, before this current Big C.

Funny, how the C-word has always been a dirty word. I am hoping when this is all over, we can all see "C" differently in the world. Just as you can look at a C-Word differently, you can look at the world differently too. Remember; C is also for Caring, C is for Children, C is for Conservation, C is for Compassion, C is for Considerate, C is for Consolidate, C is for Categorize, C is for Celebration, C is for Culture, C is for Community, C is for Change, C is for Clean, C is for Clear, C is for Calm, C is for Can Do.

SMIZE everyone.

3 May 2020 - Who Is That Masked Woman?

We have been very busy, working sun-up till sun-down, busier than before Rona's visit. That is because hubby was searching for a broken water pipe, which turned into a full redesign of the whole backyard... It had started to look like Hubby had tried to conceal a dead body or two in the backyard. Lucky it is a very small yard, as it turned out to be a mammoth task. As we must be locked in, it seemed the perfect time to redo the backyard. Well, no, it seemed the perfect time to fix the backyard, after Hubby dug it up like a gopher, and the rains came.

Oh, how I love rain, as we then have water, it just did not suit the giant holes in the backyard. Although we could have turned it into natural mud pools, there would be no clients, as everyone was locked in.

Tip, if you ever want to use large white river pebbles in your garden, don't. Over the years, we had accumulated more white river pebbles than I had realized. When the giant holes swallowed them up, and they got stuck in the mud, it took at least four weeks to dig them out and wash them. *Don't forget Hubby is Dutch, there was no way he was just going to let the earth swallow up those pebbles; he paid for them.*

That's what we have been up to, pebble washing. I was lucky to escape pebble washing at times, with dog food cooking and feeding. My only time out of the house was for the dog feeding. Neighbours would ask, where Hubby was, and my answer every day was either "Digging a hole" or "Pebble washing." They think I am a little strange anyway.

Now, with our lock-in, note, some areas aren't as locked in as others, we just happen to be in the red zone. Not that I was aware we were in the red zone until Facebook told me. If it were not for Facebook, I don't think many people in the world would have even realized there was Corona. A letter from the Adat Government for our area was posted on Facebook, saying that we would not be able to leave our area, without a letter from the village head. You would need to report when, why, how and who, etc., and that no one could have visitors. Which was fine, we had not had any visitors anyway, apart from a neighbour who pops in every single day. *I would be sending this to him immediately, as he always forgets his mask. I spray him down, but he just likes to wander in, to see how the hole digging is going, cigarette in his mouth (I guess it's hard to wear a mask then), he is just bored.*

I showed the screenshot of the letter to Hubby, and he said "Good, but how will they let everyone know?"

Well, at first, I thought, stupid question really, who does not have Facebook? So, I said, "Maybe they will put a letter under our doors?"

But then I realized some of the people in our area cannot read, so a letter or Facebook was not going to work...

We had a neighbour that kept sitting on our doorstep for the first few weeks of all of this. Hubby had to keep explaining to him that he could not do that anymore, he kept forgetting daily. The neighbour across the road commented the guy does not have a TV, so does not know about Corona, and the next time he said, the guy did not go to school. Eventually, the sitting neighbour got it. He still tried to shake Hubby's hand the other day when they both ended up at the local warung to buy water at the same time.

Well, the night the official letter was posted on Facebook, the Pecalang came to the Balinese entrance door to our property.

Not exactly to the door, one of our dogs was not letting them at the door. Hubby had obviously trained him to not let anyone, sit or stand, or knock on that door, as he was getting frustrated with the neighbour who liked to sit there. He's not exactly our dog, he belongs to the street, we all feed him, he chooses where he will sleep, depending on who left their gate open or who's got the best dinner that night. We managed to get a collar on him only two months ago, it only took four years. Obviously, holding a grudge from when the vet and I netted him and cut off his balls. Everyone in the street has a different name for him, but he does not come when you call any of them. He's huge, he reminds me of Scooby-Doo, he's our security, he will not let anyone in our street that does not belong there, without barking, a very deep bark. He should be called Pecalang.

Now, Pecalang, a word not often heard by the average tourist to Bali. Some tourists have chosen to stay in Bali during this time, I will not get started on them, or that will be a vent that will probably make the Australian news. However, these delightful tourists, *not,* have started to learn who the Pecalang are. I like to refer to these tourists as 'Instagram Influenzas', and I will leave it at that. For those of us that live here, we certainly know who the Pecalang are. We respect them, sometimes fear them. (This is due to the fact their word is final, no judge, no juror, no jail, punishment can be on the spot.) So, we don't mess with these bad boys. In times like this, everyone's a little jumpy. We do what they tell us to do, no questions asked.

The Pecalang are our Guards, it is a voluntary role, and it is a traditional role that stems back to keeping demons from the villages. However, in modern times, their role comes into play under a directive from the Administrative Adat Government for each area, working together with the Customary Adat Government. Ibu's village in the north only has Customary Government, and only Pecalang, no Police. Our village in the south has both. They work together to protect our area. Police may also come into our village. *I've only seen a Policeman once here in this village, I think he was just visiting a friend.*

The Pecalang are the guys that closed the beaches and put up the roadblocks... Usually, you only see roadblocks during ceremonies. These guys have been busy trying to keep the Influenzas off the beaches. It has been a daunting task for them, as the Influenzas constantly question the Pecalang's authority. It seems if you are not wearing a uniform, only traditional clothing, you have no right to stop an Influenza from surfing. It seems Influenzas think there is a thing called 'freedom to do what you want or go where you want'. *Ah, wrong country guys.*

On Nyepi a foreign jogger was stopped from jogging, chaining the tourist may be the new norm.

Back to the Pecalang visit. We were in the middle of eating dinner, the barking was not stopping, this was a serious invasion to our peaceful street, and to our dinner time.

I went to investigate, I put on a mask, and went out the front and opened the big door to our property. Six Pecalang were standing in perfect formation 1.5 metres away from each other, in a semi-circle facing our Balinese Door. They were wearing masks, five were in traditional outfits, one was in an Army camouflage outfit. *I guess they thought they needed a uniform, and some backup to talk to a Bule.*

They were all standing in the dark, looking at me with some confusion and suspicion, then one asked if Pak Sibran was home. They knew Hubby by name, but they did not seem to know who I was. I put my hands together and gave the old Om Swastiastu, Smized, told the dog to stop barking, as these people were here to protect us, not harm us and asked them to please wait. They did not seem happy.

Hubby put on his mask and came to the door, and one of the Pecalang asked him quite sternly who I was, completely ignoring the fact that I was standing right there. Hubby answered, "Oh, this is my girlfriend."

I glared at Hubby. I did not feel, that during these times, especially when he was not to have visitors, that he should be pretending, he had a girl over. But Hubby likes to joke around, so he kept going with that one, 'the wife's' buried in the backyard, etc'. *Geez, that's it, they will ask to come in and see these huge newly covered graves in the backyard. Hubby will be taken away for murder, and I will be arrested for prostitution.*

Eventually, Hubby realized they were taking this a little too seriously, and he said I was his wife. They weren't taking this lightly and questioned why they have never seen me before. He told them I had not left the house in six weeks.

It took a lot of convincing, as they unanimously agreed that they had never seen me before, they were very suspicious. One mentioned that the young guy on my right, was the new village head, and asked if I had met him (as everyone should meet the village head). I knew hubby had met him recently to get our new ID cards, but I was in the north at the time. *Well, no, I had not, but I can assure you I am who I say I am.*

This guy looked young enough to be my son. The new young village head started to ask me questions and then commented on how well I spoke Indonesian. We went on to speaking Balinese, so I finally won him over. *Phew, I will not be arrested for prostitution tonight.*

When I explained to the panel of men, that I did not leave the village, but I did walk around every morning before sunrise, and before sunset feeding dogs, one man proclaimed, "Oh, you are the Vet!"

I explained I am not a Vet, but yes, I did get all the neighbours' balls chopped off, do medicate the dogs, and feed them. So, finally, they believed me, that I was, 'The Wife', and the tone started to change.

Then one asked about his dog's skin problem. So, I said I would go inside, and get some medicine for that. Another wanted something for ticks, then another for something else. *Turns out they all had three dogs each. So, I have something to work with.*

I asked them to please wait.

I left them outside, with Hubby still standing in the doorway with this semi-circle of guys facing him, like a panel of executioners ready to determine our fate.

It took me a while to find some small bottles for them to take the medication home with them, some syringes, and I wanted to sterilize everything. It felt like I was taking far too long, I was getting a little nervous. Then I heard laughter, lots of laughter, so I knew they will still there. *Was Hubby though?*

When I came out, Hubby was talking dirty talk in Balinese, and oh boy, had the tone changed. It was like a bunch of fourteen-year-old boys giggling over porn magazines they had found under one of their fathers' beds. I handed over the different bottles of meds, with my gloved hands. First, I gave them a quick second spray of Dettol in front of them, just to make sure they knew we were always careful, which was the whole point of their visit in the first place. *Which we have not actually discussed yet.*

I told them that the medicine (Ivermectin) I was giving to the man with the hairless dog, was currently being tested for treatment for Coronavirus. So, if it comes back as safe to use on humans, they can all come over, and I will inject them all. Then the one holding the syringe meds for his hairless dog looked at it in his hand, pondered it for a short time, and then asked me, "Can I use this on my hair, so my hair will grow?"

I looked at him, and I pointed to Hubby's thinning hair and said, "Don't you think I would have already tried that with Hubby?"

Everyone laughed, and they thanked us, lots of goodbyes, back on their motorbikes, and off they went.

26 May 2020 - Release Forms

Just a tad excited, we got our paperwork organised today to visit the village in the north tomorrow. Taking up lots of rice and some masks. I sent Bapak a message and he sent one back and called me brother and looks forward to seeing me. *So, won't Ibu be surprised, as I don't think they realise we are coming?*

Will get some photos of Ibu tomorrow.

To be perfectly honest, my excitement is purely based on the fact I have only been out of this village twice in two months. Once, to buy two months of baby supplies for a new-born in this village. Once to the hardware store to buy a pipe.

Tomorrow I will be breaking Groundhog Day.

28 May 2020 - Breaking Groundhog Day

So, yesterday was the big outing. We had our Surat Jalan (letter to travel) from our village head here in the south. We had WhatsApp permission from the village head in the north. We were ready to go and headed off at 8.00 am.

Then we had to go back home and put in a bag of bras a guest had given me on our very last tour, way back in February, as I had received a WhatsApp, as we were about to leave the village. It was from one of the girls in the village head's office reminding me to not forget Oleh Oleh ('souvenirs', but in our case its code for donated clothes). I sent back a message that we only had bras, she then asked if we had any trousers. I replied, no, as we have had no guests, so bras it is!

First stop was to our local warung, as we like to buy the rice supplies from the lovely lady there, as her husband lost his job. We piled up the bags of rice in the car, and then had to show her and her husband the Surat Jalan, as they too would like to leave the village to visit their family in Karangasem. You can never just 'pop in' anywhere in Bali, there will always be a long conversation. *Oh well, at least now I would have a better indication of what is open and what is closed as it is later in the morning.*

So, finally out of our village and headed down Jalan Uluwatu. I was impressed that every single person was wearing a mask. Having not ventured this far in a while, this was one of the first things I wanted to see. Did not see one Westerner, so all locals, all wearing their masks and going about their day. Every open shop had a hand washing station, so they were following the rules. A lot of shops were closed, but you could still buy a mobile phone at six stores on the same street. You could still go to the supermarket, and most of the minimarts were open. One was closed with black plastic on the window, but apart from that, it appeared fifty per cent of small shops were open.

It was too early to tell if restaurants were closed temporarily or would open later.

Passed our Border crossing, the guys were having coffee, obviously too early to check people. *Kopi Dulu.*

Down the hill into Jimbaran, and that was when I noticed closures. All the hotels boarded up; the minimarts all closed. McDonald's was open, I could not tell if the Pizza Hut would be open later.

Onto the highway, very quiet, everyone wearing masks, including people in cars. I had mine in my lap.

Passing all the little shops, you know the mom and pop ones, they all seemed open, but the larger places were all closed. *Looks like anyone that had staff has closed, but if you just run a shop outside your home then you can stay open?*

Hotels closed, hotels on the highway that before Rona were only occupied by locals, usually business hotels or one was a 'Karaoke' hotel. I did once meet a lovely Australian at that hotel, to collect some donations. We had a giggle over the hotel she had chosen. It was closed now. *I guess the men could wear condoms, but the sexy girls may not look as good in hazmat suits.*

Past the roundabout, near Kuta. Okay, it is now a tunnel, but it will always be the roundabout to me.

Too early to tell if Bali Galleria was still open.

Past BMIC hospital. They seem to be doing well, lots of cars in their parking lot.

Still had not seen a Westerner, and had only seen one old lady not wearing a mask so far.

The big music store closed, hotels with chains across the driveway, we continued towards Sanur.

As we travelled along the highway, I realized you could buy a woven basket, you could buy wooden furniture from a little wholesaler, but not from a retail store. You could not get your pool pump serviced, we could not buy supplies for our canoes, or build a bike, but importantly you could buy wine. It started to hit me how many people were out of work, and not just in tourism.

Further, towards the turn to Ubud, you could buy grass. If you wanted to go to the big Karaoke bar on the highway, you would need to take a machete to get through the grass. *That's a lot of sexy girls out of work, oh, and gardeners.*

You could buy pots, and you could buy water features, you could buy statues, but you could not get any snacks. *Good thing I brought lots or Hubby will get hangry later.*

The turn onto Prof Dr Ida Bagus Highway, you could still buy a shrine, but you could not get a drink or any nibbles, as all the minimarts had plastic over their windows and shut. You could get Babi Guiling, fresh off the BBQ if you parked at the stoplights.

We finally came to a temperature check station, but it was on the other side of the highway. *I guess we will go through that later, lucky we have our letter.*

Past a Police Post, but they were all lined up for their morning inspection (Attention), so straight through.

They were re-doing the bridge, again, so all traffic had to go across to the other side. This would have been banked up for hours in the past, but easy, straight through on the single lane.

Past the Safari Park; a fence across the driveway. A few security guards sitting on plastic chairs at the entrance.

We took our turn off the highway to go up through the little villages, the first village we went though there were a few people without masks, this was the first time we had not seen masks.

We came to a market, all wearing masks.

Continued to the Gianyar border. Saw a little tiny pup needing medicine and food, so took a note to get to it on the way back as we couldn't take a pup up into another region.

Crossed the Gianyar/Bangli border, no one around.

Arrived at the border of Taman Bali, we expected a check at this point as the village has recorded a lot of cases and is in currently in 14-day lockdown. *Hmmm? Must be coffee time.*

For a village in lockdown, the few people on the street were not wearing masks.

Continued to Bangli city.

Now, Bangli Region has the highest cases on the Island, so surely, we would go through a checkpoint. The city did not look like anything was closed, everyone was wearing masks, but nothing was closed.

Past the Psychiatric Hospital. The number of cars parked in and outside that hospital seemed to indicate everyone went a bit stir crazy with self-isolation. *I guess I can't get an appointment today?*

Out of the city, and up the long road to Kintamani. *Someone needs to cut the grass at the high schools.*

Continued through the small villages. 90% wearing a mask, 9% wearing them under their chin, and one old lady sitting on a bench on the side of the road not wearing a mask, had an itchy boob. I felt for her. *I know what it is like when you can't see what's under your boob.*

She was determined to find out the cause of her itch and had one breast out and was pulling it as far as she could to look under. *See if you do not wear a mask lady, this is the result.*

As we were ascending the caldera, we noticed a brand-new sign that said Kedisan Village. *Umm, this is not our village, this is too far down; did someone put the sign in the wrong place?*

As soon as we passed that sign, we noticed hand washing stations in front of every single building, including driveways to homes. They were made from various ingenious materials, buckets, pots, water gallons, etc.

We reached the top of the caldera. The museum closed, everything else closed. The bank was open, and there was a sensible social distancing line of people waiting to go in. *Ah, the first day opening after the public holidays.*

We approached the viewing point on the rim of the caldera, the view as beautiful as always. Mt Batur was saying Hello across the black scar from the 1963 eruption. Due to rain the previous night the sky was clean and bright blue and large white clouds were in amazing formations. *I still am in awe of this view, no matter how many times I see it.*

Turned at the Penelokan police station, no one around, and down to the lake. As the lake came into view, we could see the water was like glass and looked perfect for Wayan to take tourists canoeing. *Oh, well, one day.*

We arrived in the village, well the outskirts, everything was open, everyone wearing masks, every building with a hand washing station. We could turn left to Ibu's hotel or right to the village. *We better go to the hotel first, Kopi Dulu.*

We pulled into the hotel and noticed one of the staff sweeping, wearing a mask. Ibu has had all her staff on a rotating roster so that they could get a day's work with her, then they worked in their family farms. We parked the car and saw one of the twins, now Head of Housekeeping, wearing a mask. Ibu's new rooms had a nice new roof. So, the building has continued.

We walked around to the restaurant; a brand-new sink built quite tastefully in stone right next to the reception. *Ibu will most likely wash her hair in that one.*

We said Hello to little Wayan as she was sweeping, and we walked into the empty restaurant.

My office was dark from no activity, the door closed. Walked past the kitchen servery and heard Ibu yell out Hubby's name. Ibu was out the back-washing dishes, I could see Nenagh, the cook in the kitchen, she was not wearing a mask, nor was Ibu.

We went to greet Ibu, Hubby's first words to her were "Ibu, why are you not wearing a mask?"

Ibu's first words, to me, were, "You got fat." Then she did the normal polite greeting.

Bapak came around the corner, no mask, and said that I looked fat. Bapak threw that in with the polite greetings and instead of asking if I was well, he commented I must be well, as I had gotten fat.

Ibu wanted to show me the new renovations, the problem being that 'social distancing' had not reached her vocabulary, yet, or she had forgotten about it. So, she grabbed my arm and pulled me over to see the progress.

I made sure she opened the doors to the rooms, so I did not touch the door handles, and I followed her in. *They look amazing, let's hope one day someone will use them.*

Her building workers were not wearing masks. All women, apart from the foreman, who did have a mask under his chin. She explained they were all family and she wanted to give them work and when we came back, we could use them to build our house on the land she gave us. *Here we go again.*

I just nodded in agreement. One day that house will be built, on a good day.

We chatted some more, keeping our distance, Ibu said they had guests coming for lunch, the Geopark government team. *Yes Ibu, we arranged the meeting with them for later.*

Ibu then said she had a tourist staying in a room. I questioned that and clarified it must have been a local. She said, "Bule", but then said he lived in Bali and was married to a local. Ibu said, "We will be open in June as it's all safe here."

"Umm Ibu, you will not be opening in June. It may be safe here, but no one can come, and then, of course, this is in Bangli region, and Bangli has the most cases, so the reputation may be a problem."

Oh no, Ibu assured me, Bangli had hardly any cases. I gave up.

Hubby and I sat down for coffee, alone, and then Ibu's daughter arrived on her motorbike, telling us she had seen us stop in Bangli, when she had finished her night shift. (Ibu's daughter is an obstetrician and works at the Bangli hospital.) She started saying how busy it was and how stressful it was to work there and seeing so many cases come in, it was scary. I said, "But Ibu thinks there are none."

Ibu's daughter shushed me and said, "We do not tell Ibu and Bapak, or they will get stressed."

Oh, dear!

Now, I understood the reasoning behind this denial with Ibu. Ibu stressed is worse than Mt Agung erupting, but if people are not aware, then how do they keep safe? She assured me Ibu did not leave the hotel, ever, so she would be fine. *Okay, that's fine that Ibu is also having Groundhog Day, but these workers are coming and going, what about the Bule staying etc.?*

We excused ourselves, as we had to report to the village head, and then go check our equipment storage. I was dreading checking it, as I presumed everything was covered in mould from being locked up.

As we drove towards the village heads' office, everything seemed open, all with washing stations, some had used electric water dispensers, minus the electricity. Everyone was wearing masks. However, there was no one in any place open (they are all just little shops outside people's homes,) but they were all empty. Although tourism is not big there, fifty percent of the village live away and work on the beach, the Bitch ladies and the drivers etc. Money has always been sent home, so, although they can grow vegetables here, it is too cold to grow rice, so rice is what they needed, and they needed to buy it, so that's why we only brought up rice and masks. I noticed the warungs that previously had large bags of rice for sale at the front did not have any.

We parked outside the village heads' office, and hubby said for me to go in. He would wait in the car; otherwise, it would take too long as they would all want to talk.

I walked in and was sternly told to walk back out and wash my hands.

Once I found their washing station, which was tucked away off to the left, I went back in. I gave one of the girls the bag of bras and told her Putu had asked for them.

The village head came out, and he asked how many he could have. We all had a huge laugh and made fun of him for a while, about the fact he wanted a bra, and that if he had two heads, it might work, or he could sew one into two masks.

Hubby must have thought I was taking too long, so he came in, went out, washed his hands, and then came back in.

Then another village head came out to explain that we now have a village head for Customary, and one for Administration. He wanted to talk to Hubby, he does not like talking to a woman. He explained that the new administrative border for Kedisan was a lot larger now, thus the new sign. He announced that we could open in June. Hubby laughed and said, "Well, there will be no tourists in June."

Hubby had to explain what was happening in the rest of the world, as it seemed they thought, if we open, they will come.

He asked how our business was going in the south. *Umm? We do not have a business in the south, we only have one here in this village, we have been locked in our house, and we have no income.*

He asked for our Surat Jalan. *Finally, someone wanted to see it.*

He asked how long we would be there when we were leaving, etc., *so at least he's on that.*

After leaving the village heads' office 45 minutes later, we headed towards the harbour.

We were stopped by guys spraying vehicles with disinfectant. We knew them all, so, they wanted the windows wound down to have a chat, yet they sprayed us before we could put the windows back up.

We called one of our girls and said meet us at the Balai Banjar, so we could get this rice handed out. We did not want to go in the small rabbit warren gang of the village, so we organized for a friend, who had a motorbike to take bags of rice in, and for our girls to come to us. Air hugs and lots of 'I miss you'. I didn't cry as we have been talking on WhatsApp and video calling the girls daily.

Finally, to our office/warehouse and relieved to find that although it was locked up for two months, it didn't smell. This was because we were blessed and the strong winds last year took the whole roof off, and we had to replace it, which we needed to do anyway, as the year before it flooded from a leak.

The Mangku came down and helped Hubby cut the grass at the front of the office, as Wayan seemed to have not been keeping it maintained. *Maybe his cows don't like this type of grass?*

Then we got out our new bikes, as the villagers are going to use them since we can't. I know they will be returned all broken, but it is selfish to leave them locked up when people can use them, that can't afford fuel now.

We left the bikes with the Mangku, rang Wayan to organise handing them out, and we went back to the hotel. Where the government had all arrived for lunch. No social distancing amongst the group, no masks.

I walked past the men and said, "Selamat Makan," and hoped they would put on their masks before we were to chat.

I went into the kitchen, and Ibu was cooking. She wanted to know what Hubby wanted for lunch, and she would make Hubby some chicken, since he had gotten skinny because he was only eating rice. *He must have complained to her, he is not doing well being a forced vegetarian. She did not offer to make me any lunch, I guess I was too fat.*

I told her we had brought food, it was okay, and we would be leaving straight after this meeting.

One of the guys from the Government (Geopark) came to the serving window and asked me a question about tourism. He had been sitting with the ex-Camat (Head of the District), whom I had not noticed, but Hubby had.

The ex-Camat came up once before, when I had a Geopark meeting and I had forgotten to tell Hubby that the Camat was now out of jail, as he was at my meeting last month. *I guess if you go to jail for corruption and serve your time, you can still stay in Politics?*

We ended up having our meeting with the group through the kitchen serving window. *Well, at least that was social distancing.*

They seemed to be unaware, just as everyone else that foreign tourists would not be flocking here on the 1st of June 2020.

We said goodbye to Ibu, and then went to say goodbye to Bapak, who commented that it was very quiet up here, and Kuta must be so busy. "Umm, Bapak, Kuta is like Nyepi, everything is closed?"

Bapak nervously laughed when I told him that. *Oops, his daughter, the Midwife, will not be happy we told him that.*

We left, both a bit quiet, taking it all in, how they lived in a bubble, but torn as to whether we burst that bubble or not.

It was a quiet drive home.

We stopped and looked for the pup on the way back, we could not see it, but we did find a feeding mother, so hoped the pup belonged to her. She would not let us get close, but she was the same colour, type, etc. *So annoyed I forgot the Ivomec, as we passed quite a few hairless dogs in that village. That little pup would have been fine with some Ivomec. Gets rid of parasites, cures the Mange, it's liquid gold. I am running low, no idea how I will get the next lot with Australians not coming. Ivomec is apparently a cure for COVID, but I am not sharing it with any humans when so many dogs need it.*

We came to the part of the highway that we had to be tested, it was 2.00 pm, but the testers had all gone home, so we continued all the way home, not being stopped once.

When we reached the edge of our village in the South, we had to stop at the Apotek (pharmacy) on Jalan Uluwatu. Something seemed to have bitten me under my chin, and it looked like I had a goitre. *Maybe that was there before I saw Ibu and Bapak and that's why I looked fat? I really must learn to look in a mirror before I leave the house.*

We had to swerve to avoid a Westerner with a surfboard on his motorbike, on the wrong side of the road, with no mask or helmet. Hubby was so angry, as he goes to the market every morning, he sees what's happening in the streets. He's been complaining about the 'bloody tourists' for a month now. He tells me about the 'bloody tourists' that obviously have stayed to surf, yet the beaches are closed, the bloody tourists that do not wear masks, or helmets. The bloody tourists that break down fences to get to the beach, or complain on Facebook about the rules here... *Not sure Hubby should own a Tourist Business anymore.*

When we took our dogs for a walk later that afternoon, we came across two of our male neighbours with their young kids cooking in the bushland, they were bored, so they took their kids 'camping.' We talked with them for quite some time. Both men have lost their jobs, they both worked in hotels. They had some strong ideas as well and were singling out one country. I had never seen Balinese talk about one country like this. They were very opinionated about Bules breaking the closed beach rules to go and surf as well. They were shocked to hear that the friendly Australians may not be here for six months.

What will happen with tourism in Bali in the future, the when, the how, etc. is not something anyone can predict at this moment when Indonesian COVID cases are still on the rise.

Stay safe everyone.

7 June 2020 - Gotong Royong

This morning, our village here in the South is having Gotong Royong bersihkan (community clean up). The village has a lot of empty blocks of land. Well, not empty, as nature has taken over the land. There are also a lot of empty houses, where nature has also taken over, inside the buildings.

The area was developed ten years ago. The developer built some small basic houses, affordable for young local couples. However, mains water never came, and no one bought those houses. Now trees are growing through them, and they sit there as a reminder of how development can fail without proper planning. The area is one big dry sandstone rock, and without running water, it is hard to live cheaply. Water trucks charge IDR 250,000-300,000 for 5000 litres. *Mind you, you never get 5000 litres, as they spill most of it on the way up the steep hill to the village.*

So, each street of the little village now, has only those homes occupied, that have either paid for a thin water pipe, to go across vacant land to get to their home, or has rainwater tanks such as we do. There is one farmer who has a spider web of pipes coming from the only water connection in the village, leading to various homes in different streets. Each street now has approximately five homes occupied, there are approximately 200 people at the most in the village, so everyone knows everyone.

In our village in the north, there are approximately 1500 residents, nearly 2000 when all are back in the Kampung, they also do Gotong Royong. As do most villages in Bali. To be honest, I am not sure it is done in places such as Canggu, where the residents are 95% foreigners, who probably think it is better to just pay someone to clean up.

The way Gotong Royong works is, the Banjar send out an official notice (or talk to those that cannot read). We do not have letterboxes here, so, you get a notice under your door, or handed to you if you are out gossiping with neighbours on the street. Everyone is allocated an area.

Hubby and I were allocated Temple duty this morning, but there were too many in the small Temple, so we moved to the surrounding paddocks.

Hubby and an old man are somewhere in the bushes with their sickles at present. *I have gone home for a coffee.*

They will need to clear a whole vacant block of overgrown shrubs. No idea who owns the land, but that does not matter, this is about cleaning the whole village, not your own land.

I have been picking up plastic, an old man told me there was lots in front of his house. *Thanks for that.*

I've picked up the rubbish in front of his house, it looks like it may have come from another house and was dragged there by dogs. No Whipper Snippers, all manual labour, everyone's rubbish is everyone's, including sticks, weeds, offerings and grass. So, I am done for the day, five hours is enough for me, and it is getting hot now.

I walked back home, past a house that a Bule, married to an Indonesian, used to live in years ago, and it reminded me of him. We became friends with the couple when they lived there. One day I was in front of his house, with two other neighbours, picking up large rocks that had washed down the night before in the rains, so we could get our car through. He came out, stood in his driveway and said in his booming deep voice, "In America, we've got people to do that!"

Shortly after, one of the Pecalang came by on his motorbike. He handed us all the letter for a Goyong Rotong for the following day. I said, "Well, at least everyone can help tomorrow."

The Bule looked at the letter and asked, "What's this?"

I walked up to him and translated it and explained it to him.

When I said, "You bring your sickle, broom and hoe, and we will all weed and clean the streets together."

He answered, "I'm American, I don't have a Sickle! And, besides, I keep my property clean, I'm not cleaning up anyone else's shit!"

Let's just say he only lasted one year in our village.

16 June 2020 - Ibu's Bubble

Ibu rang me last night extremely excited that we would be coming back now. *Huh?*

"Oh yeah, everything is back to normal, the war is over."

Well, that's what it seemed like, that Ibu was announcing the Corona War was over, and it was all back to normal.

Poor Ibu, she should watch more on her TV besides Indian Soap Operas. Not that I know if the TV news is providing the correct information since we do not have a TV. I had only just been reading in the local news, how the police had pulled over a lot of local 'tourists' from Denpasar, on Sunday in the Kintamani area. They had gone up for a weekend drive, and when police pulled them over and asked why they had come to an area where all tourism facilities were closed, they answered, that 'they were bored in their homes in Denpasar.'

Now, Denpasar is having a huge local transmission rate and these 'bored people' decided it would be a good idea to go to Kintamani without masks for the weekend. I had also read that a certain Hot Springs in the area had opened. The government had said that was prohibited, but they seemed to be still operating. Typical, we do not have a contract with that Hot Springs due to reasons such as this, pure greed. Ibu then told me we could open as the Hot Springs had opened and it was all normal. So, it was, "Busy, back to normal," as Ibu put it. Not even a mention of 'new normal', it was just normal.

Being June, which is usually the start of the busy season, I can only imagine how many people up there were giving, not only false hope, but an increased risk of the spread of Corona.

Ibu also told me that Australians were coming back in July this year, this is true as her son's friend told her. I ever so gently told her that this was not the case. Ibu told me all the beaches in Kuta were open. I ever so gently told her that this was not the case.

When I explained, we may not be opening for a long time, Ibu started to say how sad it was for us, and that she would be fine, as it was all normal, but sad for us and asked about our staff etc. I had wondered why Wayan sent a message on Sunday night asking how we were, he probably thought he could open on Monday.

I got off the phone and nearly cried.

I just hope Ibu's bubble pops before she does.

My Bali family

I know many of our stories I share may be humorous, that is due to life being funnier than fiction. However, there is a serious side to our relationship with Ibu and Bapak that I should also share.

Many people talk about their 'Bali families.' Some married into a Balinese family, some have relatives married into a Balinese family, etc.

They say you can't choose your family... We chose ours, or somehow, they chose us, or somewhere in some alternative universe we were brought together and all that lah lah stuff. Many years ago, Ibu and Bapak became our parents, this came about after it was decided they would be. *Who decided? I have no idea. I was not sure what was going on as I did not speak the language back then.*

Well, I presume Ibu decided, it was so long ago, and it will be in my Book – The Epiphany.

To become 'Family', there were many BIG ceremonies, and even BIGGER ceremonies, oh and THE BIG ceremony. I just remember being dragged everywhere for weeks and being so tired. My ankles and knees hurting from all the sitting in prayer position, thinking, '*What the hell are we doing?*'

When Ibu has her mind set on something; it is pretty much known that Ibu has spoken, it is like the coffee pots.

Back in those early days, I did not speak the language, so we had a Guru for three months (a relative of Ibu's). I am hopeless with language; I did not pick up much of the language from him at all. So, it took a long time to learn. (He spoke to me in English the whole time laying out the rules.) Hubby picked up the language in what felt to me, about five minutes. However, I did find all the other stuff very interesting. I love rules, I love traditions, and there are so many rules, so my interest in the culture started back then.

So, all these ceremonies needed back then, all these offerings, all the clothes needed, different ones for each ceremony. Not once, have we paid for anything, as they are our family and this was important to them and was their choice, *as we have no choice when it comes to Ibu.*

Blessings at Besakih Temple, blessings everywhere. And in more recent times blessings of our car, blessings when we move offices. *Well, she*

247

should pay for those ones, as she moved us enough.

I also remember once, we were at Temple, and I was climbing the stairs, and a girlfriend who had moved to Denpasar smacked me on the bum and said: "You got fat, business must be good."

At the school, later that day, a child commented the same. I told Ibu, and she said that someone had also commented that day, that she was fat. So, that minute she put us both on a diet. Not, the reason in the Western world, but so the villagers did not think that we were eating more than them, and not sharing. *I failed to tell Ibu, it was all from Bintang.*

Ibu taught us that every time you can do something to help the community, you do it. It is your responsibility when living in a community. So, if she has more money than others in the village then it is her role to do something for the community. So, she may do more offerings than some others may be able to afford, etc., because she is lucky enough to be able to do that.

Ibu has the 'Ceremony/offering Scale', and we have a different scale, we call it: 'The Bintang Scale', we say, "Well that's fewer Bintangs this week."

So, if we pick up a few new pups or a new child to feed, we just go without Bintangs, because we are lucky enough to be able to give up that luxury.

Ibu taught us, you do not give money to anyone, especially if they are poorer, as this takes their pride away. It is very poor taste to flash around money or give money to someone, it puts them down like they are now lower than you. I saw an example of this once, in the next village, a high caste Balinese from Nusa Dua came up with a friend of mine to deliver a wheelchair. She gave our little disabled, now, 'Instagram famous' friend Yoko, IDR 100,000, when no one was looking. His father got very angry and screamed, "Who gave my son this money? Do you think you are better than me, and that I cannot provide for my son?"

It was fine to give him gifts of clothes and a wheelchair, as these were gifts, but giving money to the child, especially without the father's permission, was very insulting.

To this day, we have never once been asked for money by anyone in the village. However, we have been asked if we have oleh oleh (souvenirs), as it is a common custom for someone, when they leave the village, to come back with a souvenir. *I mean they went travelling (Denpasar is so far away), so it is expected you bring something from your travels.*

I used to hate the spoons my grandma bought me when she travelled. I dislike clutter and souvenirs, never got the concept myself.

Another example, in the early days; we wanted to pull down the house of a woman who lost her husband, and re-build it. (It was terrible that house.) She was struggling to feed her children. We were told when her son is older, he will get a job and do that. If you do it now, he has nothing to look forward to, you will take his chance of pride away. So, we fed and clothed her daughter instead. Never giving them money, so the mother's pride was also not taken away (as she was working full time selling bracelets to do what she could). We just had her daughter for meals every day for ten years. It did not upset the village way, as many of the children rotated around the village, going to anyone's home that had spare food (leftovers are never kept); especially when there is a ceremony, so this was not a problem.

Ten years later he started building a new, very simple house for his mum. Oh, he is just so proud, and his smile is beaming, it is contagious.

Now, during Covid-19 many people are helping their local friends, this is very different from the above, this is not normal times. If it is clear to your local friends that this is temporary, that you want to help them until they get their jobs back, then, thank you to all of you. The outpouring of help so far has been incredible. Just make sure you tell them it is temporary.

Ibu has, of course taught me patience, well, Bali has, but Ibu has taught me the Balinese core values. Some of these values seem a little lost in some parts of Bali. I do hope one day the Balinese that have lost those core values do find them again.

You can read more about how we became family in the latest book *The Epiphany* and the continuing story, *The Measurement of Wealth.*

There may be another book in the future, maybe more, as we are still learning. We can continue to share the valuable lessons we have learnt. (The majority we learn by making mistakes.)

Until I become just like Ibu, there will always be stories to share.

About The Author

Rachel Bergsma is the writer of the Facebook blog, Ibu Chronicles, a blog about living in Bali with her Dutch husband and working in a traditional village in North Bali.

Rachel (Rach) and her husband have been living and running a tour and travel business located in a Balinese owned hotel, at Lake Batur, Kintamani since 2008. Closed in March 2020, due to COVID.

Twenty years after she vowed never to return to Bali, she now follows the Balinese faith. She lives a simple life in Bali, Indonesia, with her husband, her rescue dogs, and her extended Balinese family.

Now a Series

I have never called myself an author, however, due to the overwhelming response from my readers, I have now written two more books...the prequesl to The Ibu Chronicles...

The Epiphany - Released November 2020

The Epiphany is Rachel Bergsma's personal anecdotes commencing with her first visit to Bali in 1998 and follows her ten years of travel until she finally returned to Bali. The book ends with starting their tour business in 2008.

In this book Rachel shares her travel stories that contributed to her personal growth. Well, mainly her travel mishaps, the story of meeting her husband and moving permanently to Bali... and how they met Ibu.

It is also the story of how an epiphany in Rome, Italy, helped her see a different side to Bali, and a very different side to herself.

In this honest and self-reflective book, Rachel openly details the person she once was, the tourist she once was, and how Bali helped her find meaning behind the traditional trappings of success.

The Measurement of Wealth - Released May 2021

The Measurement of Wealth is the continuing story from 2008 until 2015 and it is all about living and running a business in Bali. Rachel shares her life in Bali, and how her good intentions may not have been for the good of the people she wanted to help.

Printed in Great Britain
by Amazon

84932553R00150